LET'S FIX AMERICA

Copyright, 2022, All Rights Reserved.
OUR NATIONAL CONVERSATION

Let's Fix America

Commentary about *"Let's Fix America"*

"Recent years have been challenging for those who believe in truth, integrity, balance, fairness and civility in media. With OUR NATIONAL CONVERSATION (ONC), America's youth is taking the lead on a new way forward. In ONC's first book, "Let's Fix America," we see that nonpartisan problem-solving really is possible if we just sit down and talk. Let's give OUR NATIONAL CONVERSATION the chance it deserves."
 Tom Johnson, retired President, CNN; former Publisher, Los Angeles Times

"Today's America has become so politically divided that now, people want to prove themselves right and the 'other side' wrong more than they want to solve real issues. "Let's Fix America" seeks to break down barriers and open a dialogue in which all can participate. It is incredible to witness this effort come about during a time of such intense conflict."
 Gabriella Klimov, High School Student (interning with OUR NATIONAL CONVERSATION)

"It feels like the world has broken away from its moorings. Democracy is on the decline. Reality is under attack with those on different sides of the political divide disagreeing over even basic facts. Our politics have become so fraught that families can no longer talk peacefully at the dinner table. But a group of young people has stepped into the breach with a bold attempt to straighten things out— publishing a book of 34 nonpartisan proposals, called 'Let's Fix America.' Even if it doesn't fix everything, it begins an important conversation we need now more than ever."
 Leo Wolinsky, former Managing Editor, Los Angeles Times

"This book provides the American people with a glimpse of hope for unity without political polarization. These students and experts represent the American voice that has been overshadowed by political division. An excellent piece of work led by a true visionary and my friend, Jeff Hall."
> **Deaven Rector, Student at Howard Law School (and former ONC intern)**

"Jeff's students have produced proposals to combat polarization, gun violence, socioeconomic inequality, climate change and failing educational outcomes — just to name a few. Let's hope this movement grows like what some of us older folks saw in the late 1960s, with young people demanding an end to war and racism. Bravo to Jeff and team!"
> **Randy Hull, BS Mechanical Engineering/MBA, semi-retired energy executive, author, "Political Malpractice in America: Republic at Risk," proud son of WWII veteran/machinist/union worker**

"It is time that Americans come together and build bridges across a broken political system. 'Let's Fix America' and create a better America for generations to come."
> **Brian M. Thomas, M.D. (Founder, The Candidates Network; National Co-Chair, ONC)**

Let's Fix America

Table of Contents

Introduction

1. Welcome to OUR NATIONAL CONVERSATION 1
2. Our Methodology...11

Policy Proposals

Governance
3. *Reforming Congressional Rules*..23
4. *Restoring Trust in Elections*..30
5. *Increasing Electoral Competitiveness*................................36
6. *Increasing Lobbying Transparency*..................................42

Economics
7. *Addressing U.S. Debt and Deficits*...................................49
8. *Creating Sustainable Tax Reform*....................................54
9. *Reducing Poverty Through Welfare (and Zoning) Reform*...........60
10. *How to Save Social Security*...65
12. *Mitigating Inflation*..70

Infrastructure

13. Rethinking Transportation in America..........76
14. Creating Affordable Housing for the Future..........83
15. Building a Disaster-Resilient Infrastructure..........89

Social Issues

16. Reforming the Polarizing Media Landscape..........96
17. Incentivizing National Service..........103
18. Combating Homelessness in America..........109
19. New Foundations for K-12 Public Education..........115
20. Promoting Entrepreneurship as a Pathway for Equality..........125

Justice and Public Safety

21. Balancing Gun Control and Civil Liberties..........132
22. Improving Relations Between Law Enforcement and Minority Groups..........137
23. Creating a More Egalitarian Judicial System..........143

Healthcare

24. Reducing the Cost of Healthcare..........151
25. Improving Access to U.S. Healthcare..........157
26. Getting Serious About Mental Health..........165
27. Reforming Women's Reproductive Healthcare..........172
28. Tackling Obesity in America..........178
29. Addressing Our Nation's Substance Abuse Epidemic..........183

Foreign Policy and Defense

30. Reforming U.S. Immigration Policy.................................*190*
31. Boosting Cybersecurity.................................*197*
32. Mitigating U.S./China Tensions and Reducing the Potential for Military Conflict.................................*203*
33. The Israeli-Palestinian Conflict: Can We Achieve a Breakthrough? *209*
34. Preparing NATO's Long-Term Response to a Belligerent Russia *217*

Science, Environment, and Technology

35. Tackling Climate Change in America, Starting with Carbon Emissions *224*
36. Incentivizing Environmental Protection.................................*232*
37. Protecting Our Habitats and Endangered Species.................................*239*

38. **Economic Scorecard: Do the Numbers Add Up?**.................*246*

Conclusion

39. The Baby Boomers & Gen Z: Many Similarities, Many Differences.................................248
40. Let's Fix America: Only a Conversation Starter.................................259
41. Acknowledgments: Plenty of Appreciation to Go Around.......267

Let's Fix America

Welcome to OUR NATIONAL CONVERSATION

According to a 2022 poll conducted by Monmouth University, a whopping 88% of Americans say our country is on the wrong track. Eighty-eight percent is a very big — and very troubling — number.

Our political leaders and media outlets are held in very low esteem. Everything has become so ugly and partisan. Everyone seems angry. Some say America is headed for some kind of divorce — maybe even a civil war. Young Americans, especially, fear for their future.

We all have our own ideas about how and why things got this way, but assigning blame won't get us anywhere. How many hearts and minds are won over by calling someone you disagree with an idiot — or a criminal, even? Some see the other side as actually *evil*.

Most Americans, whatever their political beliefs, can probably agree on the following:

- Too many elected officials no longer solve problems based on give-and-take or the public good. Politics is now mostly about winning — at the other side's expense.

- Too many media outlets have chosen a side, adding fuel to the fire. Too many of us get only one side of the news, which is a very different version than what the other side gets. (Trust in traditional media is at an all-time low, according to a poll published by Gallup in October of 2022.)

- With social media, the loudest, angriest and most purposely untruthful voices often prevail. Too many friends — and even family members — no longer want to even *talk* to one another.

- All this division might be good for generating cable TV ratings, clicks, 'likes' and campaign contributions, but most Americans agree: the political/media ecosystem that has emerged in recent decades is *bad* for our country.

Is it too late — or are we too hopeless — to do anything about this? Are we too far gone? We've been in tough places before. History tells us we're up to the challenge. Will making the necessary changes be hideously difficult? Of course. *Anything* worthwhile takes hard work.

So, let's get started — and, finally, begin turning things around. Reading this book is our collective first step in the proverbial journey of a thousand miles. It's time we moved forward.

Greetings. My name is Jeff Hall, Editor and CEO of OUR NATIONAL CONVERSATION, the publisher of "Let's Fix America."

I'm a newspaper guy going way back. I've worked for a big newspaper (the Los Angeles Times), a medium-sized newspaper (the Kansas City Star) and a tiny newspaper (the Brentwood News, a community newspaper I started in West Los Angeles). As everyone knows, the newspaper industry is in decline, so I've been going digital in recent years.

I'm an aging Baby Boomer — I'm 71 now. We Boomers were very idealistic in our day; *ours* was the generation that was supposed to change the world. We did some things right, but we could have — and should have — done better.

Many of my Boomer friends and I want to do what we can in the time remaining to make things as right as we can. We want to prepare young Americans — America's future leaders — for the challenges ahead. It's time to pass the baton.

There are plenty of reasons Gen Z and Millennials might not want to hear what Boomers and other older generations have to say. I think it's fair to say many Baby Boomers feel bad about the current state of the planet. We wanted to do something. That something is what you will read about in this book.

For the last two years, several older Americans and I have been working with an army of student interns from all across America. Together, we wrote this book, built a website (OurNationalConversation.org) and more. Our goal is to get America talking again, with a focus on problem-solving instead of finger-pointing.

If you watch cable news — which is mostly "opinion news," really — chances are good you aren't getting all sides of the story. At OurNationalConversation.org — we call ourselves ONC for short — our news aggregator shows how Fox News, Huffington Post, New York Times, The Blaze, BBC and other media outlets are all playing the same story at the same time, side by side.

OurNationalConversation.org doesn't have an algorithm that shows you news only from the sources you like. Everybody who visits our website will see exactly the same thing. We think people *should* be exposed to news from multiple sources.

Similarly, at ONC, you will find a wide range of opinion pieces on a lot of topics, written by liberals, moderates and conservatives. At OurNationalConversation.org, we *welcome* a robust, thoughtful and inclusive debate.

According to a poll published by Gallup in January of 2022, 37% of Americans described their political views as moderate, 36% as conservative and 25% as liberal. Surely, some liberals want to know what conservatives are saying — and some conservatives want to know what liberals are saying. Moderates almost always like hearing all sides.

In 2020, 154.6 million Americans voted. Let's assume 60% of American voters would actually *like* to be exposed to a full range of news sources and opinions. That's 92.8 million people. Where can these folks currently turn in order to learn all sides of an issue? *Now, they can turn to OurNationalConversation.org.*

ONC goes beyond showing different perspectives. Our focus is on conversations that lead to *nonpartisan solutions* that most people can agree on. It's time for common sense, not mud wrestling. We also want to do what we can to help prepare America's future leaders to solve the country's — and the world's — most vexing issues.

If we are going to think about the future, we need to include the voices of those who are about to inherit it. "Let's Fix America" is filled with 34 public policy proposals put together by high school, college and grad school students from across the nation.

Approximately 485 students, guided by 175 experienced professionals, wrote this book, built a website, started a podcasting operation, wrote editorials and explainers, assembled a video production team and more. Our students actually put together over 350 policy proposals, but they couldn't all fit into this — our first book. You will find more at our website.

The exchange between older and younger generations was invigorating and healthy. Together, we solved a lot of problems — on paper, anyway. *You* are now invited to join the conversation.

Let's Get America Talking Again

At OUR NATIONAL CONVERSATION, our goal is to build a new media outlet based on nonpartisanship, truth, fairness, accuracy and balance. Using our new media platform, we can come together as a country, engage in a civil, intelligent and respectful conversation and come up with common-sense solutions to our country's problems. Just about everyone we talk to says ONC is the right idea at the right time. People are sick of all the partisanship.

ONC isn't just for students; all Americans of good will are invited to join in. As was noted, several older Americans are working with our students. The oldsters in our group came up with a slogan to reflect our attitude toward this project: "We're not done yet."

These older professionals included doctors, journalists, former government officials, academics, two police officers, a housewife (and a mother of two in the military), business CEOs and more. They included liberals, moderates and conservatives. We had Democrats, Greens, Independents, Libertarians and Republicans. We wanted to explore the best thinking we could find, whatever the source.

We didn't tell our students what they could or couldn't propose in "Let's Fix America." We did, however, ask that they talk to a wide range of liberal, moderate and conservative experts before writing their proposals. We helped line up experts for our students to interview. As they finalized their proposals, our students forged the necessary compromises, crunched the numbers and focused on ideas they thought would be acceptable to a minimum of 60% of American voters.

The proposals you find in "Let's Fix America" are, by design, short, simple and easy to follow. Even so, policy conversations can be deadly dull. So, please don't try to read too many proposals all at once. Take your time with this book — skip around. Read one or two proposals of interest, put the book down and pick it up later.

If you work in politics, academia, government, public policy research or political journalism, I hope you will view this book as a reference tool. If, in a year or two, you suddenly need to know about one of the topics covered in this book, grab your copy of "Let's Fix America" and see what's there. I'll be surprised if you don't find something of value. But, even if you don't find it in the book, go to OurNationalConversation.org.

If you are a true policy wonk and have been studying any of these issues for many years, our students' proposals may lack the detail, specificity and sophistication you might hope to see. I ask that you cut our students some slack. First of all, they are students — they don't yet have real-world experience. Plus, our students were *asked* to keep it all very simple.

While our students' policy proposals might seem pretty basic, as you read all these proposals, it will become obvious to you that *a lot* of work went into "Let's Fix America." We think our "short and to the point" and "show all sides" approach will prove very beneficial for young Americans just starting to learn and think about all this.

You might not like all of these proposals, but you might like enough of them. If you are on the far left or far right, you might not like any of them. But if you struggle with the issues and see things as being complicated — with many shades of gray — and you just want to see the problems get solved — we think you will find "Let's Fix America" useful.

We aren't claiming to have all the answers. What we wanted to do was *get a conversation started*. Our slogan is "let's get America talking again." You are now invited to weigh in. You don't have to be famous or have a Ph.D. in order to write articles or post comments on OurNationalConversation.org (but if you are famous or have a Ph.D., you are welcome, too!).

Our hope is that all these policy proposals will, over time — after being reviewed and refined by thousands of citizens — become so well thought-out and fine-tuned that people in high places will simply *have* to pay attention — and then actually *implement* ideas found in "Let's Fix America."

The moment we publish this book, our proposals will begin to age. Some are already aging; we've been working at this for quite a while. Proposals made today might look silly a year — or even a couple of months — from now. Our proposals are constantly subject to updating, based on what's happening in the news.

We can't change the text of this book (which went to the printer on Nov. 8, 2022) — but we can update future editions — and we can update our website all the time. Given the glacial pace at which

Congress tackles things, many of the proposals you find in this book might still be relevant years from now — when they are finally taken up by those in charge.

In order to have an impact, OUR NATIONAL CONVERSATION needs to build a big following. As a wonderful bumper sticker says, "*When the people lead, the leaders will follow.*" This is a quote from Mahatma Gandhi, one of my students told me. The same thinking surely applies today. Our political leaders and media company CEOs have failed us; it's time for us to lend them a hand, and help get things back on course. ONC is as much a *social movement* as a media company. ONC is *our* media company — and our social movement.

In addition to our social media efforts, we need to market ONC via paid ads. This will take money. In our second-to-last chapter, "Conclusion," I discuss how you can *invest* in our company, should you be interested. Soon, you will no longer have to curse the media; you can *be* the media!

Before we dive into the students' proposals, I want to explain our methodology. By explaining how we went about doing this, I hope to convince as many of you as I can that this was about as pure and nonpartisan an effort as is humanly possible.

We know we have our skeptics. Some think we simply *must* have a political agenda — that we are some kind of front for liberals (or conservatives). Some think, even if we *don't* have a partisan agenda, ours is a lost cause before we even begin. "How can *anyone* fix the partisan divide?" this line of thinking goes.

Others say, if we show all sides, that's a problem right there, because the other side is surely lying. We bend over backwards to not say one side or another is right or wrong. We just put it all out there for your consideration; you can decide what to make of all this.

By the way: ONC won't endorse candidates for office. We leave voting choices up to you, the voters, to decide. Some will find a media company that doesn't endorse candidates to be a breath of fresh air; some will think we're wimping out. I think, the moment we start taking sides, that will be the beginning of the end for ONC. It's our neutrality that will cause people to give us ONC a chance.

In an attempt to keep this as nonpartisan as possible, we had some older individuals check in with our students now and then — liberal, moderate and conservative established professionals. Many were experts, but some experts don't like the label, "expert." We decided to call our older mentors "established professionals."

Some of our adult conservatives say our students' proposals are too liberal, and some of our adult liberals say our students' proposals are too conservative. I view myself as a political moderate, and I find many of the proposals *way too moderate!* Maybe this difference of reactions means we are on the right path. You can't please everyone.

To our skeptics who say we simply *must* have a partisan agenda — or who say this whole idea is too idealistic and doomed to failure — I ask: *Have you got a better idea?* If yes, we're all in. Let's join forces. If no, don't we owe it to America to at least give ONC a try? What's the downside, really? That we lose a little time on this project? The potential upside is that we might actually get America talking again. That would lead to all kinds of benefits.

At the end of the book, I make some observations about the similarities and differences between Baby Boomers and Gen Z; I also discuss ONC's next steps, including ways *you* can participate. I then include several pages of acknowledgments. Quite a few individuals have helped so far (with very little arm-twisting required). Nobody — except for our programmers — is getting paid. Everybody involved is doing this because they love America.

As soon as we can, we do want to pay for a core staff, pay some small stipends to our students, pay for some additional programmers and pay to market the hell out of ONC. So, we do need to raise some money, but the best marketing of all is organic — and free. If you are into social media, you can find our social media handles below.

Maybe *you* would like to join the team or help in some capacity. We look forward to hearing from you. Send an email to info@OurNationalConversation.org. Together, let's make America the country we know it can — and should — be.

Jeff Hall, Editor & CEO

Find Us on Social Media

Before we continue, here are our social media channels:

– Twitter: @OurNatlConvo
– Facebook: http://facebook.com/ournationalconversation
– Instagram: @ournationalconversation
– TikTok: @ournationalconversation
– YouTube: OUR NATIONAL CONVERSATION
– Snapchat: @ournatlconvo
– LinkedIn: Our National Conversation (ONC)

How We Did This: Our Methodology

Just so everyone can know who we are and how we did this, this chapter will provide some background on how this came about and how we came up with our proposals. A full list of everyone who has helped so far — and a little bit of background information on them — can be found at the back of the book.

In early spring of 2020, I ran an ad on Chegg.com, a site that pairs students with internship opportunities. I was looking for students who would help me make progress with OUR NATIONAL CONVERSATION. I had been kicking around this idea for a new, nonpartisan approach to politics and media for several years and had already hosted a handful of interns over several summers who helped brainstorm ONC.

In a normal year, I'd get four to five inquiries from my Chegg ad, and maybe two or three interns would actually come to LA (where I am located). Pre-COVID-19, our office was two blocks from the beach, which made the internship a fairly easy sell. In January and February of 2020, I received the normal trickle of responses to the ad. Then, starting in March of 2020 — when COVID hit — we saw a *massive* increase in applications coming in via Chegg.

Many of the students who were suddenly contacting me had just seen their other internships, summer jobs and summer school classes evaporate. Because we were willing to do this internship virtually, overnight, we found ourselves *drowning* in applications. Over 2,000 applications came in by June. We couldn't even look at them all.

We quickly whittled our applicant pool down to 92 students who participated as interns in the summer of 2020. I know this sounds odd, but COVID actually made OUR NATIONAL CONVERSATION possible. Sometimes, a crisis is an opportunity in disguise. I figured, with all these interns suddenly available, we now had the ability to build the *machine* that would be required to build ONC.

Some of our students went to world-renowned colleges; some came from community colleges; many went to state schools; some were still in high school; we had a few graduate students; one intern was a recent grad of one of America's military academies. We did everything virtually, using Zoom, Slack and Google Drive.

In mid-summer of 2020, as the dust began to settle, we took a poll of our interns. Our first class of students was 52% white, versus the country's 62% white. Gen Z, the generation of most of our students, is more non-white than previous generations, so our student population was nicely representative of where Gen Z is now — and where America is headed in coming years as the population ages.

Our initial team of interns came from 22 states, from every region of the country, with 71 colleges and a handful of high schools represented. We skewed female (60% versus 40%). Our student team was about two-thirds liberal, with the remaining one-third equally divided between moderates and conservatives — an accurate reflection of what one would find among today's college students, according to polling data.

We built in mechanisms in an attempt to maintain political balance. All proposals were reviewed by a three-person student editorial review team, made up of one liberal, one moderate and one conservative. Our adult advisors spanned the political spectrum. We were — and still are — a very balanced group, politically.

Getting Organized

Our policy students organized themselves into eight teams: Governance, Economics, Foreign Policy and Defense, Justice and Public Safety, Healthcare, Social Issues, Infrastructure and Science, Environment and Technology.

The students then read up on their topics and sought out experts from across the political spectrum. Our students were asked to follow an "Eight-Way Test" when assembling their policy proposals.

ONC: THE EIGHT-WAY TEST

1. **COMMON-SENSE:** Does the proposal make sense? Does it seem practical, well thought-out and designed to actually solve the issue it addresses?

2. **BIG ENOUGH:** Is the proposal visionary enough to make a real difference?

3. **SIMPLE ENOUGH:** Is the proposal easy to explain and easy to understand? Would fifth-grade students understand it and be able to explain it to others?

4. **NONPARTISAN:** Does the proposal draw upon thinking from across the political spectrum? Have we done our best to remove partisan politics from the equation?

5. **FAIR:** Does the proposal promote "the greatest good for the greatest number of people?" Have we done enough to embrace the idea that we are all created equal? Does the proposal eliminate the influence of special interests?

6. **COST-EFFECTIVE:** Is the proposed funding sufficient for the job and yet still affordable? Has wasteful spending been eliminated? Have we identified the source of the money?

7. **POPULAR SUPPORT:** Will the proposal be met with approval from most Americans? Will the proposal, if implemented, make us proud as a nation?

8. **INTEGRATED:** Do all our proposals, taken together, seem coherent? Are they part of a bigger system that makes sense? Will all our proposals, taken together, result in a balanced federal budget within 10 years?

Students were quick to point out the internal tensions created by this eight-way test. "How can we think big," some asked, "when we have to control spending, too?" "How do we take incredibly complex problems and explain them in simple terms?" And then there was the question of what "fair" really meant — fairness of opportunity? Or fairness of result?

Politics is complicated, let's face it. Humans are involved. That automatically complicates things. It was left up to the students to figure this all out. This was, by design, a *learn by doing* experience. We are training future leaders of America to lead; the best way to learn how to lead is to gain actual leadership experience.

If we simply told our students what we wanted them to do and propose, they'd be followers, not leaders. They'd, essentially, be *stenographers* for the oldsters. We oldsters did our best to provide general guidance, but we didn't dictate any outcomes.

Our student healthcare team met (via Zoom) with doctors, pharmaceutical company executives, insurance company executives and a former assistant secretary of Health and Human Services (HHS).

Our foreign policy and defense students met with a retired nuclear submarine commander and a former special ops agent (U.S. Army Ranger) who now works for the Department of Homeland Security and serves on the National Security Council (NSC).

Our infrastructure students met with a big name in architectural circles, multiple transportation agency executives and an energy executive with experience in green hydrogen.

Our students studying the excesses of social media met with the retired president of CNN, a former managing editor from the Los Angeles Times and a former TV journalist now heading up a podcasting company.

We conducted hundreds of meetings like this. The candor, the innovation, the inspiration — each was an amazing exchange. Without a doubt, our young Americans appreciated the exposure to our older Americans — and vice versa.

We set the tone for team civility early on, and everyone happily complied. Members of our budding community really *like* hanging out in a place where ideas could be explored in a logical, inclusive and non-confrontational setting. At ONC, we all get along exceedingly well.

Several students said it was much easier to conduct a truly open and honest conversation in the ONC environment than it was back on their college campuses. Numerous conservative students told me they felt welcome at ONC, but not back at school. Even though our conservative students are outnumbered by our liberal students, we go out of our way to make sure they are heard.

One of our best conversations took place, I think, when a Black Lives Matter activist — Deaven Rector, a student from Morehouse College — participated in a podcast with a sergeant from the Los Angeles Police Department, Tom Datro. This discussion took place right after the killing of George Floyd. I hope you will listen to the podcast we recorded that day. I think you will come away filled with hope for the future.

Dollars & Poll Numbers

We initially set a goal of having all of our proposed solutions, taken together, result in a balanced federal budget after 10 years (on paper, anyway). Toward the end of the summer of 2020, our economics students concluded this simply wasn't practical, especially considering the impact that the 2017 tax cuts and coronavirus-related spending will have on our economy for years — and maybe even decades — to come.

However, our student economists did their best to bend the curve in a good way. The new spending proposals you will find in "Let's Fix America" are offset by revenue increases from specific tax increases or cuts to other programs that our students identified. Projected new revenues climb a little faster than projected new spending, resulting in *some* deficit reduction (around a $300 billion decrease in the annual federal deficit). See our "scorecard" — presented in Chapter 38.

Maybe future student teams, aided by input from all interested Americans, can achieve more deficit reduction — and maybe even a balanced budget. This is my bias, but I don't think we always need to spend more money in order to solve problems; we need to spend the money we spend more wisely. We need innovative solutions that can cost *less* than typical government programs. I am an entrepreneur, and entrepreneurs learn how to do more with less. Creativity is free — and, yet, it is priceless.

We also had a team of student pollsters look at all of our proposals. We wanted to focus on proposals that would likely be met with strong approval from the majority of the American people. We defined this as 60% approval or greater. We didn't want to come up with proposals that we knew would be predictably divisive. We focused on ideas we figured would unite rather than divide.

To gauge the support of each proposal, our student pollsters made estimates based on existing polling data from Gallup, Pew, Quinnipiac, Rasmussen and others. We were simply not in a position to do original polling of our own, but, by looking at existing polls, it was reasonably easy to find the data we needed.

Because we took a consciously nonpartisan approach to this assignment, our students felt a bit pressured to come up with proposals that might strike you as fairly moderate in nature. As I started seeing the proposals come in, many seemed unexciting — to me, anyway. I like big, bold plans that capture the imagination.

But the students stood their ground and told me they wanted to focus on ideas that could actually get approved by Congress. Remember, we started in the summer of 2020 — when Donald Trump was president, Republicans controlled the Senate and Democrats controlled the

House. The students didn't want to waste time on provocative proposals like the "Green New Deal," or dumping the Electoral College in favor of the popular vote — ideas that likely wouldn't make it to the finish line in the real world, they argued.

They also didn't recommend getting rid of the filibuster, but they were willing to modify it. They were in favor of more national service opportunities, but they didn't want to make national service mandatory. They didn't want to build any walls, and nobody suggested overturning Roe v. Wade. They also didn't want to tax capital gains at the same rate as ordinary income.

The students didn't suggest term limits (popular with the public, according to polls), and, while close to two-thirds of Americans like the idea of a third (centrist) party, the students viewed this idea as impractical, pointing to the many failures of third-party movements in America.

Our students did propose voter IDs, increasing the retirement age for Social Security and maintaining a strong defense posture when it comes to China and Russia. And the students did achieve some deficit reduction. These are viewed as traditionally Republican positions.

While our students didn't call for defunding the police, they did urge a shift in the direction of community policing and more services for those in lower-income communities, including spending more on education in our inner cities. They proposed a tax on carbon, as well. These are positions often taken by Democrats.

But our students seemed, in the main, to play things pretty much right down the middle. As far as I can tell, they never took a position based on what either of the two major political parties were promoting. In fact, party politics almost never came up in our conversations. *Our students, in the main, are very practical and pragmatic.* They just want to solve the problems.

At first, I found their pragmatism a bit curious — and certainly contrary to my own life experience. We Boomers liked to dream big dreams and put forward bold ideas. In the sixties and seventies, "anything went." But I have come, over time, to appreciate the practical approach of today's students. They are less about the talk — and more about the action.

They are quite comfortable playing within the 40-yard lines. If something is too divisive, they are happy to set it aside for now. The students, I have found, are very nonconfrontational (maybe to a fault). They are amazingly collaborative (also maybe to a fault).

But maybe our students' more practical approach is what Americans truly want right now. Some progress based on compromise is, surely, better than no progress at all. And maybe the Baby Boomers, had they been more practical — and more committed for the long haul — could have achieved more.

But the two generations are different, that's for sure. I spend more time exploring the similarities and differences between the Baby Boomers and Gen Z toward the end of the book (see chapter 39). I might even write an entire book on this topic one day; I find it quite interesting.

While many express disappointment in the Baby Boomers as a generation, I think there are things young Americans can still learn from us — just as we oldsters learn from the students. More on that later.

A Noted Gap in Our Approach

There is at least one big gap in our approach, which we're working to overcome: Ours is a college crowd, to be sure. Our students are all either in college or graduate school, or headed there. But only 34% of Americans over the age of 25 have earned a four-year college degree, so we can't really claim our student group is truly representative of America.

The divide between college graduates and non-college graduates is real. Generally speaking, college grads are more liberal and earn more than those who don't go to college, and non-college grads surely resent being "talked down to" by those who graduated from college.

We are entering a new era, in which elites can no longer stand on privilege and pedigree alone. I think this is a healthy development — long overdue. The elites who have been running things for a long time got a lot wrong in recent decades.

I think non-academics often have a "sixth sense" about our political system that the college crowd does not. They have good "B.S. detectors." Many who didn't go to college possess extraordinary intelligence and common sense.

Non-college grads also have practical skills that are in great demand. Carpenters, plumbers and electricians are in short supply and make good money. We have a housing crisis in America; it's not the English and philosophy majors who are going to solve this problem. Our country desperately *needs* Americans with practical skills. It's clear to me that not all young people should go to college. They'd be much better off going to a trade school or getting a job.

We are working on an idea that will (we hope) bring college students and non-college young Americans together to solve real problems in real communities, starting in Los Angeles in the summer of 2023. We want to team up college students, non-college attendees, inner city residents, homeless individuals and adult mentors from the building trades for the purpose of building a small village of housing for homeless people. What a great way to break down divides! I'm already talking to some who might sponsor us, and the response, so far, has been positive.

With that, it's finally time to see our students' proposals. In the next 34 chapters of this book, you will see proposals on just about every issue you can think of — voting rights, Social Security, infrastructure, health care, police and minority relations, global warming, balancing the budget, national service, our energy grid — you name it. There are many *more* proposals on our website, OurNationalConversation.org, and many more to follow.

This project was never intended to be just for Baby Boomers and our army of Gen Z students. OUR NATIONAL CONVERSATION is now officially open to *all* Americans. If you want to add a proposal of your own, we want to hear from you.

Remember: Don't try and race through this book; that could cause serious brain damage. Policy conversations — even well-conducted ones — can be wonkish and dry. Skip around. Take your time. Future books (we have quite a few planned) will be far more exciting, I promise. But "Let's Fix America" lays an important foundation and gets us started.

Jeff Hall, Editor & CEO

Governance

"Life under a good government is rarely dramatic; life under a bad government is always so."

- Oscar Wilde

Reforming Congressional Rules

Big Picture:
With the increased divide between party lines, present House and Senate rules, such as the Filibuster, have caused severe delays in passing legislation. The laws and procedures used by Congress must be reformed if America is to grapple with the increasingly complex political climate in which it operates. This proposal outlines a few policy changes that can be implemented to increase congressional effectiveness.

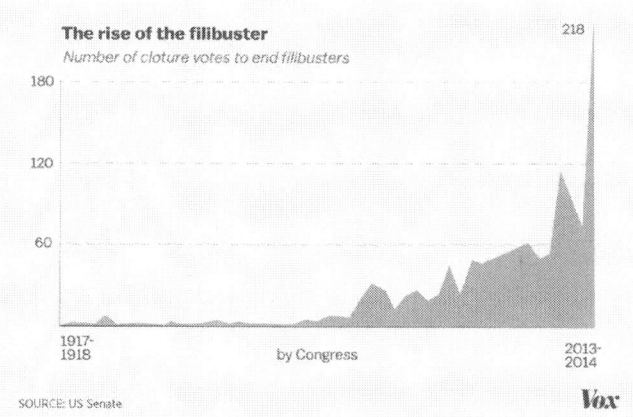

Graphic From: Klein, Ezra. "7 Myths About The Filibuster." *Vox*, Vox, 27 May. 2015. This figure illustrates the increased motion for filibusters passed in Congress from 1917 to 2015.

Operative Definitions:
1. **Congress:** The Legislative branch of the United States that is composed of the Senate and the House of Representatives and is responsible for making laws.
2. **Senate:** The upper house of the United States Congress that is composed of 100 members (2 from each state).

3. **House of Representatives:** The lower house of the United States Congress is composed of 435 members (based on each state's population).
4. **Filibuster:** Political tactic used by the minority group in the United States Senate that attempts to delay or entirely prevent the passage of a bill.
5. **Proxy Voting:** Occurs where a member of Congress delegates their vote to someone else, sometimes another legislator and sometimes an outside actor.

Important Facts and Statistics:
1. Between 1991 and 2008, Democrats successfully filibustered 63 times and Republicans, 89 times.
2. During the 2019 and 2020 Congressional term, a record-breaking 328 filibusters were used by the Democrats in the minority.
3. 57 members of Congress have violated a law made to prevent insider trading and conflicts of interest.
4. As of May 2022, a minimum of 20 congressional representatives or their spouses held stock ranging from $1,000 to $15,000 in weapons sales related to the Ukraine-Russia War. Many fear that this stock has the potential to motivate decisions influenced by financial conflicts of interest. This is just one of many examples.

6-Point Plan:
1. **Restore the talking filibuster.**
   Before 1970s rule changes, senators had to speak continuously to filibuster, and such disruptive and strenuous tactics were only used in extreme cases to protect Senate minority rights. Now, 60 votes are required to overturn the written objections that senators can file to merely threaten filibuster, letting obstructionists block proposals from reaching the Senate floor with just the stroke of a pen, instead of the arduous task of continuous speaking. As a

result, debate on new laws can be completely avoided for increasingly partisan reasons. Returning to the old "talk-till-you-drop" formula could help avoid deadlock in all but extreme cases and allow the filibuster to defend Senate minority rights when needed.

2. **Enforce stricter germaneness requirements on longer speeches.**
Germaneness requirements compel senators to keep their speeches related to the topic at hand. However, such rules mostly go unenforced, allowing senators to lengthen speeches with completely irrelevant material. For example, in 1935, Sen. Huey Long (D-LA) read aloud fried oyster recipes in a 15-hour-long filibuster against a law on appointing executive officials. More recently, Sen. Ted Cruz (R-TX) made headlines reading Dr. Seuss's *Green Eggs and Ham* in opposition to the Affordable Care Act. Establishing stricter germaneness standards would enable the chair or other senators to end a speech if it goes excessively off-topic. This would prevent using filibusters in bad faith, but not eliminate it for those making a genuine, substantive and responsive political stand.

3. **Require Members of Congress to relocate stocks to a blind trust while holding office.**
Congress members owning stock creates glaring conflict-of-interest problems. First, their immersion in nonpublic information enables insider trading. In the 2008 recession and the Covid pandemic, lawmakers used knowledge from closed-door meetings to make millions off economic disaster while average Americans lost jobs and life savings. Furthermore, lawmakers can directly profit off the companies they regulate — a loophole that, as the War in Ukraine has revealed, is especially significant in cases

where governments rely on private contractors to make and export weapons (see key facts and statistics). Several legislators allegedly profited from stock sales made after learning of the expected ravages of COVID, acting on information not yet available to the public. We must address the numerous opportunities that public office grants to profiteering. Members of Congress should be compelled to temporarily move their assets to a third-party blind trust fund during their time in office, ensuring that they are motivated to serve their constituents and not line their pockets.

4. **Establish clearer rules for Congressional proxy voting.**
   In March of 2020, Congress introduced proxy voting to reduce the number of members on the House floor at one time. Nancy Pelosi originally proposed this rule to reduce the spread of and exposure to Covid; however, members of both parties have misused proxy voting for distinct reasons, ranging from campaigning to attending book tours, allowing policymakers to avoid being present for debates and voting for nonessential reasons. As workplaces continue to evolve in a mid/post-pandemic society, the importance of proxy voting is understood. However, rules that establish valid uses of proxy voting and consequences that punish the misuse of the practice should be adopted by the House.

5. **Incentivize state legislatures to adopt Independent Redistricting Commissions.**
   Partisan gerrymandering allows politicians in the state legislature to give their party a competitive edge at the expense of democratic representation. This decreases electoral competition, and it increases both political extremism and partisan gridlock. Electoral competition and bipartisanship increase when the redistricting

process is overseen by an Independent Redistricting Commission — a group that draws districts with zero regard for the districts' partisan makeup. States can be motivated to adopt these redistricting commissions if the federal government conditions certain block grants on their cooperation, with the precise amount determined by the state's expressed willingness to establish a redistricting commission.

6. **Tie salaries of Congress to the annual median income in the nation.**
   In uncompetitive states and districts, elected officials have little incentive to work with members of the opposite party; they tend to drift toward the ideological extreme of their party. This causes gridlock and, in turn, economic hardship for average Americans. Currently, the median annual income for U.S. citizens is $67, 521. If the salaries of elected officials increased and decreased commensurate with the median household income of the nation, then elected, officials would be incentivized to work together to increase economic opportunity for all Americans.

Why This Initiative is Important:
Congress is one of the most important and powerful branches of the United States government and is responsible for the creation and passing of laws. Despite its immense powers, Congress remains paralyzed in addressing the nation's most urgent problems. All Americans are affected by the action and inaction of Congress. A reform of Congressional rules will effectively address the lack of action residing in Congress now and incentivize Members of Congress to pass needed legislation efficiently. This initiative can prioritize reforms that ensure Congressional productivity for years to come.

Economic Impact (from our student economist team):
- A more efficient Congress with fewer loopholes creates a more effective government, meaning people's tax dollars will be going to better use.
- The economic impacts of this are exceedingly difficult to calculate and our student economist team could provide no meaningful numbers.

To learn how our student economists came up with this economic impact, send an email to info@ournationalconversation.org and ask for a more thorough description of their methodologies.

Final Thought for Now:
"The very weaknesses of human nature are what make it so important that we keep a constantly watchful eye on our government, and that in turn our government watches us with equal care." – Eleanor Roosevelt (1942, My Day)

Acknowledgments:
The following student(s) worked on this nonpartisan proposal: Suha Chowdhury, University at Buffalo; Yesica Martinez, University of California, Berkeley; Robert Gan, University of California, Berkeley; Jett Young, Miami University.

The following individuals worked with our student interns and contributed expertise, wisdom and moral support to the development of this proposal:

1. Catherine Coleman: Retired professor of Lawyering Skills, USC. Los Angeles, CA.

2. <u>Alan Kopit:</u> Executive vice president and general counsel, MediLogix, LLC; President of the ABA Retirement Funds; alumnus, White House Fellows program. Cleveland, OH.
3. <u>David M. Webster:</u> Lawyer in private practice. Lake Forest, IL.
4. <u>Brad Phillips:</u> Superior Court Judge in the County of Los Angeles.

Note: Not all participants agree with every aspect of this proposal. To arrive at a proposal that takes multiple views into account requires compromise and difficult decisions. For individual commentary on this proposal and more detail, go to OurNationalConversation.org. We invite you to add your comments as well.

Sources:

"About Filibusters and Cloture." *U.S. Senate:*, 24 Mar. 2021, https://www.senate.gov/about/powers-procedures/filibusters-cloture.htm.

"Income and Poverty in the United States: 2020." *US Census Bureau* 1 Mar. 2022, https://www.census.gov/library/publications/2021/demo/p60-273.html.

Elving, Ron. "Senate Democrats Plan A Vote to Change the Filibuster. So What Is it?." *NPR*, 17 Jan. 2022. https://www.npr.org/2022/01/17/1072714887/filibuster-explained.

Haberkorn, J. "House members are using proxy voting for reasons far beyond its original intent." Los Angeles Times. 16 Feb. 2022, https://www.latimes.com/politics/story/2022-02-16/house-proxy-voting.

"Fact Brief: Did Democrats Make Record Use of the Filibuster in the Last Congress?:" *Repustar*. 27 Jun. 2021 https://repustar.com/fact-briefs/do-both-political-parties-have-a-history-of-using-filibusters.

Leonard, Kimberly. "American-Made Javelin and Stinger Missiles are Heading to Ukraine. At Least 20 Members of Congress Personally Invest in the Defense Contractors Behind Them." *Business Insider*, 11 Mar. 2022, https://www.businessinsider.com/congress-war-profiteers-stock-lockheed-martin-raytheon-investment-2022-3.

Levinthal, Dave. "57 Members of Congress Have Violated a Law Designed to Stop Insider Trading and Prevent Conflicts-of-Interest." *Business Insider*, 15 Feb. 2022, https://www.businessinsider.com/congress-stock-act-violations-senate-house-trading-2021-9.

"Median Household Income by State 2022", *World Population Review*, 9 Jun. 2022 https://worldpopulationreview.com/state-rankings/median-household-income-by-state.

Let's Fix America

Restoring Trust in Elections

Big Picture:
Free and fair elections establish the foundation of a stable republic. America must ensure that the ability to exercise voting rights is as accessible as possible. Low turnout can result in less competitive elections, giving the incumbent a significant advantage. The reforms mentioned in this proposal will not only make it easier for people to vote, but will implement measures that reassure citizens no foul play occurs.

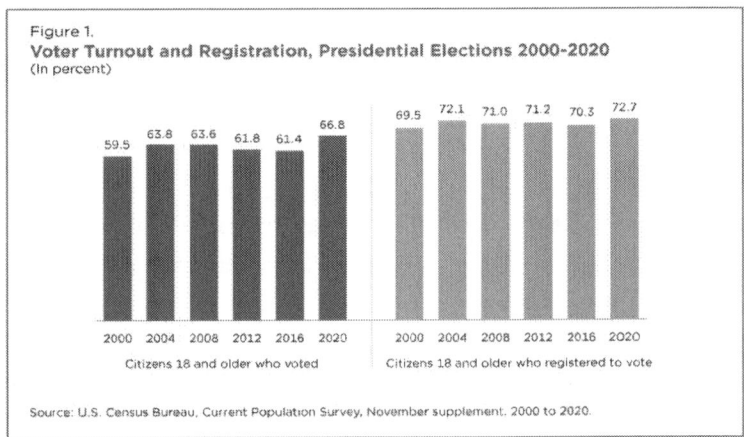

Graphic From: U.S Census Bureau, *Despite Pandemic Challenges, 2020 Election Had Largest Increase In Voting Between Presidential Elections on Record*. U.S Census Bureau. 29 Apr. 2021. This graph shows the change in voter turnout for the U.S presidential elections between 2000 and 2020.

Operative Definitions:
1. **National Voter Registration Act of 1993 (NVRA):** Also known as the "Motor Voter Act," NVRA sets certain voter registration requirements for federal office.
2. **Signature verification:** The process through which the signature on the back of a voter's ballot return envelope is

compared with the voter's signature, which is then scanned into state voter registration system databases.
3. **Gerrymandering:** The practice of drawing electoral districts in such a manner that one party is given an unfair advantage over another in elections.
4. **ACE Electoral Knowledge Network:** The largest online repository of electoral knowledge. ACE provides comprehensive information on electoral processes all around the world.
5. **State-by-State Vital Statistics:** State-level data on births, deaths, marriages, divorces, and migration.

Important Facts and Statistics:
1. About 67% of eligible voters cast ballots for the U.S. 2020 presidential election. In recent decades, on average 60% of eligible voters vote in Presidential elections and about 40% of eligible voters vote in midterm elections.
2. Voter registration is mandatory in 122 countries, including Israel, the Netherlands, Germany, Japan and South Korea.

7-Point Plan:
1. **Tie voter registration to the Census and State vital statistics.**
   Every 10 years, all citizens with a valid Social Security number 18 years or older who do not submit their census response will be automatically removed from the state voter rolls. Once the data is finalized, voters that are removed will receive a notification via mail. Upon receiving the notification, voters will have one month to return a correction with a copy of state or federal ID. Tying voter registration to the census will also allow states to better cooperate with the federal government by maintaining up-to-date voter registration rolls. The voter registration process will also require that one's state vital statistics are up to date. During

registration and the voting process, voters will provide information relevant to state vital statistics, which will then be transferred to the proper state-level agencies for incorporation into official vital statistics. To further ensure that these state vital statistics are up to date, each state will create a public database, modeled after that which currently exists in Pennsylvania. This database will make all public information on registered voters within the state readily accessible and verifiable by voters and political parties. This would help in efforts to ensure that voter databases are accurate and updated.

2. **Require voter confirmation.**
When voters register for Federal Elections via the census or in accordance with the NVRA, voters will receive a physical voter registration confirmation card which can be used to vote at their respective precinct.

3. **Allow same-day voter registration.**
If removed from the voter rolls, prospective voters can be given a provisional ballot and vote with a voter registration confirmation card. This will increase voter turnout by allowing the maximum number of prospective voters to cast their vote.

4. **Make voting as convenient as possible.**
Allow early voting. Early voting will begin on the fourth Monday before a primary or election, ending the week before election day. The week before election day will be used to count early votes and allow voters to amend their votes up to one day before election night by midnight local time. These measures will ensure that voters have sufficient time to cast their ballots, regardless of their professional and personal responsibilities, and have enough time

to potentially revisit and evaluate the full merits of all candidates before finalizing their votes.

5. **Restore the voting rights of felons upon returning to civilian life.**
   The right to participate in civil society is fundamental ad participation must be restored once individuals have finished their sentence. Only once a felon has completed their sentence, paid their fine(s) and completed any necessary probation off-paper will they be able to begin registering to vote.

6. **Encourage all states to establish non-partisan redistricting commissions.**
   State electoral maps for Congressional races must be drawn by nonpartisan commissions. The commissions will be made up of five members. Two members will be selected by each of the two largest parties, for a total of four. The chair will be selected, only with unanimous consent, by the four appointed members.

7. **Prevent polling station shortages.**
   On August 6, 2021, the FCC announced that it would be "rolling out a new mapping tool that [would] empower consumers with better data on mobile broadband coverage in America." The Federal Elections Commission should similarly "map out" the United States every 2 years. The result of this "map" would show where the longest wait times occur during elections. Using this new coverage map, municipalities and states, in coordination with the federal government, can better allocate resources to reduce wait times, spot inconsistencies with voting machines, and troubleshoot issues that cause increased wait times.

Why This Initiative is Important:

Maximizing the citizenry's access to the ballot and increasing its democratic representation is vital to maintaining a vibrant and stable Union. By securing elections, the American people will restore faith in the electoral process. Both political parties mistrust the election process, so our proposals would ensure the maximum number of voters can equally have the opportunity to cast a vote, assuring no foreign or malevolent forces attempt to influence the outcome of the elections. *See Limiting Outside Influence policy.*

Economic Impact (from our student economist team):

- Estimated effect on the annual federal deficit: + $34.5 million.

To learn how our student economists came up with this economic impact, send an email to info@ournationalconversation.org and ask for a more thorough description of their methodologies.

Final Thought for Now:

"The whole art of government consists in the art of being honest. Only aim to do your duty, and mankind will give you credit where you fail." – Thomas Jefferson (1774, A Summary View of the Rights of British America)

Acknowledgments:

The following student(s) worked on this nonpartisan proposal: Fiona Simpson, Lafayette College; Diego Romero, Seton Hall University; Marco Wertheimer, Lafayette College; Ryan Anderson, University of Mississippi.

The following individuals worked with our student interns and contributed expertise, wisdom and moral support in the development of this proposal:

1. <u>Catherine Coleman:</u> Retired professor of Lawyering Skills, USC. Los Angeles, CA.
2. <u>Alan Kopit:</u> Executive vice president and general counsel, MediLogix, LLC; President of the ABA Retirement Funds; alumnus, White House Fellows program. Cleveland, OH.
3. <u>David M. Webster:</u> Lawyer in private practice. Lake Forest, IL.
4. <u>Brad Phillips:</u> Superior Court Judge in the County of Los Angeles.

Note: Not all participants agree with every aspect of this proposal. To arrive at a proposal that takes multiple views into account requires compromise and difficult decisions. For individual commentary on this proposal and more detail, go to OurNationalConversation.org. We invite you to add your comments as well.

Sources:

Montanaro, Domenico. "Poll: Despite Record Turnout, 80 Million Americans Didn't Vote. Here's Why." *NPR*, 15 Dec. 2020, www.npr.org/2020/12/15/945031391/poll-despite-record-turnout-80-million-americans-didnt-vote-heres-why.

Stewart, Emily. "2018's Record-Setting Voter Turnout, in One Chart." *Vox*, 19 Nov. 2018, www.vox.com/policy-and-politics/2018/11/19/18103110/2018-midterm-elections-turnout.

"Same Day Voter Registration." *National Conference of State Legislatures*, 4 May 2022, https://www.ncsl.org/research/elections-and-campaigns/same-day-registration.aspx.

"Frequently Asked Questions." *Arizona Independent Redistricting Commission*. 9 June 2022, https://azredistricting.org/About-IRC/FAQ.asp

"ID to vote." *Elections Canada*. 9 Jun. 2022, https://www.elections.ca/content.aspx?section=vot&dir=ids&document=index&lang=e.

"Liste electoral: inscription d'office a 18 ans - Jeune vivant en France." *Service-Public.fr*. 28 Apr. 2022 https://www.service-public.fr/particuliers/vosdroits/F1961.

"Elections and voting in Finland" *infoFinland.fi*. 5 Mar. 2022,

"National Voter Registration Act of 1993" *Department of Justice*. 9 Jun. 2022, https://www.justice.gov/crt/national-voter-registration-act-1993-nvra

"About ACE" ACE *The Electoral Knowledge Network*. 9 Jun. 2022, https://aceproject.org/about.

Let's Fix America

Restoring Electoral Competitiveness

Big Picture:

Elections are the cornerstone of democracy, giving citizens the power to hold their elected leaders accountable. If a politician fails to represent their constituents, then those constituents have the democratic power to find a more suitable representative. However, citizens can only exercise this power when elections are competitive.

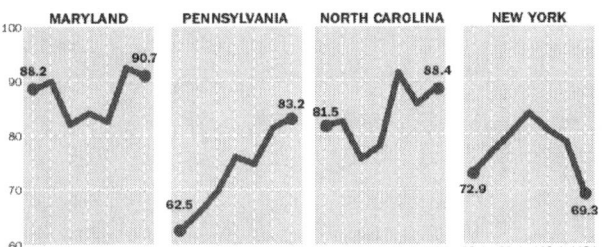

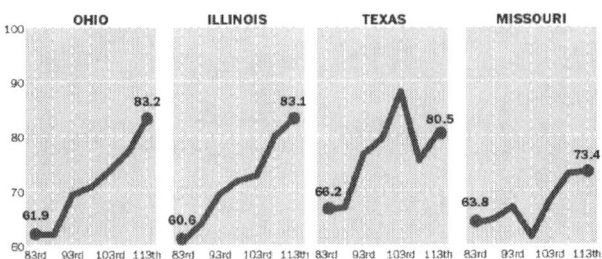

Graphic From: Wofford B. *The Great Gerrymandering Debate*. Brown Political Review (July 2014). This graph shows that states are generally becoming more gerrymandered with time.

Operative Definitions:
1. **Partisan gerrymandering:** The intentional manipulation of legislative/congressional district boundaries to achieve an unfair advantage for one's political party.
2. **Independent Redistricting Commission (IRC):** A redistricting method that disregards partisan implications of district boundaries.
3. **Ranked choice voting:** A type of voting system that allows voters to rank candidates, rather than choose a singular nominee.
4. **Political efficacy:** The belief that (1) every person's vote makes a difference and (2) the views of individual citizens are heard and understood by their representatives.

Important Facts and Statistics:
1. Less than 10% of federal congressional districts are considered competitive.

5-Point Plan:
1. **The Supreme Court should consider a partisan gerrymandering case.**
   The Supreme Court of the United States has been historically reluctant to make a ruling on partisan gerrymandering, often reasoning that the Justices have no business meddling in partisan politics. However, partisan gerrymandering affects the Supreme Court's principle of "one man, one vote." Politicians can dilute the power of voters from the opposite party, thus devaluing their individual votes. Is it incumbent on the Supreme Court to defend "one man, one vote" and take up a partisan gerrymandering case.

2. **States should adopt Independent Redistricting Commissions.**
Electoral competition and bipartisanship increase when the redistricting process is overseen by an Independent Redistricting Commission — a group that draws districts with zero regard for the districts' partisan makeup. These commissions strengthen political representation and reduce hyper-partisanship. If states do not adopt these commissions on their own, the federal government may exert pressure by making various sources of funding — such as educational, healthcare, or welfare funds — conditional on the creation of independent redistricting commissions.

3. **States should implement ranked-choice voting.**
States have the power to determine how they administer their elections. Most states have adopted a winner-takes-all election system, but this is not constitutionally mandated. The winner-takes-all system forces voters to choose just one candidate from the ballot. Ranked-choice voting allows voters to rank the candidates relative to each other, rather than choosing just one. If a candidate does not receive 50% of the votes, the candidate who received the least number of votes is eliminated. If a voter had ranked that eliminated candidate first, then their second choice receives their vote. Votes continue to be tallied this way until a candidate has received a simple majority of the votes. This will help ensure that elected officials are representative of the wants and needs of their constituents.

4. **Reduce restrictions for third party candidates.**
America has a two-party system; this means that the Republican Party and the Democratic Party dominate politics at every level of government. This also means that the Republican and

Democratic parties have vested interests in discouraging third party — or Independent — candidates from running for office. For that reason, politicians have created legal barriers for these candidates. To even appear on the ballot, third-party candidates must receive a certain number of petition signatures. Although it varies by state, this number is typically a percentage of the voting-eligible population of the previous election. This means that, in some states, third-party candidates must collect tens of thousands of signatures. These rules make it impossible for a third-party candidate to drum up enough support to challenge either major party.

5. **Adopt an open primary to general runoff election system.**
Primary elections consist of rank-and-file voters within each party nominating the candidate that they think has the best chance of winning in a general election. Primary elections often consist of the party's most loyal or extreme voters. Sometimes, partisan primaries produce politically toxic candidates that harm the foundations of American democracy. To reduce the toxicity of primaries, state election administration officials should adopt an open primary-to-general runoff election system. In this system, rather than having the extreme base of each party choose the candidates for a general election, independents would be able to vote in primary elections. The two candidates who receive the most votes would then proceed to the general November election. Although this system could just result in the same two-party system, it is a chance for independent voters to participate in the primary process, as they are often excluded from closed primaries.

<u>Why This Initiative is Important:</u>
Electoral competition is vital to a healthy democracy. Without it, voters feel apathetic to all parts of the political process and politicians

begin to take advantage of said voters. When elections are competitive, candidates are beholden to their constituents and their campaign promises. Also, candidates are less likely to hold radical or extreme views. If elections are competitive, candidates must appeal to a wide range of voters, and this is only achieved by adopting moderate, well-informed issue positions.

Economic Impact (from our student economist team):
- A meaningful economic impact could not be calculated for this proposal.

To learn how our student economists came up with this economic impact, send an email to info@ournationalconversation.org and ask for a more thorough description of their methodologies.

Final Thought for Now:
"A politician thinks of the next election. A statesman, of the next generation." – James Freeman Clarke

Acknowledgments:
The following student(s) worked on this nonpartisan proposal: An anonymous student intern who asked not to be identified.

The following individuals worked with our student interns and contributed expertise, wisdom and moral support in the development of this proposal:
    1. David Shorr: Owner, AdvocacyCraft. Stevens Point, WI.
Note: Not all participants agree with every aspect of this proposal. To arrive at a proposal that takes multiple views into account requires compromise and difficult decisions. For individual commentary on this proposal and more detail, go to OurNationalConversation.org. We invite you to add your comments as well.

Sources:

Born, K. "Increasing voter turnout: What, if anything, can be done?" *Stanford Social Innovation Review* 26 Apr. 2016, https://ssir.org/articles/entry/increasing_voter_turnout_what_if_anything_can_be_done.

"Americans are united against Partisan Gerrymandering." Brennan Center for Justice. 15 Mar. 2019, https://www.brennancenter.org/our-work/research-reports/americans-are-united-against-partisan-gerrymandering.

"Enacted maps and 2022 ratings" Cook Political Report. 18 Feb. 2022, https://www.cookpolitical.com/redistricting/2022-maps-and-ratings. Daley, D. *Ratf**ked*. Liveright Publishing Corporation, 2016.

"Redistricting rundown: Georgia" Democracy Docket. 2 Dec. 2021,https://www.democracydocket.com/news/redistricting-rundown-georgia/.

Increasing Lobbying Transparency

Big Picture:
Proper political lobbying depends on complete public transparency. Elected representatives should be held accountable when lobbying them to vote against the interests of their constituents. This proposal allows lobbying firms and lobbyists to continue to perform their functions while increasing transparency by creating a comprehensive online database detailing each lobbying proposal, by whom it is done and a general idea of public opinion on the relevant issue.

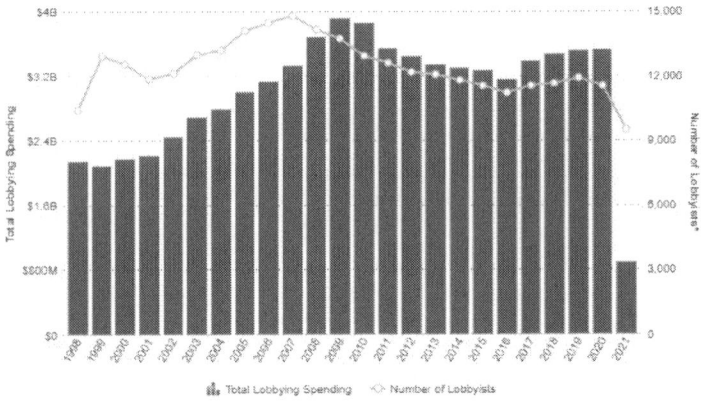

Graphic From: *Lobbying Data Summary (adjusted for inflation), 1998-2021*. Center for Responsive Politics, *opensecrets.org*. 4 April 2021. Though the number of registered lobbyists has declined from its peak back in 2007, total lobbying expenditures have risen, showing the growing power of these entities. 2021 is especially low because the data was collected partway through the fiscal year. (Numbers have been adjusted for inflation).

Operative Definitions:
1. **Lobbying:** The lawful act of persuading government officials, which includes meticulous planning and preparation, as well as prior research and other relevant background work. Making financial contributions to political campaigns and causes endorsed by candidates is a big — and controversial — part of this process.
2. **Lobbyist:** An individual who is hired by a client to represent their interests by lawfully attempting to influence legislators and public officials. Lobbyists use persuasive tactics to get laws and policies passed that further their client's agenda. Clients may be people, corporate entities, or foreign governments.
3. **Transparency Policy:** Public requirements that aim to increase public knowledge regarding the inner workings of organizations, including lobbying groups, to mitigate negative impacts that could arise from a group having parts of itself hidden.

Important Facts and Statistics:
1. There are approximately 11,500 unique, registered and active lobbyists.
2. Registered lobbyists consistently contribute upwards of $3.2 billion yearly towards lobbying efforts and spent $3.49 billion in 2020.

5-Point Plan:
1. **Create a virtual forum to address the influence of money in politics.**
   Establish a virtual forum that is accessible to the public on which registered lobbying and interest groups must submit formal proposals on existing legislation in Congress. This forum will work in conjunction with the Library of Congress' database of bills, available on Congress' website. At the head of each bill, there

will be a list of active lobbying groups who have submitted proposals regarding a specific piece of legislation that can be selected by the user, with their specific proposals hyperlinked to corresponding sections of the text.

2. **Create an "upvote" and "downvote" framework on the forum.**
   This feature will allow for interested and engaged citizens to express their support for, and opposition to, specific policy suggestions from lobbying groups. This system will be available only when the viewer filters "by lobbying proposal." The goal of this feature is to allow the most favorable proposals to become the most visible to legislators through hierarchical organization.

3. **Allow lobbyists to register on the newly stated forum.**
   On the newly established forum, lobbyists will not have to make financial contributions to register. Registration requirements will be consistent with those established in the Lobbying Act of 1995, including the name and address of the firm seeking registration, organizations that have provided $10 thousand or more in a six-month period to the lobbying firm, and any foreign organizations that hold a connection to the domestic applicant.

4. **Allow all viewers of the forum to filter by bill, legislator, lobbying proposal or lobbying group.**
   This feature of the virtual forum will provide easy and clear access to all relevant information regarding legislation. Multiple filters can be applied at once, allowing users to view individual bills, as well as the legislators and lobbyists working on them. When a user filters by bill, the most recent pieces of legislation in the House or on the Senate floor will be filtered to the top of the page. When sorted by legislator, names of legislators will be sorted

alphabetically, with their sponsored legislation appearing once their name is selected. Using the lobbying proposal filter can show the most recently added policy suggestions from various lobbying groups. The lobbying group option provides the most recently active — or most relevant — lobbyists and lobbying groups.

5. **Prevent former executive branch officials or members of Congress from immediately being involved in lobbying or "strategic consulting" positions.**
A position in a presidential administration or Congress is a privilege given to a select few. Serving on behalf of the American people should never be a steppingstone for one's career. Yet, many who work in government land lucrative jobs lobbying for many organizations with which they once worked. This fosters distrust, making political office seem more like a stepping-stone to self-elevation than public service. By placing a two-year lobbying ban on members of Congress, executive branch officials and former staff, the people can regain confidence that the government is working for them and not for a select few.

Why This Initiative is Important:
People have ample misconceptions about what a lobbyist's job is, stoking distrust and anger. By centralizing all lobbying efforts into one government resource, this proposal allows for greater transparency by organizing bills by section(s), subsections, lobbyists and firms in a way that is accessible. Elected representatives will be given a clearer view of public opinion on proposed legislation and a backlog of previous legislation. The forum will simplify the lobbying process and reduce the opportunity for corruption and selfishness in American politics.

Economic Impact (from our student economist team):
- Estimated effect on the federal deficit within a decade: + $2.061 million.

To learn how our student economists came up with this economic impact, send an email to info@ournationalconversation.org and ask for a more thorough description of their methodologies.

Final Thought for Now:
"Lobbying is the world's second-oldest profession" – **Bill Press**

Acknowledgments:
The following student(s) worked on this nonpartisan proposal: Benny Rosenzweig, Princeton University; Andrew Smith, The George Washington University.

The following individuals worked with our student interns and contributed expertise, wisdom and moral support in the development of this proposal:
1. An anonymous expert who asked not to be identified.
2. Catherine Coleman: Recently retired Professor of Lawyering Skills, USC. Los Angeles, CA.
3. Alan Kopit: Executive vice president and general counsel, MediLogix, LLC; President of the ABA Retirement Funds; alumnus, White House Fellows program. Cleveland, OH.
4. David M. Webster: Lawyer in private practice; alumnus, White House Fellows program. Lake Forest, IL.

Note: Not all participants agree with every aspect of this proposal. To arrive at a proposal that takes multiple views into account requires compromise and difficult decisions. For individual commentary on this proposal and more detail, go to OurNationalConversation.org. We invite you to add your comments as well.

Sources:

"Frequently Asked Questions." *The Transparency Policy Project*, 9 Jun. 2022, http://www.transparencypolicy.net/FAQs.php

"H.R. 2261 — 104th Congress: Lobbying Disclosure Act of 1995." *GovTrack* 1995. February 21, 2021 https://www.govtrack.us/congress/bills/104/hr2261

"Lobbying Data Summary." *OpenSecrets*, 22 Apr. 2022 www.opensecrets.org/federal-lobbying/summary?inflate=Y.

"Lobbyists: Money to Congress." *OpenSecrets.org*, 22 Mar. 2021, www.opensecrets.org/industries/summary.php?ind=k02&cycle=2020&recipdetail=H&mem=Y.

Economics

"The most important single central fact about a free market is that no exchange takes place unless both parties benefit."

- Milton Friedman

Addressing U.S. Debt and Deficits

Big Picture:
Entrepreneurs can borrow loans to fund successful businesses, and successful businesses sometimes incur debt to expand their services. Likewise, the U.S. government frequently sustains debt to fund successful programs and expand their services to Americans. However, over the past few decades, the yearly deficits have risen, and our total debt is approaching unsustainable levels, as compared to our nation's GDP. With no defined crisis threshold, and debate over how high the deficit can sustainably rise, politicians often place debt solutions on the backburner. Immediate action should be taken to discourage more unsustainable debt growth.

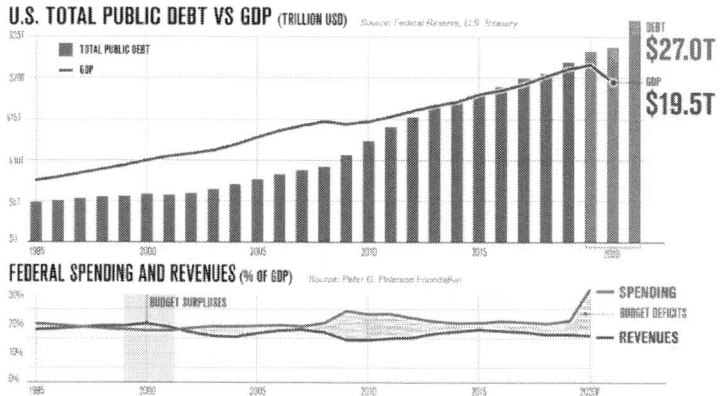

Graphic from: *Charting America's National Debt: $27 Trillion and Counting.* VisualCapitalist.com. 30 Oct. 2020. America's national debt has risen drastically over the past few decades and is now higher than the nation's annual GDP.

Operative Definitions:
1. **Debt ceiling:** A legal limit on the amount of national debt that the treasury can incur in a given fiscal year.

2. **Gross domestic product (GDP):** A monetary measure of the market value of all final goods and services produced in a given area in a given time frame.
3. **Debt-to-GDP ratio:** The proportion of the United States current national debt to its annual GDP.
4. **Sequestration:** Automatic spending cuts that occur across all government programs. Used to control the annual budget.
5. **Value-added tax (VAT):** Taxes imposed at every step of an item's production. More efficient at taxing products than sales taxes.

Important Facts and Statistics (as of April 2021):
1. National debt: $29.7 trillion.
2. Debt per U.S. citizen: $89,300.
3. Debt-to-GDP ratio: 126.9%.
4. Annual deficit of 2021: $2.77 trillion.

4-Point Plan:
1. **Control spending with maximum debt-to-GDP ratios:**

Year	Ratio
1	120%
2	115%
3	110%
4	105%
5	100%

The amount of government debt should not exceed a certain threshold of the United States' annual GDP. If this ratio gets too high (it is currently around 125%), it could lead to spiraling interest rates and slower economic growth. Once attained, year five's level will remain the standard. Further economic research into debt-to-GDP thresholds is needed. However, this ratio will serve as a valuable measure of debt sustainability.

2. **If Congress fails to abide by debt-to-GDP ratios, cut discretionary spending across the board.**
Sequestration ensures national debt is considered in future spending decisions. This will be enacted as presented in the Office of Management and Budget's sequestration report, which cuts each account across the budget by the same percentage.

3. **Increase tax revenue to offset the rising deficit.**
To increase tax revenue, lawmakers should reverse the Tax Cuts and Jobs Act tax cuts on corporate income tax, raising it back to the 35% level from before the act was passed. As well, raising the top two tax brackets created by the TCAJ by 1% would raise federal revenue by upwards of $20 billion. Another possible tax could be a "Wall Street Sales Tax," in which every Wall Street transaction is taxed at a small percentage.

4. **Require that Congress and the Executive Branch give projections on costly programs such as healthcare and national defense.**
Increased fiscal transparency will allow Americans to see how their tax money is being used, and, therefore, be more educated when making decisions about what policies to be in favor of and who to elect to office.

Why This Initiative is Important:

This plan will not go into effect until stable, pre-COVID-19 economic levels have returned, which will ensure that our total debt remains sustainable. By introducing a value-added tax and other revenue management measures, we can fund social programs and meet our financial obligations without increasing debt. A complete and thorough reform of budgetary spending is the only way to effectively address our overwhelming debt levels.

Economic Impact (from our student economist team):

- The Congressional Budget Office, a nonpartisan organization, estimates that adding a 5% VAT to a broad base, meaning the majority of goods and services, (after exclusions and rebates are accounted for) will generate $320 billion in 2022 and more in subsequent years.
- Maintaining a low debt-to-GDP ratio will help ensure inflation rates stay low.
- Estimated effect on the annual federal deficit: - $116 billion

To learn how our student economists came up with this economic impact, send an email to info@ournationalconversation.org and ask for a more thorough description of their methodologies.

Final Thought for Now:
"To contract new debts is not the way to pay old ones." – George Washington (1799)

Acknowledgments:

The following student(s) worked on this nonpartisan proposal: Mitchell Clarke, Virginia Polytechnic Institute and State University; Brennan Merone, William and Mary College.

The following individuals worked with our student interns and contributed expertise, wisdom and moral support in the development of this proposal:

1. <u>Dr. Steven Sheffrin:</u> Professor of Economics, Tulane University; Director, Murphy Institute of Political Economy. New Orleans, LA.
2. <u>David Gillies:</u> Director of Government Relations, General Dynamics; 20 years of Congressional staff experience; Former Staff Member on Senate Appropriations Committee, Defense Subcommittee. Washington, DC.
3. <u>Thomas Herndon:</u> Assistant Professor of Economics, Loyola Marymount University; exposed fundamental errors in Reinhart and Rogoff's "Growth in a Time of Debt." Los Angeles, CA.

Note: Not all participants agree with every aspect of this proposal. To arrive at a proposal that takes multiple views into account requires compromise and difficult decisions. For individual commentary on this proposal and more detail, go to OurNationalConversation.org. We invite you to add your comments as well.

Sources:

"Impose a 5 Percent Value-Added Tax." *Congressional Budget Office*, Congressional Budget Office, 13 Dec. 2018, https://www.cbo.gov/budget-options/54820.

Hennerich, Heather. "Debt-to-GDP Ratio: How High Is Too High? It Depends." *Federal Reserve Bank of St. Louis*, 15 Sept. 2021, https://www.stlouisfed.org/openvault/2020/october/debt-gdp-ratio-how-high-too-high-it-depends.

"United States Gross Federal Debt to GDP 2021 DATA: 2022 Forecast." *US Office of Management and Budget*, Dec. 2020, https://tradingeconomics.com/united-states/government-debt-to-gdp.

Creating Sustainable Tax Reform

Big Picture:
Tax policy is one of the most important tools our government can use to bridge the gap between federal revenue and spending. It is also important for combating income inequality. To do so sustainably and effectively, our current tax system must be simplified and reformed.

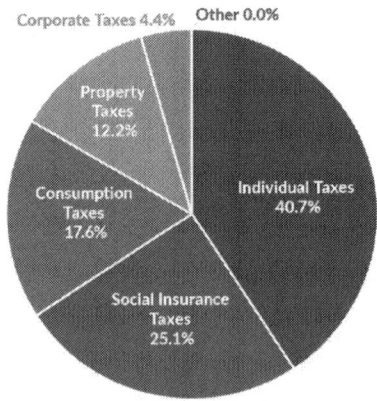

Graphic from: *OECD Global Revenue Statistics Database* (Tax Foundation; 2018). This graph shows which categories most taxes are collected from, the leader being individual taxes.

Operative Definitions:
1. **Tax code:** The federal laws that determine how much money individuals and corporations owe in taxes.
2. **Internal revenue service (IRS):** The U.S. government agency responsible for tax collection and the enforcement of the tax code.
3. **Income tax:** A tax levied on income earned by workers. The U.S. has collected a federal income tax since 1913.

4. **Corporate tax:** A tax levied on the profits of a corporation.
5. **Capital gains tax:** A tax levied on income from the sale of a property or investment.
6. **Value-added tax (VAT):** A tax levied on goods and services at every point of their production.
7. **Sales tax:** A tax levied on goods and services at their point of sale that is collected by the retailer.
8. **Progressive tax:** A tax that increases in percentage as an individual or corporation's earnings increase.
9. **Stepped-up basis loophole:** a tax loophole that allows inheritors to revalue assets at the time of death to reset the amount of gains seen on the asset, allowing the inheritor to pay no taxes on the inheritance

Important Facts and Statistics:
1. In 2021, the federal government collected $3.86 trillion in tax revenue.
2. The U.S. currently has seven income tax brackets, ranging from 10% for the lowest earners to 37% for those making over half a million dollars per year. Income is taxed marginally, meaning only earnings above each bracket's threshold are taxed at that rate. For example, if you earn $501,000, only the last $1000 earned is taxed at 37%.
3. The current corporate tax rate in the U.S. is 21%.
4. Funding for IRS enforcement efforts was $8.6 billion in 2019.
5. U.S. corporations currently hold $2.1 trillion in profits in offshore tax havens.
6. Closing corporate tax loopholes will increase government revenue by up to $90 billion per year.

4-Point Plan:
1. **Simplify the tax filing process and promote tax literacy.**
   Large tax preparation companies have continued to successfully lobby the government to keep the tax filing process as confusing as possible. Offering return-free federal tax filing, in which the IRS calculates and withholds taxes for individuals, would save Americans $2 billion a year in tax preparation expenses. On the state level, mandating basic tax literacy classes in high schools will provide Americans with the basic tools they need to understand the tax system and successfully file taxes independently.

2. **Simplify the tax code.**
   The various current tax deductions and credits can be confusing, and many taxpayers miss out on credits to which they may be entitled. Consolidating tax credit provisions for families and increasing education on these programs will help to close that gap. The Tax Cuts and Jobs Act of 2017 increased the standard deduction that taxpayers are eligible to receive. Maintaining this increase in standard deduction amounts will discourage itemizing, which will both simplify the filing process for 90% of Americans and reduce their tax burden.

3. **Reduce tax evasion through current levels of enforcement.**
   Currently, intentional tax evasion and unintentional errors on tax returns cost the federal government about $450 billion per year in revenue. With a simplified tax code, the IRS will be able to more efficiently crack down on tax evaders and reduce mistakes even with their current budget.

4. **Reform the current estate tax structure and close loopholes.**
   Closing the stepped-up basis loophole will generate $280 billion over 10 years, preventing inheritors from reevaluating the value of

their inheritance to escape taxes. In addition, a couple can currently leave $10.6 million to heirs and not be required to pay federal estate or gift tax. Lowering this cap to $5 million will encourage people to spend their assets and inject money into the economy, generating $249 billion over a span of 10 years.

Why This Initiative is Important:
Simplifying the tax process increases the system's efficiency and reduces costs for individuals and organizations. This plan includes changes to income, estate and capital gains taxes that help combat income inequality, an aspect that tax simplification alone falls short in addressing. Keeping the tax system progressive and preventing undue influence from special interests are vital to the pursuit of financial equity. The federal spending outlined above will provide returns on investment. Amending the 2017 Tax Cuts and Jobs Act, without fully reversing it, will help curb tax loopholes while maintaining bipartisan support and avoiding polarization.

Economic Impact (from our student economist team):
- Due to the 2022 Inflation Reduction Act, it is estimated that:
  - Amount of funding the IRS will receive: $79.6 billion
  - Amount of money that will be saved (due to a decrease in tax evasion): $400 billion
- Estimated effect on the annual federal deficit: - $277.9 billion

To learn how our student economists came up with this economic impact, send an email to info@ournationalconversation.org and ask for a more thorough description of their methodologies.

Final Thought for Now:
"How is it possible that a government half supplied and always necessitous, can fulfill the purposes of its institution, can provide for the security, advance the prosperity, or support the reputation of the commonwealth?" – Alexander Hamilton (1787)

Acknowledgments:
The following student(s) worked on this nonpartisan proposal: Linda Meyerson, University of California, Berkeley; Adam Brasher, Fordham University.

The following individuals worked with our student interns and contributed expertise, wisdom and moral support in the development of this proposal:
1. Leo Martinez: Professor of Law, University of California, Hastings. San Francisco, CA.
2. Jeffrey Hoopes: Research Director, University of North Carolina Tax Center; Associate Professor of Accounting, University of North Carolina. Chapel Hill, NC.
3. Karl Smith: Vice President of Federal Tax Policy, Tax Foundation. Washington, DC.
4. Chris Edwards: Director of Tax Policy Studies, CATO Institute. Washington, DC.

Note: Not all participants agree with every aspect of this proposal. To arrive at a proposal that takes multiple views into account requires compromise and difficult decisions. For individual commentary on this proposal and more detail, go to OurNationalConversation.org. We invite you to add your comments as well.

Sources:

"Fact Sheet: Offshore Corporate Loopholes." *Americans for Tax Fairness*. 2014 https://americansfortaxfairness.org/tax-fairness-briefing-booklet/fact-sheet-offshore-corporate-tax-loopholes

Lawder, David. "Explainer: The $4 trillion U.S. government relies on individual taxpayers." *Reuters*, September 28, 2020. https://www.reuters.com/article/us-usa-trump-taxes-revenue-explainer/explainer-the-4-trillion-u-s-government-relies-on-individual-taxpayers-idUSKBN26J30F

Orem, Tina. "2020-2021 Tax Brackets & Federal IncomeTax Rates." *Nerdwallet*, April 12, 2021. https://www.nerdwallet.com/article/taxes/federal-income-tax-brackets.

"Tax Policy Center Briefing Book: Key Elements of the U.S. Tax System." *Tax Policy Center*. https://www.taxpolicycenter.org/briefing-book/how-does-corporate-income-tax-work

Reducing Poverty Through Welfare (and Zoning) Reform

Big Picture:
Despite federal spending on welfare programs, more than 30 million Americans were impoverished in 2019. Economic security programs made up 8% of the U.S. budget in 2019, totaling $361 billion. During the COVID-19 pandemic, more than $1.1 trillion was spent ensuring that the poorest Americans would remain out of poverty. Modern anti-poverty legislation must address inefficiencies and enact innovative solutions rather than simply increase spending.

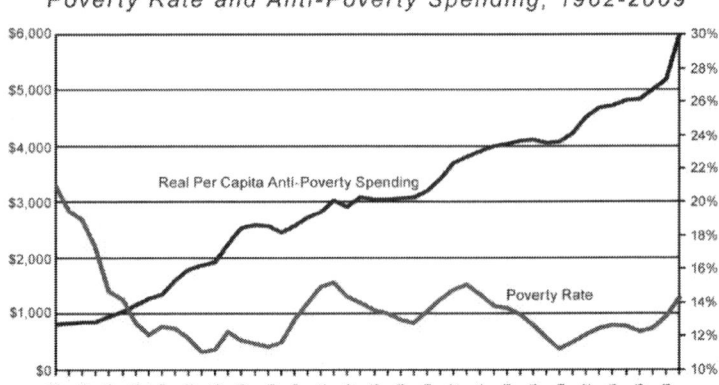

Poverty Rate and Anti-Poverty Spending, 1962-2009

Graphic From: *The War on Poverty*. 2013. Voice of Liberty. *Wichitalibrary.gov*. Dec. 23, 2013. Despite increased federal spending on Medicaid and other welfare programs, the U.S. poverty rate has remained steady, ranging from 10 to 15% for the last 50 years.

Operative Definitions:
1. **Poverty line:** A threshold set by the federal government, which varies depending on household size. If income falls below this threshold, the household is considered impoverished.

2. **Poverty rate:** The percentage of individuals living in impoverished households.
3. **Welfare:** Government assistance and benefits for those unable to meet the essential needs of living. Eligibility is often determined by level of income relative to the poverty line. The federal government operates more than 80 welfare programs.
4. **Housing Choice Vouchers (HCV):** Vouchers that enable low-income families to lease or purchase safe, decent and affordable rental housing.
5. **Supplemental Nutrition Assistance Program (SNAP):** A program that provides nutrition benefits to low-income families so that they can purchase healthy food.
6. **Universal Basic Income (UBI):** A government program in which every adult, regardless of employment status, receives a set amount of money on a regular basis. This basic living stipend will allow for every person to receive the fundamental goods and services necessary for life.

Important Statistics:
1. The 2021 poverty line for households of only one person is an income of $12,880 per year. Each additional person raises the threshold by $4,540. For example, the poverty line is set at $26,500 for families of four.
2. Over the past 20 years, the poverty rate has varied from 10.5% in 2019 to 15.1% in 2010.

6-Point Plan:
1. **Any increases to federal spending on economic security programs must be due to inflation only.**
   Any proposed expansion must be coupled with a decrease in spending elsewhere during regular economic periods, with

exceptions allowed during times of crisis, like the COVID-19 pandemic.

2. **Reform zoning regulations.**
Urban zoning regulations often make it illegal or expensive to build high-density structures. Issue discretionary tax breaks for allowing high-density housing or require a set percentage of high-density zones. This will decrease housing costs and increase housing security for low-income families. Promote planned communities with associated investment in public transportation and infrastructure.

3. **Tax acreage in urban residential zones rather than structures.**
Tax land at a rate four to five times higher than that of buildings to encourage high-density housing and allow individuals to live near work opportunities. This will also lead to increased funding for state economic security programs and public transportation systems.

4. **Expand housing subsidies in areas that implement the two prior reforms.**
Zoning reform without subsidies displaces low-income buyers. Using revenue from the tax proposed above to cover an additional $3 million with HCV, which will ensure that low-income recipients are housed in safe and decent environments.

5. **Reform SNAP to encourage healthy eating.**
Enact 30% subsidies on the purchase of produce by SNAP participants while expanding access to healthy foods in underdeveloped areas.

6. **Explore alternative methods of delivering welfare.**
   Contract out case management to reduce administrative errors, such as unclaimed welfare checks or those sent to deceased individuals. Similar errors occur in programs such as SNAP and HCV.

Why This Initiative is Important:
Reducing poverty will lower costs for related public program areas, such as healthcare, corrections and policing. This proposal is based on accurate data and survey results rather than idealisms, leading to sustainable and practical solutions. Increasing program efficiency will ensure less money is needed; increasing funding without reform is unreasonable. Promoting measures that prevent poverty, rather than outright dependence, will improve long-term solutions and help lower welfare spending in the future.

Economic Impact (from our student economist team):
- Meaningful numbers could not be calculated for this proposal.

To learn how our student economists came up with this economic impact, send an email to info@ournationalconversation.org and ask for a more thorough description of their methodologies.

Final Thought for Now:
"Today, for the first time in all the history of the human race, a great nation is able to make and is willing to make a commitment to eradicate poverty among its people." – **Lyndon B. Johnson (1964)**

Acknowledgments:
The following student(s) worked on this nonpartisan proposal: Marie Dishian, Centre College; Tim Antrim-Cashin, Columbia University.

The following individuals worked with our student interns and contributed expertise, wisdom and moral support in the development of this proposal:
1. Dave Newton, Ph.D.: Economist; Venture Consultant. Santa Barbara, CA.
2. Karen Dolan: Fellow, Institute for Policy Studies. Washington, DC.
3. Danilo Trisi, Ph.D.: Director of Poverty and Inequality Research, Center on Budget and Policy Priorities. Washington, DC.
4. Wade Killefer: Co-Founder, KFA Architecture, Los Angeles; President, AIA Los Angeles. Santa Monica, CA.

Note: Not all participants agree with every aspect of this proposal. To arrive at a proposal that takes multiple views into account implies compromise. To see their individual commentary on this proposal and more detail, go to OurNationalConversation.org. We invite you to add your comments, as well.

Sources:
De Wispelaere, Jurgen, and Lindsay Stirton. "The Administrative Efficiency of Basic Income." *Policy & Politics*, vol. 39, no. 1, Jan. 2011, pp. 115–132., https://doi.org/10.1332/030557311X546352. Accessed 8 Nov. 2021.

Schuetz, Jenny. "To Improve Housing Affordability, We Need Better Alignment of Zoning, Taxes, and Subsidies." *Brookings*, 16 Mar. 2020, https://www.brookings.edu/policy2020/bigideas/to-improve-housing-affordability-we-need-better-alignment-of-zoning-taxes-and-subsidies/.

Williams, Jeremy. "Should We Tax Land Instead of Buildings?" *The Earthbound Report*, 23 Apr. 2012, https://earthbound.report/2012/04/11/should-we-tax-land-instead-of-buildings/.

How to Save Social Security

Big Picture:
The U.S. Social Security program is not solvent and needs to be revised in order to survive. Social Security funds will nearly run dry by the middle of the 2030s. America must find effective methods of sustaining these funds for the generations to come.

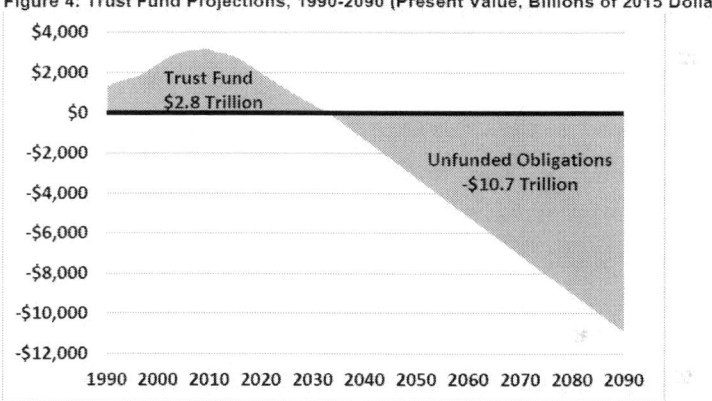

Graphic From: *Trust Fund Projections, 1990-2090 (Present Value, Billions of 2015 Dollars)*. Social Security Administration, CRFB calculations. *crfb.org*. 8 Sept. 2020. This figure illustrates the expected projection for the Social Security trust fund balance. As evident, Social Security will soon be unable to pay all retirees their full benefits unless lawmakers act.

Operative Definitions:
1. **Social Security:** A program created during FDR's administration in response to the Great Depression which provides retirement benefits, survivor benefits and disability income.
2. **Retirement age:** The age at which one is eligible to receive full Social Security retirement benefits, currently set at 66.

3. **Consumer price index (CPI)**: An index of the variation in prices paid by typical consumers for retail goods and other items.
4. **Chained CPI:** A variant of CPI that adjusts for changes in consumer behavior after the relative prices of goods change.

Important Facts and Statistics:
1. Social Security Revenue (2020): $1.118 trillion.
2. Social Security Benefits Paid (2020): $1.107 trillion.
3. Between 2000 and 2017, the CPI increased by 45.7%, while the chained CPI increased only 39.7%.

6-Point Plan:
1. **Gradually increase the retirement age.**
   Increase the retirement age from 66 to 69 by the year 2030. This will reflect demographic and life expectancy shifts, while giving individuals more time to plan accordingly.

2. **Remove the current cap on taxable earnings.**
   Currently, Social Security taxes are levied on earnings of up to $142,800 per year, with no Social Security taxes paid above this amount. Removing this cap and levying Social Security taxes on all earnings will extend Social Security solvency for 60 years. It will largely benefit low-income retirees by ensuring that they receive promised benefits to eliminate poverty.

3. **Eliminate federal and state taxes on Social Security benefits.**
   This will simplify the tax process for retirees, allowing them to enjoy retirement.

4. **Increase percentage of earnings contributions.**
   Increase worker contributions towards social security, from

6.2 % of earnings to 7.2% of earnings over the span of five years. This will provide the Social Security trust $715.5 billion over 10 years.

5. **Use progressive price indexing.**
    Benefits for low-income individuals will be constant over time, while benefits for high-income individuals will decline. By using progressive price indexing, low-income individuals will receive larger social security benefits than high earners.

6. **Transition from the Consumer Price Index to the chained CPI for calculating annual benefit increases.**
    This takes into account that consumers will tend to purchase cheaper substitute items in response to rising prices and is therefore a more accurate indicator of inflation.

Why This Initiative is Important:

Social security benefits are necessary for millions of Americans to purchase food and shelter. Over 64 million Americans received Social Security benefits in 2020, 80% of these being retirees. A sustainable Social Security system will be able to effectively address income inequality and racial disparities in elderly benefits. Improving Social Security protects the middle class since a majority of middle-class individuals aged 66 and older rely on Social Security to provide over half of their income. This initiative can prioritize Social Security benefits for Americans who need it the most and will keep the program sustainable for at least 60 more years.

Economic Impact (from our student economist team):
- Estimated effect on the annual federal deficit: - $113.35 billion.

To learn how our student economists came up with this economic impact, send an email to info@ournationalconversation.org and ask for a more thorough description of their methodologies.

Final Thought for Now:
"Should any political party attempt to abolish social security, unemployment insurance, and eliminate labor laws and farm programs, you would not hear of that party again in our political history." - **Dwight D. Eisenhower**

Acknowledgments:
The following student(s) worked on this nonpartisan proposal: Stella Bush, Emory University; Nidhi Nair, University of Connecticut; and a student who wished to remain anonymous.

The following individuals worked with our student interns and contributed expertise, wisdom and moral support in the development of this proposal:
1. Michael Campbell: Retired Administrator, University of California, Davis. Davis, CA.
2. Robert Asen: Professor of Rhetoric, Politics and Culture, University of Wisconsin; Author of "Invoking the Invisible Hand." Madison, WI.

Note: Not all participants agree with every aspect of this proposal. To arrive at a proposal that takes multiple views into account requires compromise and difficult decisions. For individual commentary on this proposal and more detail, go to OurNationalConversation.org. We invite you to add your comments as well.

Sources:

"Increase the Payroll Tax Rate for Social Security." *Congressional Budget Office,* December 13, 2018. www.cbo.gov/budget-options/2018/54805.

Konish, Lorie. "This is what the experts really want to see happen to fix Social Security." *CNBC,* 8 Dec. 2019, www.cnbc.com/2019/12/08/this-is-what-experts-really-want-to-see-happen-to-fix-social-security.html.

McMillan, Brad. "The Real Problem with Social Security." *Forbes,* 23 Apr. 2019, www.forbes.com/sites/bradmcmillan/2019/04/23/the-real-problem-with-social-security/#331d1ef4710b.

"Retirement Solutions." *Peter G. Peterson Foundation,* 9 Jun. 2022, www.pgpf.org/finding-solutions/retirement?utm_source=link&utm_medium=button&utm_campaign=lesson.

Shoffner, Dave. "Distributional Effects of Raising the Social Security Payroll Tax." *Social Security Administration,* Apr. 2010, www.ssa.gov/policy/docs/policybriefs/pb2010-01.html.

Starr, Paul. "Why We Need Social Security." *The American Prospect,* Feb. 2005, www.princeton.edu/~starr/articles/articles05/Starr-SocSec-2-05.htm.

Williams, Sean. "20 Ways to Fix Social Security, From the Logical to the Absolutely Insane." *The Motley Fool,* 19 Jun. 2017.

Mitigating Inflation

Big Picture:
The annual inflation rate that the Federal Reserve aims to maintain is one that hovers around 2%. As of August 2022, the annual inflation rate was 8.26%, based on the U.S. Bureau of Labor Statistics. The causes of the inflation we see today are complex, but some of the most glaring causes are increased discretionary government spending, the American economy opening back up post-COVID, corporate tax cuts and supply chain issues.

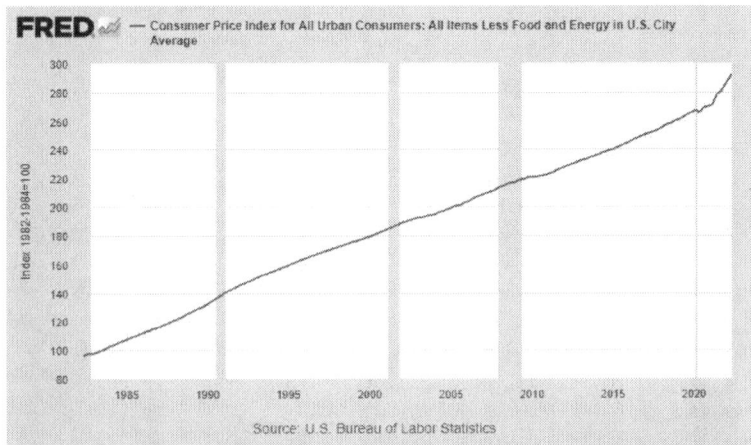

Graphic From: Federal Reserve Bank of St. Louis "Consumer Price Index for All Urban Consumers: All Items Less Food and Energy in U.S. City Average" Federal Reserve Bank of St. Louis. 8 Dec, 2021,

https://www.brookings.edu/blog/up-front/2021/11/16/what-does-current-inflation-tell-us-about-the-future/.

Operative Definitions:
1. **Inflation:** An increase in prices or fall in the purchasing power of a currency.

2. **Consumer Price Index:** The statistic the U.S. Bureau of Labor Statistics uses to determine inflation, based on the price changes of a set basket of goods.
3. **Federal Funds Rate:** The interest rate that financial institutions charge each other to loan money on a very short-term basis.
4. **The Federal Reserve:** A central banking system created in 1913 that is charged with the duties of maintaining low inflation and low unemployment through monetary policy.
5. **Open Market Operations:** A technique that the federal reserve uses to increase and decrease commercial banks' cash reserves by buying and selling bonds to and from them.
6. **Reserve Requirement:** The percentage of all deposits that commercial banks are required to hold. If the reserve requirement set by the Federal Reserve is 10%, then for every dollar consumers deposit in commercial banks, the banks can only lend out 90 cents of it and must hold 10 cents.

Important Facts and Statistics

1. As of August 2022, the rate of inflation was 8.26%, and the federal funds rate was 3 to 3.25%.
2. The current reserve requirement is 0%.
3. As of September 2022, the unemployment rate was 3.5%.

4-Point Plan

1. **The Federal Reserve should sell bonds to commercial banks, engaging in open market operations.**
   When the federal reserve sells bonds to commercial banks, the banks pay for the bonds, which are typically treasury bonds, from their reserves. Diminishing the reserves will encourage banks to charge higher interest rates on the loans they give out. While

higher interest rates slow economic growth, they are also a major combatant against inflation.

2. **Raise the reserve requirement.**
Until March of 2020, the reserve requirement set by the federal reserve was 10%, meaning that for every dollar that consumers placed in the bank, 10 cents must be held as reserves and cannot be given out as loans. Raising the reserve requirement back to 10% will decrease the overall availability of money, decreasing aggregate demand and lowering prices.

3. **Do not issue any more waves of stimulus checks.**
There are currently pushes both in Congress and among the public to have a fourth wave of stimulus checks. However, experts such as Ben Holland, an economic writer at Bloomberg, have written that such checks contributed to this massive inflation spike we are seeing today. The government and the people of the United States need to find ways of lowering unemployment and increasing economic involvement other than pumping the economy full of cash that is losing its value.

4. **Invest in America's supply chains.**
Another massive cause of inflation has been supply being unable to reach demand in many industries. This shortage is in part caused by failures in the supply chain and an overdependence on imports. Solutions such as raising wages of truck drivers, investing in America's ports, encouraging domestic manufacturing, and working to lower gasoline prices will make the supply chain more efficient, leading to decreased costs to consumers. As prices stabilize, inflation will decrease. These investments will come in the form of grants, with the money being given to companies

within the industries in the supply chain. This way the industry can still remain profitable, while still stabilizing prices.

Why This Initiative is Important

This country has not seen inflation above 7% since the late 1970s. Rising inflation makes the economy more difficult to predict, and more unstable. Inflation involving the dollar affects world markets as well because the dollar is the currency used in a large portion of foreign trade. Inflation is detrimental to Americans because their savings are losing effective purchasing power. The Federal Reserve's target inflation rate is one they believe will create sustainable growth and maintain a high level of employment.

Economic Impact

- Reducing inflation will hinder economic growth in the short term but create a more sustainable and stable economy in the future.
- These policies will bring inflation back down to the 2-3% level that is sought after by the Federal Reserve.
- Estimated effect on the annual federal deficit: + $58 billion.

To learn how our student economists came up with this economic impact, send an email to info@ournationalconversation.org and ask for a more thorough description of their methodologies.

Final Thought for Now:

"Inflation is as violent as a mugger, as frightening as an armed robber and as deadly as a hit man." – Ronald Reagan

Acknowledgments

The following student(s) worked on this nonpartisan proposal: Russell Reddecliff, University of Central Florida, FL; Michael Joseph, New Milford High School, NJ.

The following individuals worked with our student interns and contributed expertise, wisdom and moral support in the development of this proposal:
1. Glenn Lawrence: Supply Chain Manager, Hollingsworth & Vose. Wareham, MA.

Note: Not all participants agree with every aspect of this proposal. To arrive at a proposal that takes multiple views into account requires compromise and difficult decisions. For individual commentary on this proposal and more detail, go to OurNationalConversation.org. We invite you to add your comments as well.

Sources:

Amadeo, Kimberly. "How the Fed Controls Inflation." Edited by Robert C. Kelly, *The Balance*, 11 Nov. 2021.

Bragg, Bobby M. "2020 Stimulus Checks 1 & 2 - What You Need to Know for Your 202 Tax Return." *JMF*, JMF PC., 10 Feb. 2021.

Edelberg, Wendy. "What Does Current Inflation Tell Us about the Future?" *Brookings*, Brookings, 16 Nov. 2021. Holland, Ben. "U.S. Inflation Starting to Look Like a Stimulus-Led Outlier." *Bloomberg.com*, Bloomberg, 13 Sept. 2021, https://www.bloomberg.com/news/articles/2021-0 9-13/u-s-inflation-is-starting-to-look-like-a-stimulus-led-outlier.

Martínez-García, Enrique, et al. "Fed's New Inflation Targeting Policy Seeks to Maintain Well-Anchored Inflation Expectations." *Dallasfed.org*, Federal Reserve Bank of Dallas, 6 Apr. 2021, https://www.dallasfed.org/research/economics/20 21/0406.

Paton, Mike. "Buckle up: 3 Reasons Why Inflation Is Rising." *Forbes*, Forbes Magazine, 28 June 2021, https://www.forbes.com/sites/mikepatton/2021/06 /10/buckle-up-3-reasons-why-inflation-is-rising/?s h=691def192f80.

Infrastructure

"A modern, efficient highway system is essential to meet the needs of our growing population, our expanding economy, and our national security."

- Dwight D. Eisenhower

Rethinking Transportation in America

Big Picture:
The fabric of infrastructure in America is, both metaphorically and physically, crumbling. Years of neglect by policymakers, constituents and businesses have produced collapsing roads and bridges, outdated and hazardous buildings, and facilities in critical conditions across the country. The Biden Administration's recent Infrastructure Investment and Jobs Act has provided some much-needed funding, but more work still needs to be done. Compromised infrastructure systems harm the health and economy of the country. It is time to prioritize the physical network on which America functions.

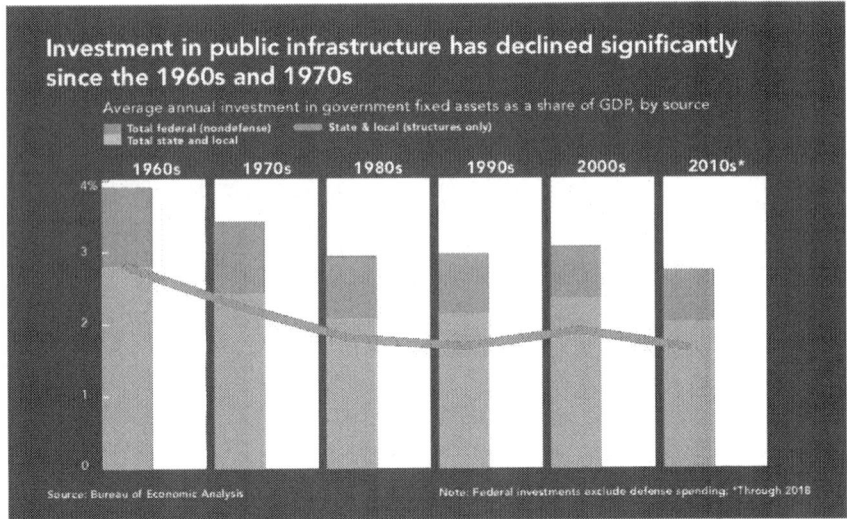

Graphic From: *Investment in public infrastructure has declined significantly since the 1960s and 1970s.* Bureau of Economic Analysis. *Ced.org.* 8 Sept. 2020. This figure illustrates the changes in government investment in infrastructure as a share of GDP since the 1960s. This number is measurably decreasing.

Operative Definitions:
1. **Transport infrastructure:** The framework that supports America's transportation system, which includes but is not limited to roads, railways, ports and airports.
2. **Private sector:** The part of the economy owned by private groups (usually as a means of enterprise for profit), rather than by the state.
3. **The American Society of Civil Engineers (ASCE):** Founded in 1852 and headquartered in Virginia, the first national-level society of engineers and the oldest professional society of engineers to date.
4. **The U.S. Department of Transportation (DOT):** The federal cabinet department of the U.S. government concerned with transportation. The DOT was established in 1966 under President Lyndon B. Johnson.
5. **Rebuilding American Infrastructure with Sustainability and Equity (RAISE):** Grant program which provides unique opportunities for the DOT to invest in infrastructure while expanding access to transportation across the country.
6. **Infrastructure Investment and Jobs Act:** Infrastructure package that included provisions related to the following programs of the Department of Transportation: federal-aid highway, transit, highway safety, motor carrier, research, hazardous materials, broadband access, clean water, electric grid renewal and rail. It was passed in November 2021 and signed into law by President Joe Biden.
7. **Value Capture:** A type of public financing that uses some (or all) of the value created by public infrastructure to help pay for the capital, debt service and/or operating costs of that infrastructure.

Important Facts and Statistics:
1. ASCE calculates that the U.S. needs to spend approximately $4.5 trillion by 2025 to fix the nation's roads, bridges, dams and other forms of infrastructure.
2. In 2021, the Infrastructure Investment and Jobs Act was passed, allocating $1.2 trillion to infrastructure projects. This is a great start, but it won't be enough, according to ASCE's calculations.
3. Over one-third of America's major roads are in poor or mediocre condition.
4. Approximately one-third of all highway fatalities are related to substandard road conditions, obsolete road designs or roadside hazards.

5-Point Plan:
1. **Revamp federal and state funding programs.**
   Dedicate $220 billion per year for 15 years to repair the country's bridges, tunnels and highways. This money will come out of the government's defense budget because crumbling infrastructure is a threat to national security in cases of invasion or insurgency. This means that the Army Corps of Engineers will work alongside the private sector in order to rebuild domestic infrastructure. Funding will go to state transportation departments, except when federal routes are involved. Mandate that states present comprehensive repair plans before receiving these funds.

2. **Attract further private sector funding.**
   Provide incentives for more private sector infrastructure financing. Increase the availability of funds (liquidity) from both domestic and international providers of capital, combining individual projects and providing a project portfolio to potential investors. Lastly, collectively address the governance and capability gaps that interfere with private sector investment.

3. **Leverage the ASCE Infrastructure Report Card in legislative decisions.**
These report cards will determine when and how to best spend federal funds. This organization stands at the forefront of civil engineering. As longtime advocates for the effectiveness of our nation's infrastructure, members of the ASCE examine current infrastructure models and conditions and provide critiques and recommendations on future projects.

4. **Improve funding models.**
In order to better finance the nation's infrastructure assets, policymakers should generate sustainable revenues with fair-usage charges and employ value capture strategies. Further, should the price of gas decline significantly from what it is as of May 2022, states should raise their gas taxes to improve infrastructure funding. Most states have not increased their gas tax rates in over a decade, resulting in losses of billions in transportation revenue. Should circumstances come to permit, gas taxes should be raised from 18.4 cents per gallon to 33.4 cents per gallon, which would produce an estimated $291 billion in revenue between 2023 and 2031.

5. **Give Amtrak a much-needed makeover.**
The railroad service will cut costly, long-distance routes and, instead, prioritize popular, shorter routes with better financial returns. This will save $233 million annually (based on federal spending in 2018), which will be used to support RAISE in cities that lose Amtrak services as a result of the implementation of these changes.

Why This Initiative is Important:
In August 2007, the I-35W bridge over the Mississippi River near downtown Minneapolis collapsed due to inadequate load capacity and design errors. As a result, 13 people lost their lives, and 145 people, including 22 children, were injured. More recently, in September 2021, an Amtrak passenger train carrying 154 passengers derailed west of Joplin, Montana on its way to Portland, Oregon. Consequently, 50 people were injured, and 3 were killed. While investigations are ongoing, rail experts suspect problems with the tracks themselves or with the wheels of the passenger train are to blame for this incident, as it has been confirmed that the train was traveling within the speed limit for the given area. These crumbling bridges, decaying roads and aging railway systems have taken a serious toll on human life. The DOT calculates that poor road designs and conditions influence approximately 14,000 highway fatalities every year. These design and condition flaws have economic effects as well. The Pacific Institute for Research and Evaluation found that injuries associated with poor road conditions cost at least $11.4 billion in 2013. It is only fair to conclude that, while the cost of repairing our nation's physical infrastructure is high, it is meager in comparison to the cost of experiencing further losses.

Economic Impact (from our student economist team):
- Increases in consumer spending will be matched by the savings provided by reduced traffic congestion and increased business growth, productivity and shipping revenue.
- Estimated effect on the annual federal deficit: $5.62 billion.

To learn how our student economists came up with this economic impact, send an email to info@ournationalconversation.org and ask for a more thorough description of their methodologies.

Final Thought for Now:
"Every citizen agrees with me that the need to bring our roads and streets up-to-date is urgent. The longer we wait, the greater the cost will be." – Harry Truman

Acknowledgments:
The following student(s) worked on this nonpartisan proposal: <u>Armin Jorgenson</u>, University of California, San Diego; <u>Joshua Ramos</u>, Texas Wesleyan University; <u>Courtney Clark</u>, Point Park University; <u>Christian Williams</u>, George Washington University.

The following individuals worked with our student interns and contributed expertise, wisdom and moral support in the development of this proposal:
1. <u>Nicholas Maldarelli</u>: Transit Route Planner, (confidential place of work).
2. <u>Wade Killefer</u>: Co-founder, KFA Architects. Santa Monica, CA.
3. <u>Jessie O'Malley Solis</u>: Program Manager, Transit Oriented Development Program, VTA (Valley Transportation Authority). San Jose, CA.
4. <u>Tamiko Percell</u>: Transportation Planner in Transit Planning & Capital Development, VTA (Valley Transportation Authority, San Jose, CA.

Note: Not all participants agree with every aspect of this proposal. To arrive at a proposal that takes multiple views into account requires compromise and difficult decisions. For individual commentary on this proposal and more detail, go to OurNationalConversation.org. We invite you to add your comments as well.

Sources:

Estevão, Marcello. "Making Infrastructure Investment More Attractive to Private Capital." *International Banker*, 1 Oct. 2018, internationalbanker.com/finance/making-infrastructure-investment-more-attractive-to-private-capital/.

"How Do Long Distance Trains Perform Financially?" *AMTRAK*, 2019 www.amtrak.com/content/dam/projects/dotcom/english/public/documents/corporate/position-papers/white-paper-amtrak-long-distance-financial-performance.pdf.

Hussain, Ali Abid, et al. "Unlocking Private-Sector Financing in Emerging-Markets Infrastructure." *McKinsey & Company*, 15 Oct. 2020, www.mckinsey.com/industries/private-equity-and-principal-investors/our-insights/unlocking-private-sector-financing-in-emerging-markets-infrastructure#.

Marshall, Aarian. "It's Not Just Clean Air: Electric Cars Can Save the US Billions." *WIRED*, 27 Oct. 2016, wired.com/2016/10/not-just-clean-air-electric-cars-can-save-us-billions.

"Public Transit New Starts Program: Issues and Options for Congress." *Congressional Research Service*, 5 Oct. 2010, www.everycrsreport.com/reports/R41442.html.

Schmitt, Angie. "Why We Need a Bus Shelter at Every Stop." *Street Blog USA*, 1 Oct. 2018, usa.streetsblog.org/2018/10/01/opinion-we-should-put-a-bus-shelter-at-every-stop-in-america/.

"U.S. Vehicle Registration Statistics." *Hedges & Company*, 2019. hedgescompany.com/automotive-market-research-statistics/auto-mailing-lists-and-marketing/

Creating Affordable Housing for the Future

Big Picture:
With a national housing shortage of 3.8 million units, extremely high construction costs and strict zoning requirements, America has an affordable housing crisis. The relatively few homes in development are too expensive for the average American, which affects citizens throughout both urban and rural communities. It is time to address this pertinent issue and increase national accessibility to houses.

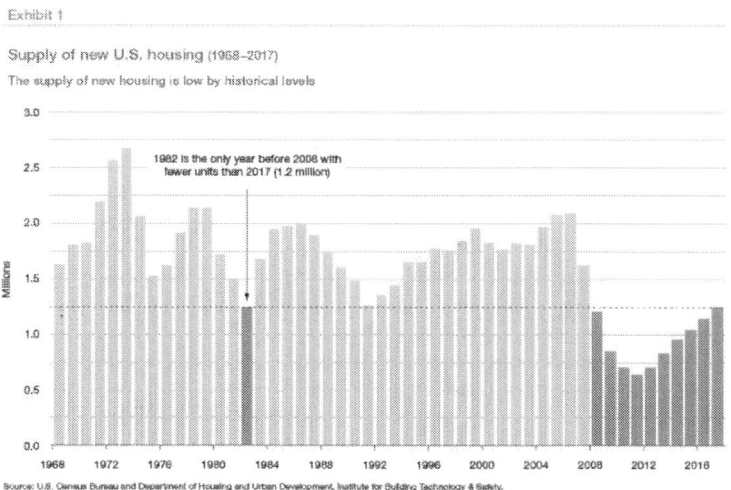

Graphic From: *Supply of new U.S. housing (1968-2017)*. U.S. Census Bureau and Department of Housing and Urban Development, Institute for Building Technology & Safety. This figure illustrates that the supply of new U.S. houses has been at record lows.

Operative Definitions:
1. **Redlining:** The historic and systemic denial of bank loans to predominantly Black and Brown communities. This has

historically impeded the ability to purchase houses and accumulate wealth and continues to do so.
2. **Zoning restrictions:** Regulations dictating what types of buildings and/or houses are allowed to be built in specific locations. Restrictions are usually decided at the local and municipal levels. Standard types of zoning include: residential (single-family, homesteads, apartments and co-ops), commercial and industrial.

Important Facts and Statistics:
1. According to data collected from Jan. 20 to Feb. 1, 2021, an estimated 13.2 million adults living in rental housing — nearly one out of every five home renters — were behind on rent.
2. Between 2000 and 2016, 61 million eviction cases were filed in the United States.
3. Across cities nationwide, people of color make up approximately 80% of those facing eviction.

5-Point Plan:
1. **Require state and local governments to impose a $2,500 vacant property tax.**
   If a property remains vacant for more than 100 days, then the owners will have to pay a $2,500 tax for every year that this is the case. This vacant property tax will raise $3.75 billion annually for states across the U.S. to fund affordable housing projects.

2. **Implement a reduced-tariff trade agreement for aluminum and lumber to lower home development costs.**
   In 2018, increases in tariffs on aluminum and lumber imports from Canada, Mexico and the European Union caused the prices of these materials to increase for construction companies. Additionally, the prices of these materials increased during the

COVID-19 pandemic. These costs burden consumers through increased housing prices. A trade agreement that scales back the Trump administration tariffs will drastically decrease the costs of these materials for construction companies, resulting in cheaper prices.

3. **Counties and cities should work with municipalities to relax zoning restrictions.**
Local and municipal zoning restrictions limit commercial and residential properties to very few areas. This interference in the market is preventing the supply of housing from meeting the demand. Since this problem is unique to each locality, cooperation between county and local governments is necessary to reach a consensus on how to relax zoning restrictions and create urban zoning areas near transit centers that allow for high-density housing. Doing so allows the supply of houses to meet the demand while reducing housing costs. Additionally, relaxing zoning restrictions, specifically in rural areas, will encourage rural development and help increase the population in rural areas.

4. **States and localities should provide tax breaks of up to 30% for landlords that reduce rental fees for tenants.**
States and localities will have discretion in determining eligibility and how much of a reduction in rental fees is required to receive certain tax breaks. If required to pay less, tenants will better be able to meet their rental payments, ultimately reducing the amount of rental assistance that the Department of Housing and Urban Development has to provide.

5. **Instruct local governments to run information campaigns in areas historically affected by redlining.**
   Many prospective homeowners, particularly in areas that have historically been affected by redlining, are discouraged by down payment prices. However, a recent survey found that 70% of Americans are unaware of available down payment assistance by state governments. Local governments should educate their citizens on these opportunities through local newspapers, media outlets and town hall meetings, inspiring people from underrepresented communities to buy houses.

Why This Initiative is Important:
This proposal will help improve almost all aspects of American lives. An increase in affordable housing will allow people to live closer to where they work, reducing transportation costs and improving job security. This lower commute time will then boost worker productivity while improving the economy. When individuals live closer to their work, they are able to spend more time with family and engage in leisure activities. Additionally, on a societal level, removing zoning restrictions will relieve overpopulation in large cities, as more people will be able to move to rural areas.

Economic Impact (from our student economist team):
- Housing makes up about 15% of America's GDP. It is necessary to further incentivize housing development, lower rent costs and increase environmental consciousness.
- Estimated effect on the annual federal deficit: - $4 billion.

To learn how our student economists came up with this economic impact, send an email to info@ournationalconversation.org and ask for a more thorough description of their methodologies.

Final Thought for Now:
"Most Americans want a decent home in a decent neighborhood for all. And so do I." – Lyndon B. Johnson

Acknowledgments:
The following student(s) worked on this nonpartisan proposal: Ashwin Prabu, Stanford University.

The following individuals worked with our student interns and contributed expertise, wisdom and moral support in the development of this proposal:
1. Ron Meyer: CEO, RMA consulting. Ashburn, VA.
2. Lynn Von Koch-Liebert: Deputy Secretary of Housing and Consumer Services, California Business, Consumer Services and Housing Agency. Sacramento, CA.
3. Wade Killefer: Co-founder, KFA Architecture. Santa Monica, CA.
4. Jessie O'Malley Solis: Program Manager, Transit Oriented Development Program, VTA (Valley Transportation Authority). San Jose, CA.
5. Tamiko Percell: Transportation Planner in Transit Planning & Capital Development, VTA (Valley Transportation Authority, San Jose, CA.

Note: Not all participants agree with every aspect of this proposal. To arrive at a proposal that takes multiple views into account requires compromise and difficult decisions. For individual commentary on this proposal and more detail, go to OurNationalConversation.org. We invite you to add your comments as well.

Sources:
"The COVID-19 Eviction Crisis: an Estimated 30-40 Million People in America Are at Risk." *The Aspen Institute*, 15 Sept. 2020, www.aspeninstitute.org/blog-posts/the-covid-19-eviction-crisis-an-estimated-30-40-million-people-in-america-are-at-risk/.

Cox-Khalfani, Lynnette. "Down payment assistance programs for all homebuyers." *HSH*, 4 Sept. 2015, www.hsh.com/finance/mortgage/down-payment-assistance-programs-for-all-homebuyers.html.

"Great Time for a Vacant Property Tax." *Center for Economic and Policy Research*, 26 Jun. 2020, cepr.net/great-time-for-a-vacant-property-tax/.

"How Zoning Shapes Our Lives." *Housing Matters*, 9 Jun. 2020, housingmatters.urban.org/articles/how-zoning-shapes-our-lives.

Irvine, Calif. "Nearly 1.5 Million Vacant U.S. Homes in Q3 2018 Represent 1.52 Percent of All Single Family Homes and Condos." *ATTOM Data Solutions*, 28 Oct. 2018, https://www.prnewswire.com/news-releases/nearly-1-5-million-vacant-us-homes-in-q3-2018-represent-1-52-percent-of-all-single-family-homes-and-condos-300739953.html

Passy, Jacob. "Trump's steel and aluminum tariffs may increase costs for home buyers and renters." *MarketWatch*, 31 May 2018, www.marketwatch.com/story/what-home-buyers-and-renters-need-to-know-about-trumps-steel-tariffs-2018-03-05.

Swanson, Jann. "Sluggish Construction Challenges the Housing Market." *Mortgage News Daily*, 6 Dec. 2018, www.mortgagenewsdaily.com/12062018_residential_construction.asp.

"Tracking the COVID-19 Recession's Effects on Food, Housing, and Employment Hardships." *Center on Budget and Policy Priorities*, 21 Aug. 2018, www.cbpp.org/research/poverty-and-inequality/tracking-the-covid-19-recessions-effects-on-food-housing-and.

Yale J., Aly. "Here's How Many New Homes It Would Take To Fix The Housing Shortage." *Forbes*, 20 Jan. 2020, www.forbes.com/sites/alyyale/2020/01/22/the-housing-shortage-is-badbut-heres-how-to-fix-it/#6ca9e70d1461

Building a Disaster-Resilient Infrastructure

Big Picture:
Our country faces numerous natural disasters every year, from fires to hurricanes to floods. Unfortunately, our responses to such crises are often inadequate and too reactive. It is time to think about how we can better prepare for natural disasters and make our infrastructure more resilient to their effects.

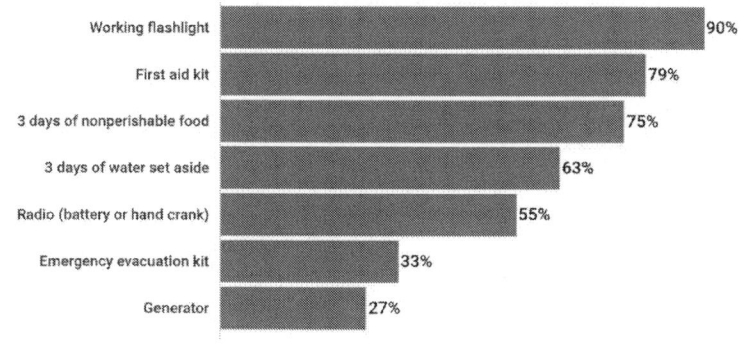

Whether consumers have key natural disaster supplies at home

Supply	%
Working flashlight	90%
First aid kit	79%
3 days of nonperishable food	75%
3 days of water set aside	63%
Radio (battery or hand crank)	55%
Emergency evacuation kit	33%
Generator	27%

Source: ValuePenguin survey of 1,577 consumers conducted in July 2022.

Graphic From: Davis, Maggie. "66% of Americans Don't Feel Fully Prepared for Natural Disasters, and 45% Don't Know if Their Insurance Covers Related Claims." *ValuePenguin*. 29 Aug. 2022. This graphic depicts how prepared U.S. residents are for natural disasters.

Operative Definitions:
1. **Federal Emergency Management Agency** (FEMA): A federal agency operating under the Department of Homeland Security. Created in 1978 under President Jimmy Carter and in charge of responding to major disasters such as fires, floods and hurricanes.

2. **Disaster Relief Fund:** The major funding source for FEMA, directed towards recovery and response efforts in areas affected by disasters.
3. **Digital Infrastructure:** Infrastructure and services that are necessary to a society's technological capabilities. Examples include broadband, cellular networks and data centers.

Important Facts and Statistics:
1. FEMA's fund-allocating approach is crafted around an "indicator," which is the minimum amount of money a state would have to spend per resident to qualify for FEMA aid. This indicator was tied to inflation rather than median incomes. But at the time of implementation (1999), the formula did not take into account inflation between 1986 and 1999. As a result, today's indicator is artificially low. THTH
2. It is estimated that only one fourth of cyberattacks get reported.
3. FEMA is underprepared for worst-case scenarios, largely due to the budget of the Disaster Relief Fund being dependent on the average yearly cost of previous disasters.
4. Congress appropriated $121.7 billion in relief for the 2005 (Katrina, Rita and Wilma) and 2008 (Gustav and Ike) hurricanes in 10 supplemental appropriations statutes.

4-Point Plan:
1. **Replace the FEMA indicator with a disaster deductible.**
   A disaster deductible would require states to invest in preparation through steps such as strengthening building codes and mitigating hazards. States would not receive FEMA aid until they make investments to reduce disaster damage. If state budgets are especially constrained, the disaster deductible may be replaced with measures such as updated building codes that take disasters into account (see point two). In these cases, state applications for

funding would be reviewed by FEMA in order to determine whether the actions taken are sufficient.

2. **Create more comprehensive building codes that take multiple kinds of disasters into account.**
   By expanding building codes, architects and builders will have a better understanding of what needs to be done to keep the building occupiers safe. Federal mandate will require these building codes to demonstrably take natural disasters into consideration, with states delineating the details beyond that. States may also incentivize building development companies, including those involved in housing, to produce disaster-resilient infrastructure beyond that required by the codes. This may be done through tax breaks, tax credits and/or partnership opportunities with government agencies. The details will depend on the circumstances of individual states. If state budgets are particularly limited, FEMA funding could be used to implement these measures.

3. **Increase funding for disaster-relief fund.**
   Rather than having to petition for emergency financial aid from Congress after natural disasters have already occurred, more money should be allocated to the Disaster Relief Fund through the federal budget.

4. **Incentivize companies to disclose cyberattacks.**
   Companies could be incentivized to comply through tax breaks and tax credits, as well as opportunities to access government-operated databases, so long as no privacy or security is breached. By providing incentives for companies to disclose cyberattacks, the federal government can build a database to better understand these attacks and develop preventive measures against future

security breaches. At this point in time, it is difficult for the government to stay ahead of digital attacks, as many companies decide not to report security breaches due to fear of public outcry.

Why This Initiative is Important:
As the number of natural disasters increases, we need strong, sound structures that can withstand extreme weather. In June 2021, the nation saw a glimpse of the damage daily, local elements such as salty air can do to old, failing infrastructure like the 40-year-old, leak-persistent Miami condominium which collapsed two years after a consulting report conveyed major structural damage, crushing 98 residents to death as they slept in their beds. The U.S. is underprepared for many of the natural disasters it faces. This initiative will ensure on-hand emergency funding and services, as well as aid in the prevention of natural tragedies, saving lives and millions of dollars in damages and repairs.

Economic Impact (from our student economist team):
- Disaster relief being more focused on state funding will save federal funds and decrease taxes for people in places where natural disasters are rarer.
- Increasing relief funding will help economies recover more quickly from disasters.
- Estimated effect on the annual federal deficit: - $5.1 billion.

To learn how our student economists came up with this economic impact, send an email to info@ournationalconversation.org and ask for a more thorough description of their methodologies.

Final Thought for Now:
"This new community center stands as a symbol of the extraordinary resilience of this city, the extraordinary resilience of its people, the extraordinary resilience of the entire Gulf Coast and of the United States of America." – Barack Obama, visiting New Orleans several years after Hurricane Katrina (2015)

Acknowledgments:
The following student(s) worked on this nonpartisan proposal: Regina Arroyo-Soto, University of Houston; Amanda Clegg, Texas A&M University; Ben Morris, Harvard University; Christian Williams, George Washington University; Ashwin Prabu, Stanford University; Sam Taylor, Brigham Young University.

The following individuals worked with our student interns and contributed expertise, wisdom and moral support in the development of this proposal:
1. Lynn Von-Koch Liebert: Executive Director of the California Strategic Growth Council, Sacramento.

Note: Not all participants agree with every aspect of this proposal. To arrive at a proposal that takes multiple views into account requires compromise and difficult decisions. For individual commentary on this proposal and more detail, go to OurNationalConversation.org. We invite you to add your comments as well.

Sources:
"13 Examples of Digital Infrastructure." *Simplicable*, 16 Oct. 2017, simplicable.com/new/digital-infrastructure.

Atkin, Emily. "America's Natural Disaster Response Is Its Own Disaster." *The New Republic*, 1 Sept. 2021, newrepublic.com/article/145019/americas-natural-disaster-response-disaster

"How Ready Are We? Natural Disaster or Emergency Preparedness." *United States Census Bureau*, 30 Apr. 2019, www.census.gov/library/visualizations/2015/comm/how_ready_are_we.html.

Frank, Thomas. "Why the U.S. Disaster Agency Is Not Ready for Catastrophes." *Scientific American*, Scientific American, 20 Aug. 2019, www.scientificamerican.com/article/why-the-u-s-disaster-agency-is-not-ready-for-catastrophes

De Vynck, Gerrit. "Many ransomware attacks go unreported. The FBI and Congress want to change that." July 27, 2021. https://www.washingtonpost.com/technology/202107/27/fbi-congress-ransomware-laws/

"Disaster Relief Fund: Monthly Reports." *FEMA*, 9 Jun. 2022, www.fema.gov/about/reports-and-data/disaster-relief-fund-monthly-reports.

Marcus, Ezra. "What Is FEMA Actually Responsible for?" *Mic,*, 6 May 2020, www.mic.com/p/what-is-fema-actually-responsible-for-22878301.

Social Issues

"The ultimate tragedy is not the oppression and cruelty by the bad people, but the silence over that by the good people."

- Martin Luther King, Jr.

Reforming Our Polarizing Media Landscape

Big Picture:

In addition to misinformation, or fake news, the polarized and biased nature of modern media commentary creates an unending, vicious cycle — one where the increasing levels of polarization and political discord feed into the rising degree of instability within our democratic system. The U.S. needs to address the issues of fake and polarizing news without undermining freedom of speech and our fundamental liberties.

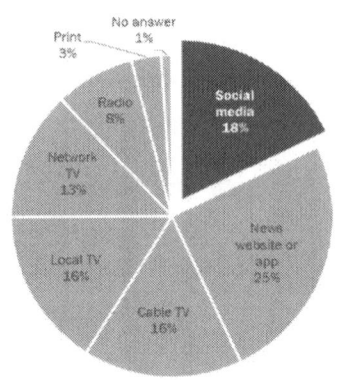

Graphic From: Pew Research Center. *"About two in ten adults get most of their political news on social media."* 28 July, 2020. This graphic indicates that social media is the second most common medium that adults rely on for their political news.

Let's Fix America

Operative Definitions:
1. **Political microtargeting:** The use of personal information, such as geographical location and interests, to tailor political advertisements.
2. **Section 230:** A part of the 1996 Telecommunications Act. Under this law, internet platforms are not legally responsible for what users post and can't be held liable for, in good faith, deleting or restricting access to anything that is deemed objectionable.
3. **Social media algorithms:** Algorithms that prioritize what social media users see in their feed. This is based on tracking their behavior and preferences.
4. **Transparency:** Disclosure of practices to consumers.
5. **Company immunity:** Protection from civil liabilities, like being sued, for internet service providers and social media companies that remove or restrict content that they deem as violent, harassment or obscene, to name a few.
6. **Content moderation:** The process of monitoring and regulating user-generated social media posts through the implementation of rules and guidelines.
7. **Federal Communications Commission (FCC):** An independent federal agency, established in 1974, that regulates the radio, television and phone industries. The goal of the FCC is to maintain standards and consistency across media and communications while protecting the interests of consumers and businesses.
8. **MediaWise:** A nonprofit and nonpartisan project of the Poynter Institute that teaches media consumers digital literacy and fact-checking skills. MediaWise initiatives directly impact all Americans.

Important Facts and Statistics:
1. In the 2019-20 presidential race, a total of $8.5 billion was spent on political advertising. $1.3 billion was spent on online ads, 59% of which went to Facebook.
2. Fake news spreads faster than true information. Falsehoods are 70% more likely to be retweeted on Twitter, reaching people six times faster.
3. In the U.S., those from the ages of 18 to 34 predominantly rely on social media for their daily news updates, while network news was the primary choice for those above the age of 65.
4. Fox News (at 16% of survey respondents) and CNN (at 12% of respondents) are the two most-named media outlets that Americans turn to for political news, according to Pew Research Center's study in late 2019.
5. Those who identify as Republican or Republican-leaning cited Fox News (93%) and ABC News (44%) as their primary sources for political and election news, while those who identify on the opposite side of the political spectrum cite MSNBC (95%) and New York Times (91%).

5-Point Plan:
1. **Address disclosure requirements for political advertising.**
Paid political messaging on platforms such as Facebook, Instagram and YouTube play a major role in campaigns and are not tied to the same regulations governing traditional advertising. Increase campaign finance transparency by ensuring advertisers of digital political ads disclose their identity and funding sources. Mandate archives of all past and current online political advertisements. Archives are to include digital copies of advertisements, a description of the targeted audience, number of views, dates and times of publication and rates charged for the ads in question.

2. **Reform Section 230 immunity and content moderation laws.**
   Amend Section 230 (c) (2)(a) in order to clarify some of the ambiguous language. Content moderation should be limited only to the following: 1) cyber-stalking, harassment and intimidation, 2) terrorism, 3) wrongful death actions, 4) defamation and 5) incitement to commit illegal acts. Preserve Section 230 protections for companies not contributing such materials and for companies engaged in reasonable content moderation. Clearly define the phrase "in good faith" to mean "without ill intent, attempting to further a demonstrably beneficial aim." This will ensure that if social media platforms purport to act "in good faith," they would potentially be held to a legal standard of proof. Establish that immunity doesn't extend to advertisements, as the provider has already directly accepted payment to host content.

3. **Increase transparency of content moderation programs.**
   Establish quarterly content reporting procedures from social media companies to the public and to government agencies with aggregate statistics describing content moderation programs; specifically, what content is being taken down and why. Users must also be given notice when content is taken down, with subsequent access to a robust appeals process. Allow researchers and regulators to access recommendations, content moderation, prioritization and advertising algorithms. Call for audits by independent companies to verify the accuracy of moderation and algorithm reports. This is essential to improve trust in media corporations.

4. **Build public awareness of media disinformation.**
   Allow all third-party fact checkers that pass a screening test (to make sure they can remain politically neutral) to fact-check material on registered social media platforms. This will form an unbiased and balanced check on content. Promote media bias charts such as Ad Fontes and All Sides to news consumers, educators, marketers, researchers and publishers. These charts are formed using a rigorous methodology and a balanced team of policy analysts. Partner with nonprofit and nonpartisan initiatives, like MediaWise, to educate people to be critical consumers of online content.

5. **Integrate digital literacy into public school curricula.**
   Lobby state policymakers to enact legislation supporting media literacy education in schools. Develop digital literacy K-12 curriculum in partnership with technology coordinators, policy specialists and local school districts. Curricula must align with standards and allow for proper assessment of students. Form expert committees and partnerships with media experts to advise education departments on the integration of digital literacy curricula. Create non-credit media literacy community college classes. Non-credit courses are financially supported by the state.

Why This Initiative is Important:
Though disinformation has been around forever, electoral disinformation has become an especially pressing issue since the 2016 foreign electoral intervention and the 2020 campaign. The need for regulation is underscored by the enormity of funds spent on political advertisements. There is also a legitimate concern that social platforms are not doing enough to control media content, leading to the unchecked spread of disinformation and to echo chambers of like-minded people. Social media transparency is needed to rebuild public

trust, and Section 230 is due for an update that strikes a balance between free speech protection and content moderation. As the new generation of thought leaders, students must be given as many tools as possible to navigate this fraught digital landscape.

Economic Impact (from our student economist team):
- Estimated effect on the federal deficit: + $60 million (one-time grant).
- Curbing fake news has various economic benefits, which include reducing stock market fluctuations, financial misinformation and election chaos.

To learn how our student economists came up with this economic impact, send an email to info@ournationalconversation.org and ask for a more thorough description of their methodologies.

Final Thought for Now:
"The democratic system is challenged by the failure in television because our evening news programs have gone for an attempt to entertain as much as to inform in the desperate fight for ratings." — Walter Cronkite (2000, BBC Hardtalk interview)

Acknowledgments:
The following student(s) worked on this nonpartisan proposal: Phyllis Feng, Centerville High School; Michelle Krolicki, California State University, San Bernardino; Diego Romero, Seton Hall University; Samuel Taylor, Brigham Young University.

The following individuals worked with our student interns and contributed expertise, wisdom and moral support in the development of this proposal:

1. <u>Tom Johnson:</u> Former Publisher, L.A. Times; retired President, CNN. Atlanta, GA.
2. <u>Luci B. Johnson:</u> President LBJ's daughter; Philanthropist; Businesswoman. Austin, TX.
3. <u>Myron Levin:</u> Founder and Editor, FairWarning. Los Angeles, CA.
4. <u>Leo Wolinsky:</u> Former Managing Editor, L.A. Times; Editor, Daily Variety; Board Member, CalMatters. Los Angeles, CA.
5. <u>Jerri Hogg:</u> Director of Media Psychology, Fielding Graduate University. West Hartford, CT.
6. <u>Christine O'Donnell:</u> Head, BrightSighted Podcasting; Former TV Reporter. Los Angeles, CA.
7. <u>Niraj Antani:</u> 42nd District, Ohio House of Representatives. Miamisburg, OH.
8. <u>Ruben Navarrette:</u> Syndicated Columnist. Carlsbad, CA.

Note: Not all participants agree with every aspect of this proposal. To arrive at a proposal that takes multiple views into account requires compromise and difficult decisions. For individual commentary on this proposal and more detail, go to OurNationalConversation.org. We invite you to add your comments as well.

Sources:

Carson, Andrea, et al. "Trust in quality news outlets strong during coronavirus pandemic." *The Conversation*, 17 May 2020, theconversation.com/trust-in-quality-news-outlets-strong-during-coronavirus-pandemic-138410.

Ellman, Matthew, and Fabrizio Germano. "Regulating for an independent media: The problems of political and commercial bias." *VOX EU*, 18 Sept. 2009, voxeu.org/article/reducing-media-bias-through-regulation.

"Legislation against fake news is open to abuses." *Financial Times*, 7 Apr. 2019, www.ft.com/content/b1d78fc2-57b4-11e9-a3db-1fe89bedc16e.

Meyer, Robinson. "The grim conclusions of the largest-ever study of fake news." *The Atlantic*, 8 Mar. 2018, www.theatlantic.com/technology/archive/2018/03/largest-study-ever-fake-news-mit-twitter/555104/.

Robinson, Nathan. "Media bias is OK if it's honest." *The Guardian*, 10 Sept. 2019, https://www.theguardian.com/commentisfree/2019/sep/10/media-bias-is-ok-if-its-honest.

Let's Fix America

Incentivizing National Service

Big Picture:
Voluntary national service programs offer experiential opportunities for individuals and create infrastructure and education improvements around the nation. Boosting America's current small-scale commitment to volunteerism will boost gross domestic product (GDP) and help mitigate some of the country's most pressing issues.

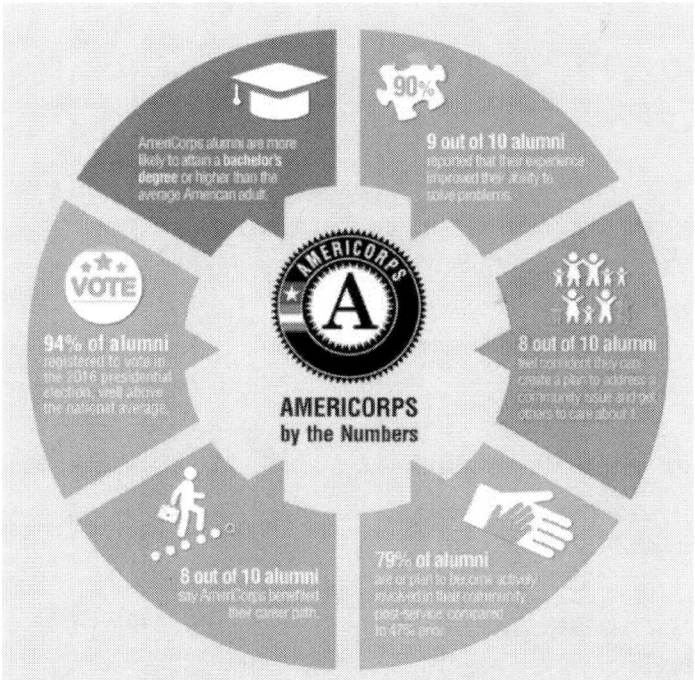

Graphic From: *National Service Benefits for the Youth.* Youth.gov. 2016. This graphic highlights six different benefits for joining AmeriCorps. That said, some 'benefits' may actually be explained by the fact that youth who join AmeriCorps were already more politically active and academically motivated than the average citizen.

Operative Definitions:
1. **Gross domestic product (GDP):** Total monetary value of all the finished goods and services a country produces within a specific time frame.
2. **National service:** Systems that facilitate government projects. In the context of this proposal, national service refers to voluntary community-based initiatives.
3. **AmeriCorps:** A voluntary civil society program funded by the federal government and comprised of various national service organizations. AmeriCorps connects volunteers with community-based nonprofits and public agencies.
4. **Segal AmeriCorps Education Award:** A monetary award which can be put towards paying tuition. For a full year of service through AmeriCorps, a person will be eligible for an award equal to the maximum value of the Pell Grant that year.
5. **Teach For America (TFA):** An organization that provides low-income communities across the country with education.
6. **Student Loan Forgiveness Program:** A program in which students are no longer required to make loan payments due to certain circumstances.
7. **The Bureau of Population, Refugees, and Migration:** This bureau serves as a humanitarian branch that works to assist refugees and migrants.

Important Facts and Statistics:
1. Interest in taking a gap year between high school and post-secondary education is growing. Gap years provide time for experiential learning and skill-building. Nearly half of all American students say they want to take a gap year in which they would volunteer.

2. TFA currently has a network of 5,450 members and 58,000 alumni. Encouraging involvement in TFA allows people to establish bonds within a professional web.

5-Point Plan:
1. **Launch a targeted outreach campaign.**
   The first step in standardizing national service is to establish a national marketing initiative, advertising national service as a top priority and attracting new members. Develop a youth public service division to encourage volunteering at a young age. Merge this division with the public school system in order to promote localized volunteer service across the country. If demand increases, Congress should appropriate additional funds to AmeriCorps, the centerpiece of American national service.

2. **Expand TFA from 5,400 members to 10,000 or more.**
   An increased TFA workforce expands education resources available to disadvantaged localities. More teachers assisting in education will benefit the economy by furthering the English, math and science skills within America's next generation of workers. This also directly benefits educators through exposure to diverse community settings.

3. **Expand the AmeriCorps national service organization.**
   With increased marketing and funding, AmeriCorps' full-time membership is expected to increase from 75,000 members to 200,000 within a decade. Establish new branches of AmeriCorps dedicated to natural disaster preparation and response, infrastructure development — including renewable energy — and community-based initiatives like geriatric care and homelessness. Reduce the amount of administrative paperwork that makes it more difficult for applicants to receive AmeriCorps

funding. Create a greater incentive to serve in AmeriCorps by offering volunteers with educational courses in relevant areas of study and workshops in various life skills. Currently, AmeriCorps offers Segal AmeriCorps Education Awards to its members, allowing them to repay loans or pay for college or trade school. Expand the Student Loan Forgiveness Program. One year of national service will be exchanged for a year of in-state university tuition.

4. **Keep total national service expansion costs to under $20 billion over the next 10 years.**
   America's Department of Defense is allotted $636 billion per year as of July 2021. An average of $2 billion a year is a small price to pay for a healthier, cleaner and more educated society. Keeping the cost under $20 billion will not put a significant financial burden on the federal government while allowing for national service expansion.

5. **Establish a human resources department within AmeriCorps dedicated to achieving diversity and inclusivity among volunteers.**
   This branch will focus on diversity and inclusivity amongst volunteers and team leaders to maximize social cohesion, as well as to help immigrants adjust to life in America. Because increased marketing and incentives will draw diverse populations to AmeriCorps, expanded volunteerism holds the potential of bringing various ethnic groups together. The Bureau of Population, Refugees, and Migration must connect immigrants and able-bodied refugees with civilian national service opportunities.

Why This Initiative is Important:
Expanded AmeriCorps programs will locally address the growing need to care for the aging "Baby Boomer" population, a phenomenon that will devastate the American economy if not confronted. An expansion of national service will increase GDP because future workers will develop professional skills, become more educated and gain valuable work experience. Expanded loan forgiveness programs will challenge the mounting student debt crisis and improved social cohesion will result in diverse volunteering groups collaborating on community initiatives.

Economic Impact (from our student economist team):
- Estimated effect on the annual federal deficit: - $20 billion

To learn how our student economists came up with this economic impact, send an email to info@ournationalconversation.org and ask for a more thorough description of their methodologies.

Final Thought for Now:
"Ask not what your country can do for you — ask what you can do for your country." - **John F. Kennedy (1961)**

Acknowledgments:
The following student(s) worked on this nonpartisan proposal: John Strezewksi, Johns Hopkins University; Marianne Swan, State University of New York College at Oneonta; Lucas King, Washington and Lee University.

The following individuals worked with our student interns and contributed expertise, wisdom and moral support in the development of this proposal:

1. <u>Leslie Lenkowsky, Ph.D.</u>: Professor Emeritus of Public and Environmental Affairs, Indiana University. Bloomington, IN.
2. <u>Barbara Stewart</u>: Former CEO, AmeriCorp. Washington, DC.
3. <u>Richard Harrill, Ph.D.</u>: Professor of Hospitality and Tourism, University of South Carolina. Chapel Hill, NC.

Note: Not all participants agree with every aspect of this proposal. To arrive at a proposal that takes multiple views into account requires compromise and difficult decisions. For individual commentary on this proposal and more detail, go to OurNationalConversation.org. We invite you to add your comments as well.

Sources:

"Member Race and Ethnicity National Figures." *AmeriCorps.* 2020, https://data.americorps.gov/National-Service/AmeriCorps-Member-Race-and-Ethnicity-National-Figu/as6e-6nns/data

"Gap Year Volunteering." *Student Training & Education in Public Service.* Aug. 2020, .https://www.publicservicedegrees.org/volunteering/for-a-gap-year/

"Who We Are." *Teach For America.* 9 Jun. 2022, https://www.teachforamerica.org/what-we-do/who-we-are

Combating Homelessness in America

Big Picture:

Homelessness in the U.S. has reached a critical point. Major cities throughout the U.S. are seeing record homelessness rates, all worsened by the COVID-19 pandemic. This proposal envisions providing assistance and affordable housing without making people perpetually dependent on federal or state governments.

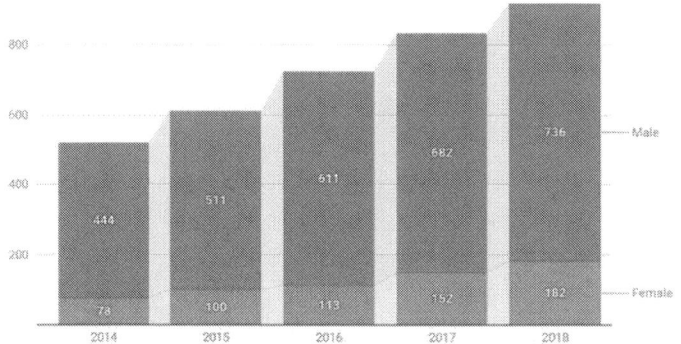

Graphic From: Gorman, Anna and Harriet Blair Rowan. "The Homeless Are Dying In Record Numbers On The Streets Of L.A." *Kaiser Health News.* 24 Apr. 2019. This figure illustrates the increase in death of homeless citizens, both male and female. This particular figure focuses specifically on statistics collected from Los Angeles County, California.

Operative Definitions:
1. **Sheltered Homeless:** Homeless Americans who live in shelters instead of on the street or in encampments.
2. **Unsheltered Homeless:** Homeless Americans who live outside of shelters.
3. **Continuum of Care:** A program run by the Department of Housing and Urban Development that designates money for nonprofit organizations, state governments and local governments to provide care and housing for homeless people, with a specific focus on "self-sufficiency."
4. **Open Space Area:** In this proposal, an open space area is defined as a publicly accessible area overseen and maintained by the government and government contractors.

Important Facts and Statistics:
1. It is estimated that, at any given point in time, around 500,000 Americans are homeless, with a 30% increase in the number of unsheltered homeless since 2015.
2. Homeless Americans have a life expectancy of 50 years, which is nearly 30 years less than that of average Americans.
3. An estimated 13,000 homeless Americans die from poor living conditions each year, although death tolls vary depending on infrastructure and reporting.
4. The federal government spends $6 billion on homelessness programs annually, with individual states also spending billions of dollars. Despite the funding being poured into homelessness' eradication, the U.S. has only seen a 10% decline in homelessness since 2007, and a 1% decline in individual (i.e. non-family) homelessness since 2007.
5. Larger cities, such as Los Angeles, report a 70% incidence of drug addiction in monitored homeless populations.

3-Point Plan:
1. **Appoint a homelessness coordinator in city and local governments.**
The coordinator would be responsible for overseeing the cooperation of private contractors, government officials and civil service workers on projects aimed at addressing local homelessness. The coordinator would advocate for the provision of affordable housing and health services, and would be vested with the power to take legal action against the city if its programs are not up to par, with legally-binding goals set on the state level. Vesting these powers in a single, local individual with expertise in contracting, construction and civil service would reduce bureaucratic hold-ups that cause homelessness programs to be halted. The coordinator would also be responsible for overseeing efforts to reduce stigma against homeless populations, which can stifle homelessness alleviation projects. The coordinator would be appointed by the mayor or the highest executive figure within the relevant local government.

2. **Use city and local agencies to further encourage developers to construct affordable housing.**
City and local governments must place priority on incentivizing housing developers to produce cheap but functional housing. One way to achieve this is to put a cap on the cost of building within certain areas, naturally reducing the price of associated housing. Affordable housing could be pushed along even further as city and local governments, and higher levels of government as deemed necessary, offer tax credits, grants and rental assistance to developers and new homeowners. Government agencies can also redefine tax credits for housing developers, requiring that a higher percentage of developed housing (e.g. 10% as opposed to 5%) is adequately affordable for the developer to qualify for the

tax credit. Additionally, the bureaucracy surrounding affordable housing construction must be reduced. The longer it takes to construct housing, the more expensive the housing becomes. Many states require 10 to 15 housing inspections before completion. This should be simplified to two or three inspections at different stages in the housing development, ensuring homeowner safety without needlessly increasing costs.

3. **Prioritize mental health and addiction services.**
   This initiative highlights the need for mental health and addiction services. All levels of government, especially city and local levels, must place emphasis on assisting those with mental illnesses and addictions that inhibit self-sufficiency. Counseling and rehabilitation services would be provided in the affordable housing areas discussed under point two, as coordinated by the coordinator discussed under point one. Prevention services would also be provided to decrease the number of homeless individuals who engage in substance abuse or who develop mental illness.

Why This Initiative is Important:
Fighting homelessness is vital to the humanitarian needs of the U.S. The homelessness that grips our cities *can be solved*, but this effort will require the combined services of government officials, business owners, philanthropists and the general public. Only then can we solve, or at least make great strides in combating, the problem of American homelessness.

Economic Impact:
1. The average cost of job training for a single homeless participant is $1,485.
2. Estimated effect on the annual federal deficit: + $7.926 billion

To learn how our student economists came up with this economic impact, send an email to info@ournationalconversation.org and ask for a more thorough description of their methodologies.

Final Thought for Now:
"The test of our progress is not whether we add more to the abundance of those who have much; it is whether we provide enough for those who have too little." – **Franklin D. Roosevelt (1937)**

Acknowledgments:
The following student(s) worked on this nonpartisan proposal: Alex Joplin, University of North Georgia; Sam Taylor, Brigham Young University.

The following individuals worked with our student interns and contributed expertise, wisdom and moral support in the development of this proposal:

1. Barry Gittleman: President and CEO at Hamlet Homes, Salt Lake City, UT.
2. Elizabeth Baker: Chief Strategy Officer at the Other Ones Foundation, Austin, TX.

Note: Not all participants agree with every aspect of this proposal. To arrive at a proposal that takes multiple views into account requires compromise and difficult decisions. For individual commentary on this proposal and more detail, go to OurNationalConversation.org. We invite you to add your comments as well.

Sources:
"Continuum of Care (COC) Program." *HUD Exchange*, 9 Jun. 2022, https://www.hudexchange.info/programs/coc/.

Hall, Jeff. "A 22-Point Plan to Deal with LA's Homelessness Situation." *Brentwood News*, 10 May 2021, https://brentwoodnewsla.com/a-22-point-plan-to-deal-with-las-homelessness-situation/.

Lucas, David S. "From the Bottom Up: Rebuilding Federal Homelessness Policy." *Syracuse University*, 2019.
"Mortality Archives." *National Coalition for the Homeless*, 9 Jun. 2022, https://nationalhomeless.org/category/mortality/.
"Homelessness Statistics in the US for 2021: Policy Advice." *PolicyAdvice*, 5 Mar. 2022, https://policyadvice.net/insurance/insights/homelessness-statistics/.
"The Cost of Affordable Housing: Does It Pencil out?" *UrbanInstitute,* 9 Jun. 2022, https://apps.urban.org/features/cost-of-affordable-housing/.
"The State of Homelessness 2021." *Endhomelessness.org.* 9 Jun. 2022, https://endhomelessness.org/wp-content/uploads/2021/07/NAEH_StateOfHomelessness2021-VizPrintable.pdf

Let's Fix America

New Foundations for K-12 Public Education

Big Picture:
The current K-12 public education system is failing the American public. It neglects students of low socioeconomic status, rendering underfunded schools unable to adequately prepare America's youth for the working world. Improving the systemic and monetary foundations of our education system will address the widening gap between high and low-performing schools, and ultimately ensure that Americans can better compete on the global stage.

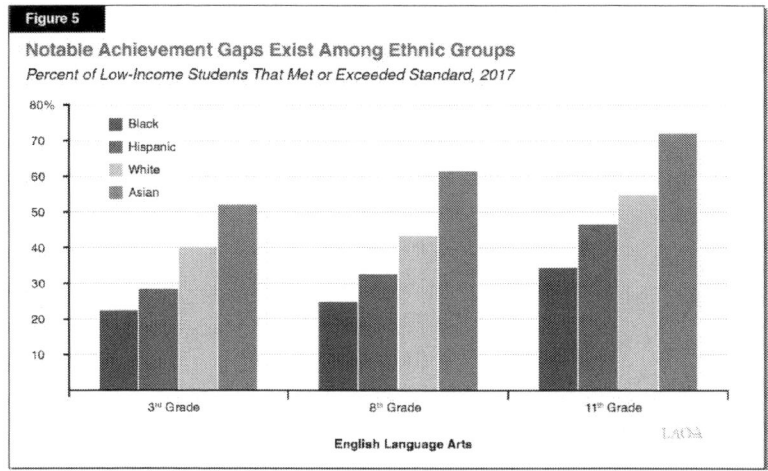

Graphic From: *Notable Achievement Gaps Exist Among Ethnic Groups.* 2018. LAO Report. *Lao.ca.gov.* 8 Sept. 2020. This graph illustrates the drastic achievement gaps between low-income Asian, white, Hispanic and black students in English language arts in three different age groups.

Operative Definitions:
1. **Federal tax credit:** A type of credit that reduces the amount of income owed to federal and state governments.
2. **Title I of the Elementary and Secondary Education Act (ESEA) of 1965 funds:** Funds that provide financial assistance

to local educational agencies for children who come from low-income families. The majority of Title I funds are allocated at the district level through four grants.
3. **Title II of ESEA:** A U.S. Department of Education grant program that provides supplemental funding to strengthen the quality and effectiveness of teachers, principals and other school leaders.
4. **Low-performing schools:** Schools that are categorized by low scores on standardized tests, as well as low graduation and high dropout rates.
5. **High-needs schools:** Schools that fall under one or more of the following three classifications: 1) more than 30% of the school population comes from low-income families, 2) the school has more teaching vacancies than 75% of schools statewide and 3) a high percentage of teachers are teaching outside of their field and/or lack teaching credentials.
6. **High-stakes testing:** A test in which the consequences are crucial. Passing a high-stakes test has important benefits.
7. **Performance assessments:** Alternative assessment models that require students to demonstrate their unique knowledge and skills through a performance task, as opposed to standardized tests in which all students are given the same exam.
8. **Science, Technology, Education and Math (STEM) skills:** Expertise in numeracy, data analysis and communication, problem-solving, ingenuity and reasoning.
9. **English as a Second Language (ESL):** Classification for students who are learning English as their second language within the K-12 education system.
10. **Teacher Loan Forgiveness Program:** A program administered by the Federal Student Aid division within the U.S. Department of Education that provides up to $17,500 in loan forgiveness for

practitioners teaching full-time for five consecutive years at low-income schools or educational service agencies.
11. **Culturally Responsive Teaching:** A pedagogy that includes students' cultural differences in all aspects of teaching and gives equitable access to education for students from all cultures.
12. **National Board for Professional Teaching Standards (NBPTS):** An independent, nonprofit organization seeking to improve the quality of teaching for all students.

Important Facts and Statistics:
1. If the national graduation rate was increased from 83% to 90%, the GDP would increase by over $5.5 billion for every year that this stayed consistent.
2. The average student loan debt of educators stands at around $55,000 as of July 2021; of those who remain in debt as of this time, around 14% owe $105,000 or more in student debts.
3. Public school teachers make 19.2% less in comparison to other workers with an equivalent amount of education.
4. Black and Hispanic children have lower achievement and graduation rates than white children due to them being twice as likely to live in poverty than their white counterparts.
5. K-12 total annual standardized testing costs states $1.7 billion per year.

8-Point Plan:
1. **Establish new school funding models with existing funds.** There is no standard method for allocating money to schools, resulting in disparate funding inequities and funding formulas. State districts should implement a system in which a fixed percentage of district resources is directly given to schools. Districts will start with 10% and increase by five to 10% each year until roughly two-thirds of district funds go directly to schools.

To flatten funding disparities, redistribute school funding coming from local property taxes. Assist K-12 schools with identifying available grants for which they qualify, and partner districts with local employers that provide students with professional development skills.

2. **Provide educators with additional resources.**
Use the federal tax code to create a $10,000 refundable federal teacher tax credit for teachers in low-income school districts, increasing wages by $192 per week. Simplify loan forgiveness program guidelines to ease the process in which teachers determine eligibility and expand the existing Teacher Loan Forgiveness Program to cover private loans and part-time teachers. Provide ongoing professional development support, through Title II ESEA funds, specifically in remote education environments, with a particular focus on teachers at high-needs schools.

3. **Address inequities at high-needs schools.**
Distribute Title I ESEA funds to low-income school districts and verify budget plans before granting funds to ensure proper utilization. Incentivize teacher recruitment, retention and equitable teacher assignments with a federal tax credit. Promote NBPTS financial incentives across all states for teachers at high-needs schools. Reduce food insecurity by supplementing federal programs with funding from school initiatives and private programs. This will improve reading and math performance levels, as well as school attendance and graduation rates.

4. **Reform standardized testing and student assessment.**

High-stakes standardized testing holds school districts and students accountable by directly influencing teacher pay and student funding. Shift the focus away from high-stakes testing and employ alternatives such as performance assessments. Implement a robust low-stakes measurement system that evaluates statistically representative samples of students, liberating funding directed toward standardized testing, and delink merit-based pay for teachers from standardized test scores.

5. **Implement STEM and ESL initiatives.**
Increase STEM initiatives through public-private partnerships and support the development of early-childhood STEM initiatives. American students are consistently outperformed by their international peers in STEM. Recruit undergraduate and graduate students majoring in STEM-related areas of study to consider applying for K-12 teaching positions. This will boost STEM engagement and participation within the education system, while instilling relative skills in children from an early onset. Build the supply of qualified bilingual teachers for dual language programs by establishing alternative certification pathways, by recruiting teachers from abroad and by partnering with teacher preparation programs. Establish peer mentorship programs to assist newcomers' assimilation to our country and its cultural norms. More often than not, children identify feeling lonely and out of place when going through life-changing events, such as moving to unfamiliar environments. Not only can this create additional leadership opportunities for students, but it can also significantly alleviate the struggles for newcomers to our country by having a bond with a peer mentor who understands their native tongues and cultures, or at least recognizes the difficulties of this transition.

6. **Strengthen collaborations with local art organizations.**
Though public support for arts programs in schools has grown significantly in recent years, budgets for these programs are still often the first to be cut when resources become scarce. As personnel costs often account for most of the expenses, promoting collaborations with local arts organizations can reduce the necessity for additional hires while allowing students to gain valuable knowledge and experiences. A set portion (which should be predetermined based on availability and quality of resources in each school and their respective communities) of funds should be allocated to facilitating and enhancing this partnership between schools and organizations.

7. **Incorporate family and community into public education.**
1% of Title I, Part A ESSA funds are allocated for parent engagement initiatives. Maintain these funds and ensure school districts submit parent engagement best practice plans to state education agencies. Hire technology advisers to improve web-based platforms supporting parent-teacher communication. Advisers will keep costs down for low-income schools without adequate resources. Expand teacher training programs for community engagement and parent communication, specifically for English language learners and racially diverse and low-income student populations. Specifically, it is necessary to expand Teach for America (TFA) to aid in training and engagement programs for low-income communities. Statewide Family Engagement Center (SFEC) Program grants are available for parent education and family training. Teachers, nurses and trained parent educators should conduct home visits with K-12 students to build community. Head Start provides home visits to children from birth to age 5 and can serve as a model for program expansion. Boost internet bandwidth and digital device access to low-income

students to address learning disparities. Utilize CARES (Coronavirus Aid, Relief, and Economic Security) Act funds and create partnerships with the private sector.

8. **Incentivize "underperforming" schools to improve outcomes.**
Recognizing that the disproportionate number of resources and funding schools have access to is a major factor that has led to the current circumstances, the allocation of funds should be assessed by education authorities to determine what each "underperforming" school is lacking and/or how the money can be better spent. Additionally, if these schools were to be able to improve outcomes, additional funding can be given as a reward. Details as to what constitutes meaningful improvement (i.e. increases in students' standardized test scores) and how long the improvement should last to be considered successful should be determined beforehand, with the help of education authorities and experts of the field.

<u>Why This Initiative is Important:</u>
Education must be prioritized due to its essential role in building the foundations of success, improving the standards of living for all Americans and remaining competitive on the global stage. This proposal suggests alternate funding models, allocating resources for low-performing schools and advising them on how to make the most out of existing budgets, further increasing graduation rates. In order to increase recruitment and retention of teachers, teacher debt and pay must also be addressed. Additionally, this proposal highlights STEM skill-building and teacher recruitment in order to account for anticipated increases in STEM job growth.

Economic Impact (from our student economist team):
- Estimated effect on the annual federal deficit: + $15 billion.
- The infusion of resources into K-12 education will be instrumental in the continued development of human capital, innovation and transmission of knowledge.

To learn how our student economists came up with this economic impact, send an email to info@ournationalconversation.org and ask for a more thorough description of their methodologies.

Final Thought for Now:
"Each child matters. Every child has potential..." — **George W. Bush (2006)**

Acknowledgments:
The following student(s) worked on this nonpartisan proposal: Santiago M. Rodriguez, University of Redlands; Royce Williams, University of California, Davis; Michelle Krolicki, California State University, San Bernardino; Marianne Swan, State University of New York College at Oneonta; Deja Jackson, Lafayette College.

The following individuals worked with our student interns and contributed expertise, wisdom and moral support in the development of this proposal:
1. Dawnelle Hyland: CEO of Senior Training and Learning Consultant, Align Leadership; Co-Founder and Executive Director, Trainer Designs Global. Raleigh-Burham, NC.
2. Jo Napolitano: Freelance Writer, Argonne National Laboratory; Author. Brooklyn, NY.
3. Keith Osajima: Professor of Race and Ethnic Studies, University of Redlands. Redlands, CA.

4. <u>Eesir Kaur:</u> Director of Schools, Rocketship Public Schools. Redwood City, CA.
5. <u>Natalie Wexler:</u> Senior Contributor, Forbes; Author. Washington, DC.
6. <u>David Rogers:</u> Faculty Director of Digital Business Strategy, Columbia Business School; Author and Consultant, Digital Transformation Playbook. New York, NY.

Note: Not all participants agree with every aspect of this proposal. To arrive at a proposal that takes multiple views into account requires compromise and difficult decisions. For individual commentary on this proposal and more detail, go to OurNationalConversation.org. We invite you to add your comments as well.

Sources:

Allegretto, S. & Mishel, L. "Teacher pay penalty dips but persists in 2019." *Economic Policy Institute*, 17 Sept., 2020 https://www.epi.org/publication/teacher-pay-penalty-dips-but-persists-in-2019-public-school-teachers-earn-about-20-less-in-weekly-wages-than-nonteacher-college-graduates/

Bahn, K., Benner, M., Johnson, S. & Roth, E. "How to give teachers a 10,000 raise. *Center for American Progress*. 13 Jul. 2018 https://www.americanprogress.org/issues/education-k-12/reports/2018/07/13/453102/give-teachers-10000-raise/

Boyle, A., August, D., Tabaku, L., Cole, S., & Simpson-Baird, A. "Dual Language Education Programs: Current State Policies and Practices." *U.S. Department of Education Office of English Language Acquisition.* Dec. 2015, https://www.air.org/sites/default/files/downloads/report/Dual-Language-Education-Programs-Current-State-Policies-April-2015.pdf

Briggs, S. "8 Alternatives to High-Stakes Standardized Tests. informED." 21 Nov. 2015, https://www.opencolleges.edu.au/informed/features/8-alternatives-to-standardized-testing/

Clark, C. & Laurence, T. "Exploring alternatives for school-based funding." *Texas Center for Educational Research.* 1998, https://nces.ed.gov/pubs98/clark.pdf

Delisle, J.D. & Holt, A. "The tangled world of teacher debt." *Education Next, 17* (4). 2021 https://www.educationnext.org/tangled-world-of-teacher-debt-rules-uncertain-benefits-federal-student-loan-subsidies/

Fry, R. and Thomas, D. "Prior to COVID-19, child poverty rates had reached record lows in U.S." *Pew Research Center.* Nov. 2020 https://www.pewresearch.org/fact-tank/2020/11/30/prior-to-covid-19-child-poverty-rates-had-reached-record-lows-in-u-s/

Hickson, M., Ettinger de Cuba, S., Weiss, I., Donofrio, G., Cook, J. "Feeding Our Human Capital: Food Insecurity and Tomorrow's Workforce." *Boston, MA: Boston Medical Center, Children's Health Watch*. 9 Jun. 2022 http://www.childrenshealthwatch.org/wp-content/uploads/FeedingHumanCapital_report.pdf

Loewus, L. "White House Rolls Out Early-Childhood STEM Initiatives." *EdWatch*. 22 Apr. 2016 https://www.edweek.org/teaching-learning/white-house-rolls-out-early-childhood-stem-initiatives/2016/04

"Public high school graduation rates." *National Center for Education Statistics*. May 2020, https://nces.ed.gov/programs/coe/indicator_coi.asp

"Review of Teacher Incentive Programs." *Hanover Research*. Aug. 2014, http://www.hanoverresearch.com/media/Review-of-Teacher-Incentive-Programs-2.pdf

Riddell, R. Curricular Counsel: "How a rural, low-income district uses partnerships to 'find a way'." *K-12 Drive*. 11 Sept. 2019, https://www.k12dive.com/news/curricular-counsel-how-a-rural-low-income-district-uses-partnerships-to/562422/

"The graduation effect: Every student's potential to impact a community." *The Alliance for Excellent Education*. Nov. 2017, http://impact.all4ed.org/US-GradEffect-Infographic.pdf

"The widening achievement gap in the U.S.: NAEP 12 grade reading scores by percentile." *National Center on Education and the Economy*. 2020, https://ncee.org/2020/11/the-widening-achievement-gap-in-the-u-s/

Thomas, P. L. "An alternative to accountability-based education reform." *Radical Scholarship*. 21 Aug. 2013, https://radicalscholarship.wordpress.com/2013/08/21/an-alternative-to-accountability-based-education-reform/

Ujifusa, A. "Standardized Testing Costs States $1.7 Billion a Year, Study Says." *EdWatch*. 29 Nov. 2012, https://www.edweek.org/teaching-learning/standardized-testing-costs-states-1-7-billion-a-year-study-says/2012/11

Entrepreneurship as a Pathway to Equality of Opportunity

Big Picture:
Business startups play an important role in increased job opportunities within local communities. In the U.S., 20% of new businesses fail within two years, 45% within four years and 65% within 10 years. The government must invest differently in small businesses to maximize success, allowing all Americans the ability to truly live the "American Dream."

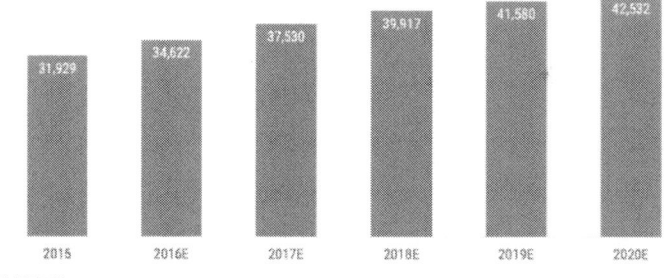

MACRO TRENDS
Small businesses in the US continue to climb
# of small businesses with 0-49 employees (in thousands)

Graphic From: *The U.S. Small Business Fintech Report. CBInsights.* 15 Nov. 2018. This graphic illustrates that the number of small businesses in the U.S. has increased within the past few years.

Operative Definitions:
1. **Small business:** A business with less than 500 employees.
2. **Small Business Administration (SBA):** A federal agency founded in 1953 dedicated to providing help for small businesses. The SBA offers various services such as counseling, and capital

and contracting expertise, to help entrepreneurs grow their businesses.
3. **Free Application for Federal Student Aid (FAFSA):** A form completed by current and prospective college students in the U.S. to determine their financial aid eligibility.
4. **Service Corps of Retired Executives (SCORE):** Founded in 1964. America's largest network of volunteer expert business mentors.
5. **Opportunity Zones:** Economically distressed communities eligible for tax relief.
6. **Association of Procurement Technical Assistance Centers (APTAC):** An organization that helps small businesses fight for contracts in the face of bigger competitors, such as the Department of Defense. It has served over 57,000 clients with $24 billion in contracts and subcontracts.

Important Facts and Statistics:
1. Around 25 million Americans are starting or already own a small business.
2. 22% of small businesses fail within their first year.
3. The biggest challenge for 33% of small businesses is the lack of capital.

6-Point Plan:
1. **Revise and simplify tax deductions for small businesses.** Use the FAFSA as an example of an application form that affords monetary support for undergraduate and graduate studies. Focusing on and expanding the need-based aspects of this kind of application is vital. For example, low-income small business owners across the country lack access to external capital, which is necessary for their businesses to reach their full potential.

2. **Create harsher punishments for large corporations breaking antitrust laws.**
   Increase maximum fines from $10 million to $50 million for firms and $350,000 to $1 million for investors when they are found guilty of breaking antitrust laws. These charges will be announced publicly. This will diminish monopolies and open new opportunities for small businesses. Affording economic mobility to all Americans is a necessary means of achieving social change.

3. **Increase incentives for entrepreneurial ventures.**
   Increase SCORE funding by $25 million (allocated from fines for breaking antitrust laws) to make funding more available for small-business owners. This will ensure that they have access to high-quality resources such as mentoring programs to learn how to write business plans and create marketing strategies, as well as the ability to attend educational workshops. Revise Opportunity Zones, allowing businesses to waive taxes on capital gains for the first seven years of business. Develop startup incubators to help students network. Dedicate $25,000 to community colleges to develop startup incubators where they do not already exist.

4. **Revise and simplify tax deductions for small businesses.**
   Transfer an additional 6% of defense contracting from large firms to small firms. Increase access and availability to the Association of Procurement Technical Assistance Centers. Incentivize businesses of 500-plus employees with tax breaks equal to 10% of supply expenses if a firm only uses small businesses as suppliers. In the face of COVID-19, many larger businesses are struggling with disruptions in global supply

chains. On the other hand, many small businesses have reported that they had increased trouble accessing their COVID-19 relief fund. There is ample space and precedent for these larger companies to reach out to small businesses, given that they treat their supply issues.

5. **Offer small businesses better access to public goods.**
   Encourage public transportation agencies to offer discounted fares to small business employees. *See Transportation policy.* This will increase access for workers of all backgrounds to commute to these jobs, allowing for greater equality of opportunity. Allow small businesses to purchase joint health insurance. Cooperation lowers insurance costs, encouraging businesses to offer health insurance and/or invest in wages. This will attract more workers to small businesses, as they will be able to offer benefits that resemble that of a larger corporation.

6. **Extend SBA low-interest loans to startup firms.**
   Expand available loans by $1 million per company. Direct 40% of new loans to startups for women, veterans, minorities and low-income citizens. Mandatory repayment will begin two years after loans are issued. Loans that target these marginalized groups are consistent with data that substantiates the disproportionate financial trouble they endure. External financing is also less present and effectual among populations of color.

Why This Initiative is Important:

Americans depend heavily on small businesses, as they provide a creative opportunity for entrepreneurs while encouraging innovation and development. At the local level, economies benefit from small businesses, as the profits remain in local communities. This proposal allows for more entrepreneurs and more job creation. Increased support and guidance for entrepreneurs, especially those who are disadvantaged by disparities in intergenerational wealth, minimizes the risk of business failure and bankruptcy. Ultimately, this plan creates more jobs and boosts the American economy at large.

Economic Impact (from our student economist team):
- Estimated effect on the annual federal deficit: + $125 million.
- Supporting America's 30 million small businesses stimulates local economies through increased tax revenue, employment opportunities and economic adaptability in communities.

To learn how our student economists came up with this economic impact, send an email to info@ournationalconversation.org and ask for a more thorough description of their methodologies.

Final Thought for Now:
"America is too great for small dreams." – **Ronald Reagan (1981)**

Acknowledgments:
The following student(s) worked on this nonpartisan proposal: Lucas King, Washington and Lee University; Jack Feenick, University of Virginia; Gad Raganas, Rutgers University; Kylie Kreitz, Pennsylvania State University; Mikel-Lorenz Ilasco, Glendale Community College; Ashley Mullarkey, Rhodes College; Ryan Dexheimer, University of Portland; Aiza Gaffar, Jasper High School; Zoe Benham, Harvard University.

The following individuals worked with our student interns and contributed expertise, wisdom and moral support in the development of this proposal:
1. Zachary Ledford: Owner, ELJUN LLC; Army veteran. Columbus, OH.
2. Randy Grooms: CEO, Samara Strategies; University administrator. Athens, GA.
3. Andrew Privitera: Entrepreneur; Army veteran. Omaha, NE.
4. Gibson Sylvestre: CEO, Infinite Possibilities; Bestselling author. Jupiter, FL.

Note: Not all participants agree with every aspect of this proposal. To arrive at a proposal that takes multiple views into account requires compromise and difficult decisions. For individual commentary on this proposal and more detail, go to OurNationalConversation.org. We invite you to add your comments as well.

Sources:

Mac, C., Wheat, C. & Farrell, D. "Small Business Owner Race, Liquidity, and Survival." *JP Morgan Chase & Co.* Jul 2020, https://www.jpmorganchase.com/institute/research/small-business/report-small-business-owner-race-liquidity-survival#finding-5.

Vaheesan, S. "How Antitrust Perpetuates Structural Racism." *The Appeal.* 16 Sept. 2020, https://theappeal.org/how-antitrust-perpetuates-structural-racism/.

"Contracting Success." *APTAC.* 9 Jun. 2022. https://www.aptac-us.org/contracting-assistance/successes/.

Marks, G. "Black Owned Businesses Are Finding New Opportunities in Today's Social Justice Movement." *The Philadelphia Inquirer.* 4 Aug. 2020, https://www.inquirer.com/business/small-business/black-owned-business-diversity-supply-chains-20200804.html.

Liu, S. & Parilla, J. "New Data Shows Small Businesses In Communities of Color Had Unequal Access to Federal Covid-19 Relief." *Brookings.* 17 Sept. 2020, https://www.brookings.edu/research/new-data-shows-small-businesses-in-communities-of-color-had-unequal-access-to-federal-covid-19-relief/.

Dragomir, S. "39 Entrepreneur Statistics You Need to Know in 2021." *Smallbizgenius.* 5 Jan. 2021, https://www.smallbizgenius.net/by-the-numbers/entrepreneur-statistics/#gref.

Justice and Public Safety

"Those who make peaceful revolution impossible will make violent revolution inevitable."

- John F. Kennedy

Balancing Gun Control and Civil Liberties

Big Picture:
Gun control refers to restrictions placed on the sale, storage and transportation of firearms. This policy proposal serves to enforce restrictions while balancing civil liberties regarding gun ownership. Gun violence is a uniquely pervasive problem in the U.S. and must be addressed.

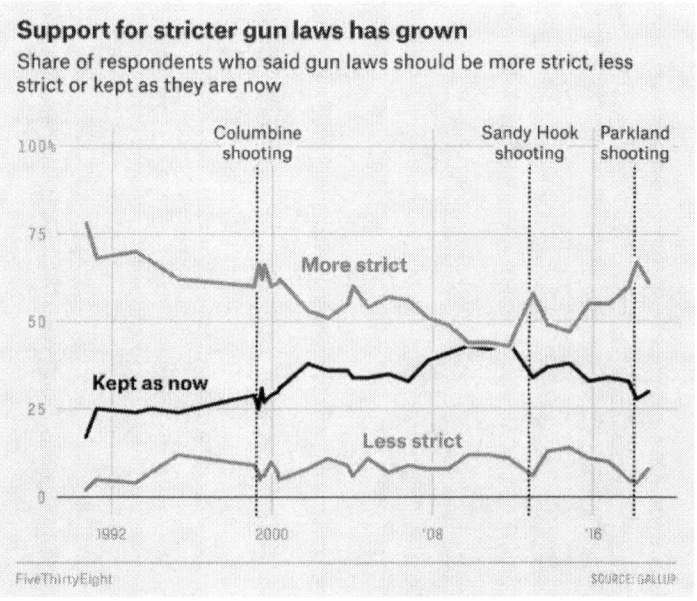

Graphic From: Rakich, Nathaniel. "How Views on Gun Control Have Changed in the Last 30 Years." *Five Thirty Eight,* Aug. 7, 2019, https://fivethirtyeight.com/features/how-views-on-gun-control-have-changed-in-the-last-30-years/. This figure illustrates the public opinion on gun control policy over time. Public opinion has consistently favored stricter gun legislation, spiking directly after mass shootings.

Operative Definitions:
1. **Vet buyers:** A joint project that requires a thorough investigation of an individual, company or other entity before a gun purchase can be approved.
2. **National Rifle Association (NRA):** An advocacy group founded in 1881 to advance gun rights and firearms safety.
3. **The Federal Assault Weapons Ban:** A ban on assault weapons in the United States, signed into law by former President Bill Clinton in 1994 and expired in 2004.

Important Facts and Statistics:
1. Gun sales increased 40% from November 2019 to November 2020.
2. About 3,010 people were injured or killed in mass shootings in 2020.
3. Every day, over 500 people across the United States are killed by guns.
4. Forty-four percent of all homicides worldwide involve guns.
5. From 2012 to 2016, there were 1.4 million firearm-related deaths worldwide.

4-Point Plan:
1. **Make gun access more restrictive.**
   It is crucial that the process of acquiring a gun be made more difficult than it currently is. By increasing the number of firearms that are federally age-restricted and requiring unlicensed gun sellers to conduct background checks on customers, the likelihood of guns ending up in the wrong hands would drop.

2. **Establish a waiting period for gun purchases.**
   Enacting a waiting period of several weeks after every gun purchase could help reduce gun violence by giving gun buyers time to reconsider impulsive feelings or behaviors. It is possible that someone might buy a gun with the intention of hurting themselves or someone else but, after having time to reflect, they may be able to step away and rethink the feelings that were causing such violent urges. They could use the time to calm down and come to understand the true severity of acting upon such thoughts. It is also true that implementing a waiting period would give a gun seller more time to evaluate the eligibility of a potential gun buyer.

3. **Confiscate all firearms from domestic abusers and violent felons.**
   Domestic abusers and those convicted of other violent felonies should not have access to firearms. This policy would keep guns from getting into dangerous hands. Perpetrators of domestic violence, or any type of violence, have proven themselves a threat to others; as such, it is unwise and unsafe to allow them access to firearms.

4. **Mandate firearm safety courses for gun buyers.**
   As a precaution before purchasing a gun, gun buyers across the nation will need to attend a gun safety course facilitated either by the NRA or local police departments. It is not uncommon for gun buyers to be uninformed of gun safety. A mandatory gun safety course would ensure that prospective gun owners know how to safely and properly handle a gun. By teaching gun owners how to responsibly and securely use and store their firearms, this course could prevent accidents from happening.

Why This Initiative is Important:
Gun violence occurs when the wrong people are able to access guns, which is why gun control is so important. To prevent potentially dangerous individuals from purchasing weapons, stricter laws and increased security for gun transactions need to be put in place. As a result of stricter gun control laws, violence caused by guns could be reduced across the nation.

Economic Impact (from our student economist team):
- Estimated effect on the annual federal deficit: + $10.5 million.

To learn how our student economists came up with this economic impact, send an email to info@ournationalconversation.org and ask for a more thorough description of their methodologies.

Final Thought for Now:
"This isn't left or right, it's about saving lives. Through unity and love we will win and end gun violence." –
David Hogg, March for Our Lives

Acknowledgments
The following student(s) worked on this nonpartisan proposal: Amane Shuman, Florida International University.

The following individuals worked with our student interns and contributed expertise, wisdom and moral support in the development of this proposal:
1. Thomas Stedina: Police Lieutenant, NYPD. New York.

Note: Not all participants agree with every aspect of this proposal. To arrive at a proposal that takes multiple views into account requires compromise and difficult decisions. For individual commentary on this

Let's Fix America

proposal and more detail, go to OurNationalConversation.org. We invite you to add your comments as well.

Sources:

Brownlee, Chip. "2020 By the Numbers." *The Trace*, 4 Jan. 2021, https://www.thetrace.org/newsletter/2020-by-the-numbers/?gclid=CjwKCAjwopWSBhB6EiwAjxmqDT-jzA-zicRqBXaGU3dbgGAyAuMmGZaBq4FmQy3R9VuNDd5Ggft69BoCU_kQAvD_BwE

"Gun Violence." *Amnesty International*, 19 Apr. 2021, https://www.amnesty.org/en/what-we-do/arms-control/gun-violence/

Pérez-Peña, Richard. "Gun Control Explained." *The New York Times*, 7 Oct. 2015, https://www.nytimes.com/interactive/2015/10/07/us/gun-control-explained.html

"Should More Gun Control Laws Be Enacted?" *ProCon*, 7 Aug. 2020, https://gun-control.procon.org/#:~:text=Gun%20control%20laws%20infringe%20upon,2.5%20million%20times%20a%20year

Thompson, Derek. "Do Americans Want More or Less Gun Control? Both, actually." *The Atlantic*, Atlantic Media Company, 17 Dec. 2012, https://www.theatlantic.com/national/archive/2012/12/do-americans-want-more-or-less-gun-control-both-actually/266312/

Improving Relations Between Law Enforcement and Minority Groups

Big Picture:
The police force serves to enforce the law as well as ensure the safety of American citizens. Insufficient training has resulted in killings as well as discord between law enforcement and minority groups. This proposal serves to provide a comprehensive approach to ensure that all American citizens are fairly and adequately protected by the police.

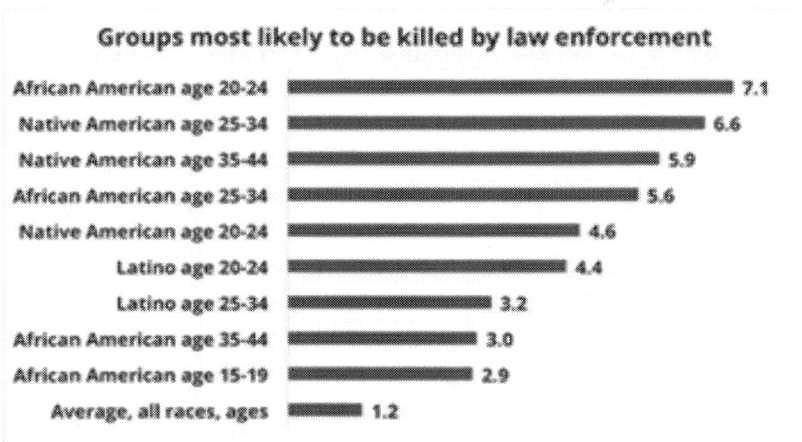

Graphic From: *Who Are Police Killing?* Center on Juvenile and Criminal Justice. *Cjcj.org*. 26 Aug. 2014. This figure illustrates the rate of law enforcement killings per million population per year between 1999 and 2011. As is evident from this graph, African American men are more likely to be killed by police than any other ethnic and gender group.

Operative Definitions:
1. **Ticket and arrest quotas:** Formal and informal measures that require police officers to issue a particular number of tickets or make a certain number of arrests, often within a specific time frame.

2. **Qualified immunity:** A judicially-created doctrine that shields government officials from being held liable for constitutional violations for monetary damages under federal law, so long as the officials do not violate any "clearly established" law.
3. **Excessive force:** Situations in which government officials legally entitled to use force exceed the reasonable amount necessary to diffuse an incident.

Important Facts and Statistics:
1. African American men are killed by police force at a rate three times higher than white men.
2. As of April 2021, only seven states, Colorado, Connecticut, Illinois, Maryland, New Jersey, South Carolina and New Mexico, legally mandate that law enforcement agents wear body cameras.
3. After education, police departments are the U.S.' most heavily funded category of local spending. Policing costed local governments a total of $193 billion in 2017 alone.

4-Point Plan:
1. **Mandate body camera usage.**
   Require local, state and federal law enforcement agents to wear body cameras from dispatch until the end of each incident. The movement of individual states strengthening their body camera legislation illustrates the general consensus that body cameras hold police more "accountable and make departments more transparent," benefiting both the people and the criminal justice system. Body cameras reportedly increase transparency, limit brute force, increase civility and lead to quicker resolutions. Investigations of misconduct can be completed quicker when such evidence is available, saving both time and money. Though it does cost money to invest in the storage of body camera footage,

these cameras' contributions to the attainment of justice will outweigh the costs.

2. **Provide more thorough training to police officers.**
Officers in all different sectors of law enforcement should be mandated to complete a 35-week police training course that emphasizes de-escalation and highlights the dangers of racial profiling. In the U.S., police training varies in length from 10 to 36 weeks in total, compared to U.S. Navy Seals who train about eight months for a six-week deployment. On average, police departments spend 60 hours on firearm training and 44 hours on self-defense. However, non-lethal weapons like tasers, which can be strong alternatives to guns, only receive an average of eight hours of training, despite manufacturers recommending a training time of 36 hours. During this time, prospective officers should also take the Harvard Implicit Bias Test, which was proven effective in informing officers of their subconscious biases in a 2018 NYPD study.

3. **Restructure the police budget and make additional investments in community programming.**
All levels of government should work together to redirect one-fourth of the national $119 billion police budget—which includes federal, state and local spending—toward further training while investing additional funds toward community programs such as life skills training and family therapy services. By redistributing the U.S. police force budget to fund body camera technology and training, future officers will have the resources they need to serve their communities to the best of their abilities, and accountability will be more fairly monitored. By investing more in community programs, the need for policing will lessen, and the overall well-being of the community will improve.

4. **Ban ticket and arrest quotas.**
   Abolish ticket and arrest quotas on federal, state and local levels and allow officers to respond to dangerous crimes, rather than simply searching to satisfy an arrest requirement. Further, many contend that quota-based systems perpetuate racial profiling. Official abolition of quota systems in policing on all different governmental levels will increase trust, productivity and justice.

Why This Initiative is Important:
The unjustified police killings of many BIPOC in 2020 highlighted the reality of police brutality and sparked further movements for racial justice and equality across the U.S. Meanwhile, many are right to point out that crime rates in inner cities are particularly high and that not all violent interactions between law enforcement and minority groups denote racism. If this policy proposal or others like it are implemented, not only will racial bias and discrimination be combatted more effectively, but police will receive the tools they need to better de-escalate situations and diminish the incidence of violent outbreaks between law enforcement and civilians.

Economic Impact (from our student economist team):
- Meaningful numbers could not be calculated for this proposal.

To learn how our student economists came up with this economic impact, send an email to info@ournationalconversation.org and ask for a more thorough description of their methodologies.

Final Thought for Now:
"The duties which a police officer owes to the state are of a most exacting nature. No one is compelled to choose the profession of a police officer, but having chosen it, everyone is obliged to live up to the standard of its requirements..." **- Calvin Coolidge**

Acknowledgments:

The following student(s) worked on this nonpartisan proposal: Olivia Bronson, Barton College; Deaven Rector, Morehouse College; Zariya Jeffers, Clark Atlanta University; Anna Birman, College of William and Mary; Paul Samberg, University of Kansas; Katelyn Owens, The Open University; Diego Andrades, University of Southern California; William Duffy, University of Massachusetts Amherst; Shreya Shesadi, Elizabeth Haub School of Law at Pace University; Amane Shuman, Florida International University.

The following individuals worked with our student interns and contributed expertise, wisdom and moral support in the development of this proposal:
1. Brian Churchill: Police Sergeant, LAPD. Los Angeles, CA.
2. Thomas Datro: Police Sergeant, LAPD; Doctoral Candidate, University of Southern California. Los Angeles, CA.
3. Sinead Younge: Professor of Psychology, Morehouse College; Director, Andrew Young Center for Global Leadership. Atlanta, GA.

Note: Not all participants agree with every aspect of this proposal. To arrive at a proposal that takes multiple views into account requires compromise and difficult decisions. For individual commentary on this proposal and more detail, go to OurNationalConversation.org. We invite you to add your comments as well.

Sources:

Allen, Keith, Brad Parks, and Hollie Silverman. "Minneapolis police officers must keep body cameras turned on during entire response to a call, new policy says." *CNN*, 2 Feb. 2021, https://edition.cnn.com/2021/02/02/us/minneapolis-police-body-worn-camera-policy/index.html

Chapman, Brett. "Body-Worn Cameras: What the Evidence Tells Us." *National Institute of Justice*, 14 Nov. 2018, https://nij.ojp.gov/topics/articles/body-worn-cameras-what-evidence-tells-us

Edwards, Frank, Hedwig Lee, and Michael Esposito. "Risk of being killed by police use of force in the United States by age, race–ethnicity, and sex." *PNAS* 5 Aug. 2019, https://www.pnas.org/content/116/34/16793

Gutierrez, David. "Why Police Training Must be Reformed." *The Institute of Politics at Harvard University*, 9 Jun. 2022, https://iop.harvard.edu/get-involved/harvard-political-review/why-police-training-must-be-reformed

HEC Paris Insights. "Why Budgets Can Be A Key To Transforming The Role Of The Police In America." *Forbes*, 3 Jul. 2020. https://www.forbes.com/sites/hecparis/2020/07/03/why-budgets-can-be-a-key-to-transforming-the-role-of-the-police-in-america/?sh=37092142e264

Kates, Graham. "Some U.S. police train for just a few weeks, in some countries they train for years." *CBS News*, 10 Jun. 2020, https://www.cbsnews.com/news/police-training-weeks-united-states/

Norwood, Candace. "Body cameras are seen as key to police reform. But do they increase accountability?" *PBS*, 25 Jun. 2020, https://www.pbs.org/newshour/politics/body-cameras-are-seen-as-key-to-police-reform-but-do-they-increase-accountability

Ossei-Owusu, Shaun. "Race and the Tragedy of Quota-Based Policing." *The American Prospect*, 3 Nov. 2016, https://prospect.org/justice/race-tragedy-quota-based-policing/

"Police departments in the US: Explained." *usafacts.org*, 13 Aug. 2020, https://usafacts.org/articles/police-departments-explained/

Rose, Joel. "Despite Laws And Lawsuits, Quota-Based Policing Lingers." *NPR*, 4 Apr. 2015, https://www.npr.org/2015/04/04/395061810/despite-laws-and-lawsuits-quota-based-policing-lingers

Sobel, Nathaniel. "What Is Qualified Immunity, and What Does It Have to Do With Police Reform?" *Lawfare*, 6 Jun. 2020, https://www.lawfareblog.com/what-qualified-immunity-and-what-does-it-have-do-police-reform

Stephens, Darrel W. "Police Discipline: A Case for Change." *ojp.gov*, Jun. 2011, https://www.ojp.gov/pdffiles1/nij/234052.pdf

Van Ness, Lindsay. "Body Cameras May Not Be the Easy Answer Everyone Was Looking For." *pewtrusts.org*, 14 Jan. 2020, https://www.pewtrusts.org/en/research-and-analysis/blogs/stateline/2020/01/14/body-cameras-may-not-be-the-easy-answer-everyone-was-looking-for

Worden, Robert, Sarah McLean, Robin Engel, Hannah Cochran, Nicholas Corsaro, Danielle Reynolds, Cynthia Najdowski and Gabrielle Isaza. "The Impacts of Implicit Bias Awareness Training in the NYPD." *The Official Website of the City of New York*, Jul. 2020, https://www1.nyc.gov/assets/nypd/downloads/pdf/analysis_and_planning/impacts-of-implicit-bias-awareness-training-in-%20the-nypd.pdf

Let's Fix America

Creating a More Egalitarian Judicial System

Big Picture:
The U.S. Judiciary was created under Article III of the Constitution to interpret and apply laws in the United States. At times, the judiciary has failed to deliver on this role due to disparities in sentencing among different races and ethnicities. The purpose of this proposal is to help ensure that the judicial system delivers fair and impartial justice to all American citizens.

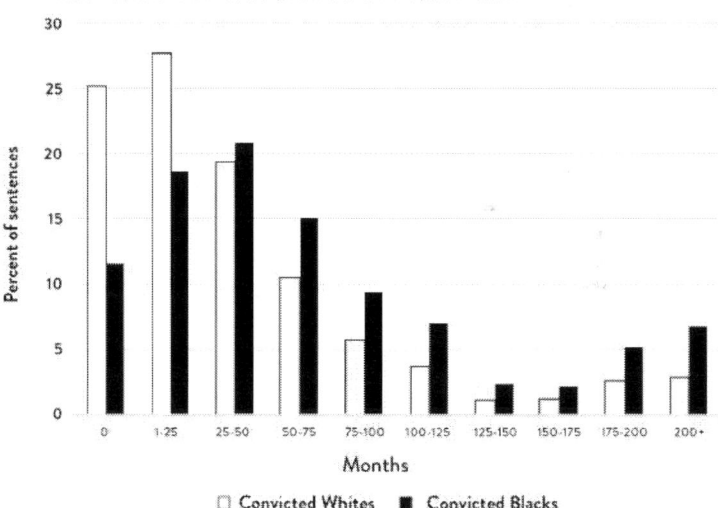

Graphic From: Kahn, Andrew and Chris Kirk. *"What It's Like to Be Black in the Criminal Justice System." Slate.* 9 Aug. 2015. This figure illustrates the difference in sentence lengths for convicted Black and white offenders. Black offenders generally receive longer sentences, reflecting the disproportionate punishment of Blacks in the American justice system.

Operative Definitions:
1. **Recidivism:** The rate at which formerly incarcerated individuals commit another crime after completing their original sentence.
2. **War on Drugs:** A campaign led by the U.S. federal government and popularized by former President Richard Nixon to reduce the drug trade in the United States.
3. **Civil forfeiture:** The process that allows law enforcement officials to take one's property based on the mere suspicion of criminal activity.
4. **"Just Say No" movement:** Launched by former President Ronald Reagan's wife, Nancy Reagan, in the early 1980s, this campaign encouraged children to reject drugs by simply saying "no."

Important Facts and Statistics:
1. In the United States, the likelihood of serving prison time is reflected disproportionately based on race, with one in 17 white men, one in six Latino men and one in three Black men being incarcerated, as well as one in 111 white women, one in 45 Latina women and one in 18 Black women. The causes of these disparities are controversial, with some pointing to systemic racism and others calling attention to disproportionate crime rates within these communities of color.
2. The non-white races and ethnicities account for 37% of the U.S. population yet comprise 66% of the U.S. prison population. This is partially the result of crime-rate differences and partially the result of sentencing disparities.
3. Black men consistently receive harsher sentences for low-level crimes than their white counterparts. According to a U.S. Sentencing Commission report, Black men receive federal sentences that are 20% longer than those white men receive for the same crimes. Black men are also 75% more likely than white men

to face a charge that features a mandatory minimum. Some attribute these disparities to racist stereotyping, others to the historical crack-down on crime in inner-city communities and still others to the fact that plea bargains might mask the fact that Black men are charged with higher-level crimes that are dropped during court proceedings but nevertheless affect the length of a sentence. Each factor probably plays a role.

4-Point Plan:
1. **Stop the abuse of civil forfeiture.**
    A criminal conviction is not required for a person to face forfeiture. While civil forfeiture was originally implemented to divert resources from large-scale criminal enterprises, it is now notorious for stripping often innocent people of their property. According to previous Supreme Court rulings, it is only constitutionally acceptable to proceed with civil asset forfeiture due to the deprivation of money with a clear demonstration of persuasive evidence and after undergoing proper due process. Regaining this property is often an expensive and lengthy process, making justice difficult to achieve. Governments must be barred from seizing the property of those suspected of committing crimes. By limiting this unjust aspect of the policing sector, the nation can create a more just society.

2. **Create opportunities for ex-convicts.**
    Most often, the greatest obstacle faced by those who complete their sentences is re-entry into society. Ex-offenders are not taught skills that can be used vocationally upon their release from prison and, as a result, often must choose between living on the streets or re-entering a life of crime. Governments must encourage businesses to consider ex-offenders for open positions and implement restrictions based on criminal history discrimination.

Additionally, training programs and trade school workshops must be readily available at accessible prices for convicts to better prepare them for the workforce, such as implementing on-site job training programs and schooling options.

3. **Reform legislation created during the "War on Drugs."**
Legislation created under multiple administrations since the 1970s has disproportionately punished people of color. For example, crack cocaine users, who were usually Black, were often charged with a minimum five-year sentence. However, their white counterparts, who typically used the same drug in powder form, were hardly punished. White individuals are more likely to deal drugs than Black individuals, but Black individuals are 3.6 times more likely to be arrested for selling drugs. Additionally, Black men are 75% more likely to be charged with federal offenses carrying harsher mandatory minimums than their white counterparts. Such inconsistencies in drug charges demonstrate the need for criminal justice reform that ensures consistent sentencing for citizens, regardless of their racial group. The state attorneys general should consider reviewing statistics on arrests and sentencing to ensure that local law enforcement is fairly protecting their communities irrespective of race and ethnicity. This reform would not only combat the discriminatory effects of the War on Drugs, but would also decrease government spending on prisons.

4. **The federal government and all states should legalize marijuana within their respective jurisdictions.**
Legalizing marijuana will reduce racial disparities in drug arrests, which will help ensure that sentences are consistent regardless of race. Its legalization will also lead to less government spending on marijuana policing and incarceration, leading to millions in tax

revenue. This money could be redirected to fund housing for the homeless, professional development programs and cost-effective addiction treatment centers. Furthermore, it will contribute to the success of banks and credit unions as the marijuana industry will be legitimized. Of course, to not cause an overreach of federal power, this legalization should be done on the state level.

Why This Initiative is Important:

Since its inception, the U.S. has been a melting pot of races, religions and cultures. The country has prided itself on its allegiance to the values of liberty, equality and justice. However, as it stands, the American criminal justice system is not a model of these values. By decreasing racial disparities in sentences, the U.S. will ensure that all citizens receive equal opportunities for justice. The U.S. must reduce the prison population and increase funds to community services such as education, rehabilitation programs and treatment centers for those with mental illnesses and substance use disorders. The U.S. must increase re-entry opportunities that reduce recidivism rates. By implementing these initiatives, the U.S. will increase public faith in the justice system.

Economic Impact (from our student economist team):

- Allowing ex-convicts to re-enter the workforce more easily will lead to more economic growth and prosperity.
- Fair wages will provide more welfare for ex-convicts and without causing unnecessary inflation.
- Estimated effect on the annual federal deficit: + $420 million

To learn how our student economists came up with this economic impact, send an email to info@ournationalconversation.org and ask for a more thorough description of their methodologies.

Final Thought for Now:
"I have always been persuaded that the stability and success of the National Government, and consequently the happiness of the people of the United States, would depend in a considerable degree on the interpretations and execution of its laws." – George Washington (1790)

Acknowledgments:
The following student(s) worked on this nonpartisan proposal: Anna Engel, Indiana University Bloomington; Shreya Shesadri, Elizabeth Haub School of Law at Pace University; William Duffy, University of Massachusetts Amherst; Anna Birman, College of William and Mary; Paul Samberg, University of Kansas; Katelyn Owens, The Open University; Diego Andrades, University of Southern California; Corina Rueles, University of La Verne.

The following individuals worked with our student interns and contributed expertise, wisdom and moral support in the development of this proposal:
1. Andrea Kupfer Schneider, J.D.: Professor of Law, Marquette University. Milwaukee, WI.
2. Benjamin Barton, J.D.: Professor of Law, University of Tennessee. Knoxville, TN.
3. Pat Nolan, J.D.: Director, American Conservative Union Foundation's Center for Criminal Justice Reform. Leesburg, VA.
4. Brian Churchill: Police Sergeant, LAPD. Los Angeles, CA.
5. Thomas Datro: Police Sergeant, LAPD; Doctoral Candidate, University of Southern California. Los Angeles, CA.

Note: Not all participants agree with every aspect of this proposal. To arrive at a proposal that takes multiple views into account requires compromise and difficult decisions. For individual commentary on this

Let's Fix America

proposal and more detail, go to OurNationalConversation.org. We invite you to add your comments as well.

Sources:

Bonczar, Thomas P. "Prevalence of Imprisonment in the U.S. Population, 1974-2001." *Bureau of Justice Statistics (BJS), U.S. Department of Justice.* 17 Aug. 2003, www.bjs.gov/index.cfm?ty=pbdetail&iid=836

Crawford, Charles, Ted Chiricos, and Gary Kleck. "Race, Racial Threat, and Sentencing of Habitual Offenders." *Criminology.* Vol. 36, 1998: 481-511.

Ingraham, Christopher. "Black men sentenced to more time for committing the exact same crime as a white person, study finds." *The Washington Post.* 16 Nov. 2017, https://www.washingtonpost.com/news/wonk/wp/2017/11/16/black-men-sentenced-to-more-time-for-committing-the-exact-same-crime-as-a-white-person-study-finds/

Moss, Stephen J. "CLEAR and CONVINCING CIVILITY: APPLYING the CIVIl COMMITMENT STANDARD of PROOF to CIVIL ASSET FORFEITURE." *American University Law Review*, vol. 68, no. 6, 2019, pp. 2257-96.

Skiera, AJ. "Removing Roadblocks to Redemption: How 10 U.S. Think Tanks Are Getting Criminal Justice Right." *Atlas Network*, Apr. 2018. https://www.atlasnetwork.org/articles/removing-roadblocks-to-redemption-how-10-u-s-think-tanks-are-getting-criminal-justice-right

Steffensmeier, Darrell, Jeffrey Ulmer, and John Kramer. "The Interaction of Race, Gender, and Age in Criminal Sentencing: The Punishment Cost of Being Young, Black, and Male." *Criminology*, vol. 36, 1998, pp. 763-97.

Waldman, Michael and Adureh Onyekwere. "Ending Mass Incarceration: Ideas from Today's Leaders." *Brennan Center for Justice*, 16 May 2019, https://www.brennancenter.org/our-work/policy-solutions/ending-mass-incarceration-ideas-todays-leaders

Chung, Ed, Maritza Perez, and Lea Hunter. "Rethinking Federal Marijuana Policy." *Center for American Progress*. 1 May 2018, https://www.americanprogress.org/issues/criminal-justice/reports/2018/05/01/450201/rethinking-federal-marijuana-policy/ (February 14, 2021).

Healthcare

"We finally declared that in America, health care is not a privilege for a few, but a right for everybody."

- Barack Obama

Let's Fix America

Reducing the Cost of Healthcare

Big Picture:
As of 2019, over 26 million Americans lack health insurance. 73% of uninsured Americans report that they are uninsured because the cost of health insurance is simply too high. It is important to note that other wealthy countries spend about half as much as the U.S. does on healthcare. In order to reduce uninsured rates and improve access to affordable care, we must implement legislation that aims to address this issue.

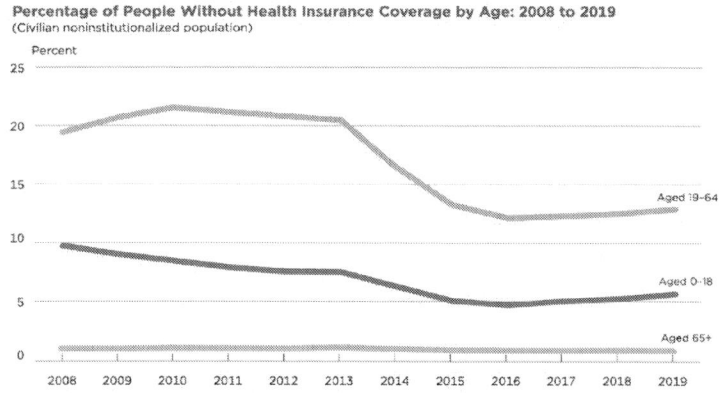

Graphic From: U.S. Census Bureau, Current Population Survey, 2020 Annual Social and Economic Supplement (CPS ASEC). This graph illustrates the percentage of each age group that is uninsured.

Operative Definitions:
1. **Affordable Care Act (Obamacare):** An act legislated in 2010 that aimed to increase affordable health insurance coverage and reform the health insurance market.
2. **Preventive care:** Healthcare services that help prevent disease, disability or death.

3. **Bundled payment billing system:** A single payment made to healthcare providers that will cover the costs of all the healthcare services in an episode of care.
4. **Value-based medicine:** A healthcare model in which the net value output is optimized, often based on improvements to quantitative measures, such as improvements in length and quality of life.
5. **Shrank's targeted interventions:** Policy measures and/or programs that specifically target one of the six domains of administrative waste that have been evidenced to be effective at reducing administrative costs, compiled in a recent study by William H. Shrank, et al.

Important Facts and Statistics:
1. Current research estimates that administrative waste accounts for approximately $935 billion — equivalent to 20-25% of the total money currently spent on the American healthcare system.

5-Point Plan:
1. **Increasing knowledge on covered preventive care for lowering individual costs for routine care.**
According to the CDC, 75% of the nation's healthcare spending can be attributed to chronic illnesses that can be avoided through preventive care. Current ACA provisions make it so that consumers under certain provider networks have access to free preventive care procedures such as screenings, tests and health evaluations. We must create digital content with accurate information on the services the ACA covers and locations where those services are offered, with the intent to increase general knowledge on how to reduce the amount of money spent on preventive care.

2. **Expand coverage of diverse treatment options to increase accessibility.**
   Encourage all insurance plans to provide access to telehealth professionals, thereby allowing nurses and physician assistants to practice telehealth and increase funding to community health centers. *See Improving Access to U.S. Healthcare policy.*

3. **Incentivize price transparency among healthcare services and fine providers that do not disclose prices.**
   Price transparency improves the patient's experience, enables patients to make informed decisions about when and where to seek healthcare, and creates market competition that reduces costs. Significant cost containment cannot happen without extensive transparency in provider prices. It is often thought among patients that more expensive treatments equate to improved health outcomes. However, recognizing price variation in healthcare allows patients to acknowledge that higher prices do not necessarily translate to a better quality of care. Additionally, market pressure that is created as a result of digital price transparency can encourage competitive behavior among providers, lowering overall out-of-pocket costs for patients.

4. **Introduce interventions that target administrative waste.**
   Through the use of Shrank's targeted interventions, the costs of administrative waste can be greatly curbed. Most notably, care-coordination, care delivery and overtreatment interventions can save up to $300 billion in healthcare costs. These treatments will focus on internal improvements in the system. Through the compilation of these interventions, a large portion of the waste will become reformed. Proper utilization of administrative resources allows for easier implementation of initiatives, increased

access to healthcare and the dramatic reduction of healthcare costs.

5. **Reform payments to reflect the bundled payment billing system.**
Implementing a bundled payment billing system will help the healthcare system move towards a value-based care model and away from a fee-for-service model. Bundled payments encourage healthcare providers to work together to improve quality and efficiency by mapping out a plan for the patient. This serves as an incentive for healthcare providers because if they collaborate, they will not go through unnecessary procedures and will get a share in the savings (bundled payment minus cost to administer services).

Why This Initiative is Important:
This plan helps both consumers and healthcare providers reduce healthcare costs. It will reduce out-of-pocket costs for policyholders while increasing insurance coverage and accessibility. It will also provide preventive care to promote long-term health. Additionally, it will increase competition between healthcare providers and drug manufacturers, resulting in lower prices for consumers. By lowering the cost of healthcare, more Americans will be able to afford health insurance.

Economic Impact (from our student economist team):
- Meaningful numbers could not be calculated for this proposal.

To learn how our student economists came up with this economic impact, send an email to info@ournationalconversation.org and ask for a more thorough description of their methodologies.

Final Thought for Now:
"We cannot be a strong nation unless we are a healthy nation."
– Franklin D. Roosevelt

Acknowledgments:
The following student(s) worked on this nonpartisan proposal: <u>Karen Huynh</u>, University of California Los Angeles; <u>Krithik Vishwanath</u>, Klein Cain High School; <u>Sana Imam</u>, The George Washington University; <u>Maui Wabe</u>, Mira Mesa High School; <u>Sophia Welsh</u>, Mira Mesa High School.

The following individuals worked with our student interns and contributed expertise, wisdom and moral support in the development of this proposal:

1. <u>Catheryn McDowell:</u> Student in health policy and economics at Vanderbilt University.; first GM of ONC's student team and advisor to the healthcare policy team. Nashville, TN.
2. <u>Ned Holland:</u> Hospital and industry association counsel and board member; private sector benefits and healthcare purchasing executive; former assistant secretary of HHS (Obama Administration). Kansas City, MO.
3. <u>Brian Thomas, M.D.:</u> Physician; founder of The Candidates Network, a group of nonpartisan public policy enthusiasts; Chief Policy Advisor, ONC. Pittsburgh, PA.
4. <u>Tom Kline:</u> Pharmaceutical executive formerly with Pfizer Inc; leader of The Kline Health Group. Hollywood, FL.
5. <u>Shelley Scipione:</u> eCommerce & FinTech marketing executive. Boulder, CO.
6. <u>Wendy Scipione:</u> Co-Founder & National Sales Director of MPowering Benefits. Louisville, CO.

Let's Fix America

Note: Not all participants agree with every aspect of this proposal. To arrive at a proposal that takes multiple views into account requires compromise and difficult decisions. For individual commentary on this proposal and more detail, go to OurNationalConversation.org. We invite you to add your comments as well.

Sources:

Beaton, T. How Preventive Healthcare Services Reduce Spending for Payers. *HealthpayerIntelligence.* 29 Aug. 2017 https://healthpayerintelligence.com/news/how-preventive-healthcare-services-reduce-spending-for-payers

"Bundled Payment: Effects on Health Care Spending and Quality." *Agency for Healthcare and Research Quality.* 21 Jul. 2021, https://effectivehealthcare.ahrq.gov/sites/default/files/related_files/bundled-payments-quality-effects_executive.pdf

Kamal, Rabah, Ramirez, Giorlando, & Cox, Cynthia "How Does Health Spending in the U.S. Compare To Other Countries?". *Peterson-KFF Health System Tracker*, 23 Dec. 2020, https://www.healthsystemtracker.org/chart-collection/health-spending-u-s-compare-countries-2/.

Tolbert, J., Orgera, K., & Damico, A. "Key Facts about the Uninsured Population" *KFF.* 6 Nov. 2020, https://www.kff.org/uninsured/issue-brief/key-facts-about-the-uninsured-population/

Robinson, A. B. J. C. "Appropriate Use of Reference Pricing Can Increase Value:" *Health Affairs.* 7 Jul. 2015, https://www.healthaffairs.org/do/10.1377/hblog20150707.049155/full/

Shih, T., Chen, L. M., & Nallamothu, B. K. "Will Bundled Payments Change Health Care? Examining the Evidence Thus Far in Cardiovascular Care." *Circulation.* 16 Jun. 2015, https://www.ncbi.nlm.nih.gov/pmc/articles/PMC4471872/.

Shrank, W. H., Rogstad, T. L., & Parekh, N. "Waste in the US Health Care System." JAMA, 322(15), 2019, 1501. https://doi.org/10.1001/jama.2019.13978

US Census Bureau. "Health Insurance Coverage in the United States: 2019." *United States Census Bureau.* 15 Sep. 2020, https://www.census.gov/library/publications/2020/demo/p60-271.html

Improving Access to U.S. Healthcare

Big Picture:
While the U.S. leads the world in healthcare research, technology and specialty care, the healthcare system lags in various World Health Organization metrics, including access to medical care. The U.S. must create a better healthcare system for its citizens that accounts for affordable, accessible and equitable care.

Healthcare Quality and Access (HAQ) Index Rating, 2016

Netherlands	96.1
Australia	95.9
Sweden	95.5
Japan	94.1
Austria	93.9
Comparable Country Average	93.7
Germany	92
France	91.7
United Kingdom	90.5
United States	88.7

Graphic From: *KFF analysis of data from: "Measuring performance on the Healthcare Access and Quality Index for 195 countries and territories and selected subnational locations: a systematic analysis from the Global Burden of Disease Study 2016," The Lancet.* 23 May 2018. This chart illustrates that the U.S. lags behind many other industrialized countries in terms of healthcare quality and access.

Operative Definitions:
1. **Medicare:** America's national healthcare insurance program for those above the age of 65 and for those who experience a disability, regardless of income.
2. **Medicaid:** A health insurance program for Americans of every age who have limited income and cannot afford healthcare

services on their own. In states with expanded Medicaid, having low income is enough to warrant the benefits of Medicaid. In states without expanded Medicaid, criteria vary. People who qualify for Medicare and Medicaid can have both.
3. **Telehealth:** Remote healthcare that is practiced either over the phone or a virtual call.
4. **Resident Physician Shortage Reduction Act of 2021:** The legislation adds 14,000 residency positions to Medicare-supported direct graduate medical education and indirect medical education over the course of seven years.
5. **The Affordable Care Act (ACA):** Signed into law by President Barack Obama in 2010 to increase health insurance coverage for the uninsured, providing insurance for those with pre-existing conditions, shifting to a quality/value-based healthcare model, as well as curbing rising costs of healthcare.
6. **Community Health Centers (CHCs):** Responsible for providing treatment even if patients do not have insurance, do not speak English or live in rural areas. These centers provide preventative and primary care services as well as health education, disease prevention and mental health treatment.
7. **The Liaison Committee on Medical Education (LCME):** Oversees institutional accreditations for allopathic medicine, along with establishing guidelines and standards for accredited institutions.

Important Facts and Statistics:
1. As of the last census in 2019, 8% of Americans do not have any healthcare insurance.
2. As of the last census in 2019, 5.5% of white Americans, 9.9% of Black Americans, 6.2% of Asian Americans and 16.7% of Hispanics are uninsured.

3. Over 70% of those who are uninsured cited affordability as a reason for not being insured.
4. Americans who lack insurance are three times more likely to not fill prescribed prescriptions compared to those who do have insurance.
5. In 15 studies that tested for racial and ethnic bias in primary care providers and their treatment, 14 of the studies concluded low to moderate levels of implicit bias from physicians against Black people and Hispanic or Latino people.
6. On average, 50,000 students apply to medical schools, but up to 60% of applicants are rejected. Over 4,000 applicants do not get into a residency program.
7. By 2033, it is estimated that the U.S. will face a shortage of between 54,100 and 139,000 physicians.
8. Fifteen percent of all Americans live in rural areas. They are at greater risk of death with the leading causes of death being cancer, heart diseases, unintentional injuries, stroke and chronic respiratory diseases.

5-Point Plan:

1. **Stabilize the individual insurance marketplace.**
   State-level approaches to marketplace stabilization can contain high insurance premium costs. Implementing state-level reinsurance programs and requiring insurers participating in the state's Medicaid managed care program to sell a minimum number of products on the marketplace can increase Medicaid enrollment. Expanding enrollment will lead to greater insurance coverage, which is critical to ensuring patient access to healthcare.

2. **Increase the number of residency slots in the Resident Physician Shortage Reduction Act of 2021 to 21,000 slots over the course of seven years.**

Increasing the number of residency slots in Medicare-supported direct graduate medical education and indirect medical education will allow more doctors to be accepted into these programs and will help the current shortage of physicians. The Government Accountability Office will continue monitoring and reporting strategies that will increase the diversity of the health professional workforce with respect to representation from minority, low-income and rural communities.

3. **Encourage the expansion of community health centers (CHCs).**
The expansion of CHCs will help improve accessibility to primary healthcare services. This will help increase accessibility to care in rural communities, as its goal is to reduce health disparities. Funding for CHCs will need to be increased by assigning $6 billion annually to renew the $4 billion Community Health Center Fund and increase discretionary allocations from $1.6 billion to $2 billion.

4. **Expand coverage of diverse treatment options to increase accessibility.**
Encourage insurance plans to provide access to telehealth professionals. This allows health professionals to practice virtually. Furthermore, barriers to accessing healthcare will decrease significantly in rural communities by offering primary and preventive care remotely.

5. **Implement a more thorough education program for state medical licensing boards to address racial, ethnic and gender biases within American medical institutions.**
Discriminatory attitudes and behaviors from healthcare providers contribute to health disparities between white, non-white and

female Americans. The Liaison Committee on Medical Education (LCME) should review standardized curriculums to include courses that address implicit bias and ways to counteract it. After licensing, physicians ought to receive continuous education and training that addresses biases among existing providers. This will combat inequalities that affect minorities and women within the healthcare system.

Why This Initiative is Important:
This plan expands on the best of public and private insurance firms to create a system better suited to the needs of Americans, increasing the efficiency of medical providers. Simultaneously, this plan encourages market competition to ease individual financial strain and allows Americans to have more freedom of choice regarding their health. It also addresses many of the inequalities that minorities face regarding the accessibility and quality of healthcare.

Economic Impact (from our student economist team):
- Estimated net annual cost to the federal government: $6.5 billion.
- There will be a significant cost to states and insurance companies associated with this proposal, which will most likely be passed on to consumers.
- This proposal will benefit consumers by increasing access to care, lowering prescription drug prices and encouraging individuals to lead healthier lifestyles.
- Estimated effect on the annual federal deficit: + $65 billion.

To learn how our student economists came up with this economic impact, send an email to info@ournationalconversation.org and ask for a more thorough description of their methodologies.

Final Thought for Now:
"This great nation cannot afford to allow its citizens to suffer needlessly from the lack of proper medical care. Our ultimate aim must be a comprehensive insurance system to protect all our people equally against insecurity and ill health." – Harry Truman (1948)

Acknowledgments:
The following student(s) worked on this nonpartisan proposal: Sophie Brown, Boston University; Allison Potter, Elon University; Catheryn McDowell, Vanderbilt University; Cole Woody, Dulles High School; Hannah Halladay, Cornell College; Karen Huynh, University of California Los Angeles; Krithik Vishwanath, Klein Cain High School; Sana Imam, The George Washington University; Maui Wabe, Mira Mesa High School.

The following individuals worked with our student interns and contributed expertise, wisdom and moral support in the development of this proposal:
1. Ned Holland: Hospital and industry association counsel and board member; private sector benefits and healthcare purchasing executive; former Assistant Secretary of HHS (Obama Administration). Kansas City, MO.
2. Thomas Kline: Personal Injury and Medical Malpractice Attorney, Kline and Specter. Hollywood, FL.
3. Gregory Hess, M.D.: President, Wabash College; CEO, Institute for the International Education of Students. Greater Philadelphia Area, PA.
4. Brooke Ellison, Ph.D.: Board of Directors Member, National Organization of Disabilities; Influencer. Greater New York City Area, NY.

5. <u>Ayana Buckner:</u> Preventive Medicine Doctor, Grady Memorial Hospital. Greater Atlanta Area, GA.
6. <u>Brian Thomas, M.D.</u>: Medical Oncologist and Hematologist, Allegheny Health Network Cancer Institute. Pittsburgh, PA.

Note: Not all participants agree with every aspect of this proposal. To arrive at a proposal that takes multiple views into account requires compromise and difficult decisions. For individual commentary on this proposal and more detail, go to OurNationalConversation.org. We invite you to add your comments as well.

Sources:

"About Rural Health | CSELS | OPHSS | CDC". *CDC*, 2022, https://www.cdc.gov/ruralhealth/about.html. Accessed 14 Jan 2022.

Blumberg, Linda J., Holahan, John and Zuckerman, Stephen. "The Healthy America Program." *Urban Institute,* May 2018. https://www.urban.org/sites/default/files/publication/98432/2001826_2018.05.11_healthy_america_final_1.pdf

Hall, W. J., Chapman, M. V., Lee, K. M., Merino, Y. M., Thomas, T. W., Payne, B. K., Eng, E., Day, S. H., & Coyne-Beasley, T. "Implicit Racial/Ethnic Bias Among Health Care Professionals and Its Influence on Health Care Outcomes: A Systematic Review." *PubMed Central (PMC),* Dec. 2015, https://www.ncbi.nlm.nih.gov/pmc/articles/PMC4638275/

"Health Care." *Biden for President,* 2020. joebiden.com/healthcare/#.

"Healthcare: President Donald J. Trump Achievements." *Promises Kept,* 2020. https://www.promiseskept.com/achievement/overview/healthcare/.

Heiser, S. "New AAMC Report Confirms Growing Physician Shortage" *AAMC*. 26 Jun. 2020, https://www.aamc.org/news-insights/press-releases/new-aamc-report-confirms-growing-physician-shortage

Jubbal, Kevin, M.D. "Rejected from Medical School. Now What?". *Med School Tutors,* 2019, https://www.medschooltutors.com/blog/rejected-from-med-school

Keith, K. "Tracking the Uninsured Rate In 2019 and 2020." *Health Affairs.* 7 Oct. 2020, https://www.healthaffairs.org/do/10.1377/hblog20201007.502559/full/

"Key Facts about the Uninsured Population." *KFF.* 13 Nov. 2020, https://www.kff.org/uninsured/issue-brief/key-facts-about-the-uninsured-population/

Porter, M. E., & Lee, T. H. "The Strategy That Will Fix Health Care." *Harvard Business Review*; 1 Oct. 2013, https://www.facebook.com/HBR. https://hbr.org/2013/10/the-strategy-that-will-fix-health-care

"State Funding." *National Association of Community Health Centers,* 2020. https://www.nachc.org/focus-areas/policy-matters/health-center-funding/state-funding.

"Health Insurance Coverage in the United States: 2019." *United States Census Bureau.* 15 Sept. 2020, https://www.census.gov/library/publications/2020/demo/p60-271.html

"Why Community Health Is Important for Public Health" *Tulane University.* 21 May 2020, https://publichealth.tulane.edu/blog/why-community-health-is-important-for-public-health/

Let's Fix America

Getting Serious About Mental Health

Big Picture:
More than 20% of Americans have a mental illness. However, mental healthcare is expensive, inadequate and inaccessible, causing a deficiency of appropriate care. We must balance mental and physical health standards and increase access to treatment.

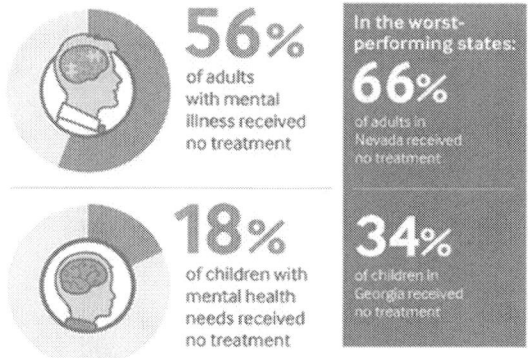

Graphic From: *The State of Mental Health Care in America, 2017*. 2013–15 National Survey of Drug Use and Health; *2016 National Survey of Children's Health*. Child and Adolescent Health Measurement Initiative. *The Commonwealth Fund*, May 2018. This graphic shows the percentage of people who need mental health treatment but have not received it, on average and in the worst performing states.

Operative Definitions:

1. **"Fail First" policy:** Insurance policies that require the cheapest drug to be prescribed to a patient first, rather than that originally prescribed by the doctor.
2. **Mental health certification:** The certification and licensure required to practice as a clinical mental health professional.
3. **Mental health access:** The factors that influence a person's ability to receive treatment, such as access to insurance, special education and workforce availability.
4. **The Mental Health Parity Act of 1996:** A federal law that requires health insurance plans to cover behavioral health benefits and physical health benefits equally.

Important Facts and Statistics:

1. Approximately half of all Americans living with a mental illness drive over an hour to receive mental health services.
2. 53% of adults seeking mental healthcare are considered low-income.
3. Medical necessity is defined differently by physicians and health insurance providers. The latter group tends to use their own criteria to deny insurance claims despite physicians' and the medical community's recommended course of treatment.
4. 37% of inmates in state and federal prisons suffer from a mental illness, and 44% of inmates in locally run jails suffer from mental illness.
5. 66% of inmates in federal prisons have reported not receiving any mental health treatment for their illness.
6. Studies have found that only 23% of high school students believe their school has sufficient resources to support students with mental health issues.

5-Point Plan:

1. **Pass stronger federal regulations to better enforce parity laws.**
   Mandate a telemedicine parity law so that all insurers are required to cover telehealth services to increase accessibility to mental health treatment.

2. **Eliminate "Fail First" policies.**
   By eliminating these policies, a doctor would be able to prescribe what they consider to be suitable treatment, rather than having to work through a list before finally arriving at the best treatment for the patient. However, insurance policies or medical standards may still require a doctor to talk to the patient about the cheapest option available, which may be prescribed at the physician's discretion.

3. **Expand the accessibility of mental health services.**
   State and local governments should hold mental health clinics and job-training programs at local institutions, such as community centers, schools and city hospitals. Fund grassroots mental health services, mentioned above, through the guidelines in the *Improving Access to Healthcare policy*. List reputable and accessible mental health professionals on local and state government websites. These professionals will be filtered by insurance providers and ZIP codes. Additionally, require schools and companies to hire mental health experts.

4. **Increase funding by 5% for prisons that offer inmates mental health services.**
   Increasing funding to public prisons will help alleviate the mental health problem. It can also serve as an incentive for other public prisons to offer mental health services.

5. **Require doctors to inform patients of available mental health screenings during primary care.**
   During patients' annual physical check-ups, doctors must inform patients of opportunities for mental health check-ups. Mental health screenings will occur more frequently, and appropriate treatments can begin sooner when found necessary.

Why This Initiative is Important:
Mental health problems are prevalent across all age, gender, ethnic and socioeconomic groups within the U.S. This plan aims to remove the barriers that prevent access to mental healthcare by alleviating the shortage of care facilities while expanding care and cracking down on corruption within insurance companies. This includes tackling the current Medical Necessity and Fail First policies, as well as ensuring that they obey parity laws. Additionally, this proposal provides services for the youth and subsequently combats the stigma surrounding receiving mental healthcare. Lastly, it helps low-income adults struggling with mental health to find adequate care.

Economic Impact (from our student economist team):
- Meaningful numbers could not be calculated for this proposal's effects on the federal deficit.
- There will be a large economic burden placed on states and businesses associated with scaling up mental health resources.
- Mental illness costs Americans up to $193 billion per year in lost earnings. Closing this gap could generate up to $40 billion in

additional income tax revenue and provide a boost to GDP but is not guaranteed.
- Expected increase in workplace productivity, employment rates, economic growth and overall levels of well-being.

To learn how our student economists came up with this economic impact, send an email to info@ournationalconversation.org and ask for a more thorough description of their methodologies.

Final Thought for Now:
"Our country must make a commitment: Americans with mental illness deserve our understanding, and they deserve excellent care." **– George W. Bush (2002)**

Acknowledgments:
The following student(s) worked on this nonpartisan proposal: Ryan Ishii, University of California, Santa Barbara; Connie Xu, University of California, Berkeley; Karen Huynh, University of California, Los Angeles.

The following individuals worked with our student interns and contributed expertise, wisdom and moral support in the development of this proposal:
1. Farha Abbasi, Ph.D.: Professor of Psychology, Michigan State University. East Lansing, MI.
2. Jennifer Lewis, Ph.D.: Clinical Associate Professor of Social Work, University of Southern California. San Diego, CA.
3. Ruth C. White, Ph.D.: Adjunct Professor of Social Welfare Policy, Fordham University; Director of Diversity, Equity, Inclusion and Belonging, Carbon Five. San Francisco Bay Area, CA.

4. Ronald Manderscheid, Ph.D.: Executive Director, National Association of County Behavioral Health and Developmental Disability; Professor, Bloomberg School of Public Health, Johns Hopkins University; Professor, School of Social Work, University of Southern California. Washington, DC.
5. Lois Weithorn, Ph.D., J.D.: Professor of Mental Health and Healthcare Law, University of California, Hastings College of Law. San Francisco, CA.
6. Rintaro Mori, M.D., Ph.D.: Regional Adviser, Population Aging and Sustainable Development, United Nations Population Fund. Japan.
7. Randall Avila: Executive Director, Republican Party of Orange County. Yorba Linda, CA.

Note: Not all participants agree with every aspect of this proposal. To arrive at a proposal that takes multiple views into account requires compromise and difficult decisions. For individual commentary on this proposal and more detail, go to OurNationalConversation.org. We invite you to add your comments as well.

Sources:

"Access to Mental Health Care and Incarceration." *Mental Health America.* 11 Aug. 2021, https://www.mhanational.org/issues/access-mental-health-care-and-incarceration

Breitinger, Scott. "3 ways to expand access to mental health care beyond adding more psychiatrists." *STAT News,* 20 Apr. 2018. www.statnews.com/2018/04/20/expand-access-mental-health-care/.

Dangor, Graison. "Mental Health Parity' Is Still an Elusive Goal in U.S. Insurance Coverage." *NPR,* 7 Jun. 2019. www.npr.org/sections/health-shots/2019/06/07/730404539/mental-health-parity-is-still-an-elusive-goal-in-u-s-insurance-coverage.

Heath, Sara. "Key Barriers Limiting Patient Access to Mental Healthcare." *Patient Engagement Hit,* 7 Aug. 2019. https://patientengagementhit.com/news/key-barriers-limiting-patient-access-to-mental-healthcare

"Mental Health". *PrisonPolicy,* 2022, https://www.prisonpolicy.org/research/mental_health/.

Marques de Miranda, Debora et al. "How Is COVID-19 Pandemic Impacting Mental Health of Children and Adolescents?". *International Journal of Disaster Risk Reduction,* vol 51, 2020, p. 101845. *Elsevier BV,* doi:10.1016/j.ijdrr.2020.101845.

"Mental Health Benefits: State Laws Mandating or Regulating." *National Conference of State Legislatures,* 30 Dec. 2015. ncsl.org/research/health/mental-health-benefits-state-mandates.aspx.

"New Study Reveals Lack of Access as Root Cause for Mental Health Crisis in America." *The National Council for Behavioral health,* 2018. www.thenationalcouncil.org/press-releases/new-study-reveals-lack-of-access-as-root-cause-for-mental-health-crisis-in-america/.

"The State of Mental Health in America." *Mental Health America,* 2022, https://mhanational.org/issues/state-mental-health-america

Reforming Women's Reproductive Healthcare

Big Picture:
Women's reproductive healthcare is difficult to access, overly expensive and, consequently, underutilized by women in America. Preventive and reproductive wellness care must be made readily available to those who need it.

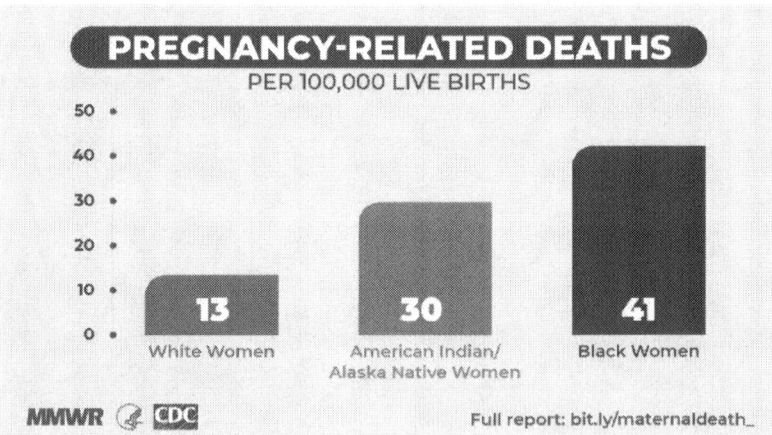

Graphic From: *Pregnancy-Related Deaths. Morbidity and Mortality Weekly Report. Cdc.gov.* 8 Sept. 2020. This graph illustrates disturbing differences in maternal death rates among racial groups. Pregnancy-related deaths are more prevalent in Indigenous women than in white women, with Black women being at highest risk.

Operative Definitions:
1. **Title X Family Planning Program:** A federal grant initiative enacted in 1970 dedicated to providing individuals with comprehensive family planning and related preventive health services.
2. **Reproductive Wellness Exams:** Exams centered around examining a woman's reproductive health. Consultations range from pelvic exams to resolving irregular periods.

3. **Medicaid:** A federal and state program that provides healthcare cost assistance to qualified people with limited income and resources.
4. **Postpartum:** The period of time beginning immediately after childbirth as the mother's body returns to a non-pregnant state.
5. **Reproductive Health:** A field of research, healthcare and social activism that explores the health of an individual's reproductive system and sexual well-being during all stages of their life.

Important Facts and Statistics:
1. Title X supported services for more than 3 million people over nearly 4.7 million visits in 2019.
2. The average woman surveyed spends $13.25 a month on menstrual products. That's $6,360 in an average woman's reproductive lifetime (ages 12 to 52).
3. On average, women pay an extra estimated $1,300 per year for essentially the same products and services that men use.
4. In 2019, close to 10 million women of reproductive age in the U.S. lived below the federal poverty line.
5. Less than 50% of high schools and about 20% of middle schools in the U.S. teach the 16 topics of sexual health education recommended by the Centers for Disease Control and Prevention (CDC).

5-Point Plan:
1. **Encourage all states to exempt female hygiene products from their respective sales taxes and encourage all 50 states to provide feminine hygiene products in public schools.**
Exempting female hygiene products will make these products more affordable. Providing these products at schools will increase attendance rates for impoverished students who might otherwise

have to stay at home during menstruation and will provide them with a necessity that they may not have at home.

2. **Restore 10.8% of Title X clinic funding.**
   This will restore funding to its 2010 level. By returning $33 million of funding, clinics will become a more significant resource for reproductive care.

3. **Expand Medicaid coverage of postpartum care from 60 days to one year and include mental health counseling.**
   For many women, recovery after birth can be physically and mentally debilitating. Providing accessible physical and mental health care will reduce maternal mortality rates and post-delivery complications.

4. **Encourage the sexual education system in all public middle and high schools to meet the CDC's 16 essential sexual health topics.**
   Reforming the sexual education system to meet the CDC's recommendations and including information and statistics about abortion will ensure schools cover topics including STI transmission and pregnancies, how to prevent them and options for care. Additionally, it will provide students with ways to access resources and services if needed. As a result, this could prevent unwanted pregnancies and sexually transmitted infections (STIs) in adolescents.

5. **Include adequate rape, incest and health exceptions to abortion laws.**
   Currently, 18 states prohibit abortion if it is after 20 weeks with no adequate exceptions for cases of rape, incest or some health complication save for a demonstrable threat to the mother's life.

By encouraging these states to provide adequate exceptions, the mental and physical health of women in these scenarios will improve.

Why This Initiative is Important:
This initiative ensures availability, accessibility and quality care for every woman in America. Women who are already covered by suitable health insurance will maintain their access to care. This plan will increase care for the uninsured, which will reduce unintended pregnancies, the spread of STIs and poor delivery outcomes. We can protect the health of our adolescents through proper healthcare and education efforts.

Economic Impact (from our student economist team):
- Estimated effect on the annual federal deficit: + $110 million.
- States and localities will incur the costs of revamping curriculum and providing feminine hygiene products in schools.
- This plan will attain economic security for women and lower long-term healthcare costs.

To learn how our student economists came up with this economic impact, send an email to info@ournationalconversation.org and ask for a more thorough description of their methodologies.

Final Thought for Now:
"The fundamental purpose of feminism is that women should have equal opportunity and equal rights with every other citizen." – Eleanor Roosevelt (1935)

Acknowledgments:
The following students worked on this nonpartisan proposal: Sophie Brown, Boston University; Claire Dormitzer, University of Maryland, College Park; Karen Huynh, University of California Los Angeles; Sana Imam, The George Washington University; Sophia Welsh, Mira Mesa High School.

The following individuals worked with our student interns and contributed expertise, wisdom and moral support in the development of this proposal:
1. Lois McCloskey, DrPH: Maternal and Child Health Center for Excellence Director; Associate Professor, Boston University. Boston, MA.
2. Chadburn Ray, M.D.: Professor of Obstetrics and Gynecology, Augusta University Medical School; member, Georgia Department of Public Health's Maternal Levels of Care; Member, Maternal Mortality Review. Grovetown, GA.
3. M. Isabelle Chaudry, J.D.: Senior Policy Manager, National Women's Health Network. Washington, DC.
4. Jane Orient, M.D.: Executive Director, Association of American Physicians and Surgeons. Tucson, AZ.
5. Kelsey Hazzard, J.D: President, Secular Pro-Life; Board Member, Equal Rights Institute. Naples, FL.
6. Sarah Gehlert: Former Dean, College of Social Work, University of South Carolina; Faculty Advisory Council, Institute of Public Health; Advisory Panel Member, Inclusion Institute for Healthcare. Lexington County, CA.

Note: Not all participants agree with every aspect of this proposal. To arrive at a proposal that takes multiple views into account requires compromise and difficult decisions. For individual commentary on this proposal and more detail, go to OurNationalConversation.org. We invite you to add your comments as well.

Sources:
"An Overview of Abortion Laws" *Guttmacher Institute.* 9 Mar. 2016 https://www.guttmacher.org/state-policy/explore/overview-abortion-laws#

"Budget and Appropriations." *National Family Planning & Reproductive Health Association,* 13 Sep. 2018, https://www.chn.org/organizations/national-family-planning-reproductive-health-association-nfprha/

Daw, R. Jamie, et al. "Women in the United States Experience High Rates of Coverage 'Churn' In Months Before and After Childbirth." *Health Affairs,* vol. 36, no.4, pp. 598-606, Apr. 2017. doi.org/10.1377/hlthaff.2016.1241.

Denford, Sarah, et al. "A comprehensive review of reviews of school-based interventions to improve sexual-health." *Health Psychology Review,* vol. 11, no. 1, pp. 33-52, 2017, DOI: 10.1080/17437199.2016.1240625.

Morgan, A. Perri, et al. "Impact of Physicians, Nurse Practitioners and Physician Assistants on Utilization and Costs for Complex Patients." *Health Affairs,* vol. 38, no. 6, pp.1028-1036, June 2019, DOI: 10.1377/hlthaff.2019.00014.

"NHPC Press Release: Schools Teaching Prevention" *CDC.* 9 Dec. 2015, https://www.cdc.gov/nchhstp/newsroom/2015/nhpc-press-release-schools-teaching-prevention.html

Scaccia, Annamarya. "The Price Young Girls Pay When Tampons Aren't Free." *Free The Tampons,* 29 Feb. 2016. www.freethetampons.org/the-price-young-girls-pay-when-tampons-arent-free.html.

Trumble, Sarah. "What You Should Know about Abortion after 20 Weeks ." *Third Way,* 19 Feb. 2020, www.thirdway.org/one-pager/what-you-should-know-about-abortion-after-20-weeks.

Tackling Obesity in America

Big Picture:
In America, one in three adults and one in five children are obese. This disease is the number one cause of preventable deaths in America and contributes to one-third of national healthcare costs.

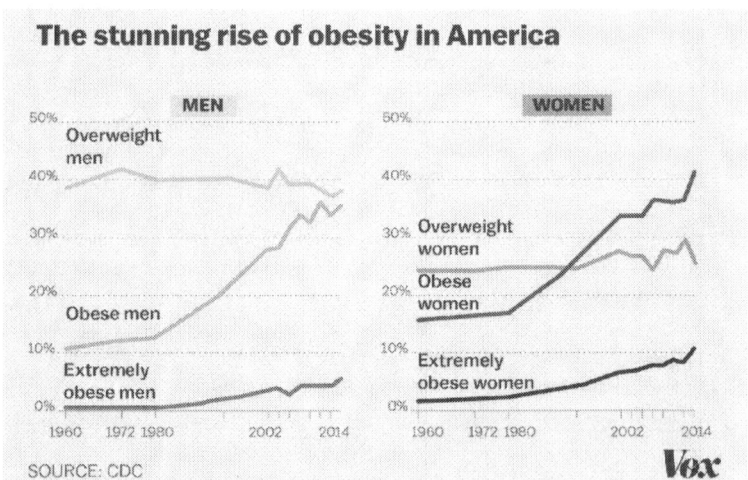

Graphic From: Zarracina, Javier. *The stunning rise of obesity in America.* Vox.com. 8 Sept. 2020. These charts illustrate the growing obesity rates among American men and women from 1960 to 2014.

Operative Definitions:
1. **Supplemental Nutritional Assistance Program (SNAP):** A program that provides food funds to low-income individuals.
2. **Early Care and Education Learning Collaborative (ECELC):** A project that aims to implement policy to help end childhood obesity.

Important Facts and Statistics:

1. In America from 1999 to 2017, the prevalence of obesity increased from 30.5% to 42.4%, and the prevalence of severe obesity increased from 4.7% to 9.2%.
2. The worldwide prevalence of obesity nearly tripled between 1975 and 2016.
3. The estimated annual medical cost of obesity in the U.S. was $147 billion in 2008. The annual medical cost for people who are obese was $1,429 higher than those of normal weight.

5-Point Plan:

1. **Implement national obesity education campaigns.**
   These campaigns will be funded by the ECELC, which educates children about lifestyle choices. Incentivize non-chain restaurants to have nutritional labels with advertising space for healthy products.

2. **Require weight control and obesity care to be included in baseline coverage plans.**
   Taxpayers and insurers will save billions annually by preventing obesity.

3. **Implement a national sugar-sweetened beverage excise tax.**
   A one cent per ounce tax on manufacturers, transporters and retailers will generate $30 of healthcare savings for each $1 invested.

4. **Pilot food prescription programs in all localities.**
   Pharmacies, farms and healthcare facilities will collaborate to let patients pick affordable food for their diet. Target "food-as-medication" efforts in food deserts, which are areas with limited access to affordable and nutritious food options, typically in low-

income neighborhoods. To address food deserts, mobile farmers' markets will be subsidized to get fresh produce in stores, and existing tax incentives for supermarkets to operate in Opportunity Zones will be strengthened. See *Small Business policy*.

5. **Encourage financial incentives for every SNAP dollar spent on fruits and vegetables.**
Offering financial incentives with the SNAP card on a federal level will encourage people to purchase and consume healthier foods. With every SNAP dollar spent on eligible fruits or vegetables, 30 cents can be rewarded back to the person's SNAP card.

Why This Initiative is Important:
Increased education and access to healthy lifestyle options help individuals control their weight. Power is transferred towards state and local governments to partner with organizations and improve community health. This initiative protects Americans by turning big businesses healthy. Food and beverage companies removed 6.5 trillion calories from the marketplace from 2007 to 2012, proving how much potential there is for dietary improvement. Medical diagnoses will now focus on encouraging a healthy lifestyle to limit the need for costly treatment.

Economic Impact (from our student economist team):
- By investing in reducing obesity, we can reduce long-term healthcare costs, increase workplace productivity and lower premature mortality rates.
- Estimated effect on the annual federal deficit: - $34 billion

To learn how our student economists came up with this economic impact, send an email to info@ournationalconversation.org and ask for a more thorough description of their methodologies.

Final Thought for Now:
"If the childhood obesity epidemic remains unchecked, it will condemn many of our kids to shorter lives, as well as the emotional and financial burdens of poor health." – Richard Carmona

Acknowledgments:
The following student(s) worked on this nonpartisan proposal: Grace Ellrodt, Bates College; Pablo Herrera, Baylor University; Catheryn McDowell, Vanderbilt University; Sophie Brown, Baylor University; Veda Kota, Rutgers University; Maui Wabe, Mira Mesa High School.

The following individuals worked with our student interns and contributed expertise, wisdom and moral support in the development of this proposal:

1. Mark Pettus, Ph.D.: Medical Education Director, Berkshire Medical Center. Dalton, MA.
2. Lisa Nelson, Ph.D.: Family physician, Family Practice Associates; Medical Director, Nutrition Center; Director of Medical Education, Kripalu Center for Yoga and Health. Great Barrington, MA.
3. Pete Gazillo: Director of Nutritional Health, Berkshire Medical Center. Pittsfield, MA.
4. James Zervios: Vice President of Communications, Obesity Action Coalition. Tampa, FL.
5. Zach Ward: Ph.D candidate; programmer/analyst for the Center for Health Decision Science, Harvard T.H. Chan School of Public Health. Boston, MA.
6. Eli Bremer: Former military officer and olympian; health and wellness entrepreneur; long-serving Colorado republican. Colorado Springs, CO.

Let's Fix America

Note: Not all participants agree with every aspect of this proposal. To arrive at a proposal that takes multiple views into account requires compromise and difficult decisions. For individual commentary on this proposal and more detail, go to OurNationalConversation.org. We invite you to add your comments as well.

Sources:

Abdelaal, Mahmoud et al. "Morbidity and mortality associated with obesity." Annals of translational medicine, vol. 5, no. 7 (2017): 161. doi:10.21037/atm.2017.03.107.

Biener, Adam et al. "The High and Rising Costs of Obesity to the US Health Care System." Journal of general internal medicine vol. 32, Suppl 1 (2017): 6-8. doi:10.1007/s11606-016-3968-8.

"Food Deserts." *Food Empowerment Project,* 9 Jun. 2022, foodispower.org/access-health/food-deserts/.

Goddu, Anna P et al. "Food Rx: a community-university partnership to prescribe healthy eating on the South Side of Chicago." Journal of prevention & intervention in the community vol. 43, no. 2 (2015): 148-62. doi:10.1080/10852352.2014.973251.

Goldman, Dana. "Obesity, Second to Smoking as the Most Preventable Cause of US Deaths, Needs New Approaches." *USC Schaeffer,* 27 Jan. 2020. healthpolicy.usc.edu/article/obesity-second-to-smoking-as-the-most-preventable-cause-of-us-deaths-needs-new-approaches/

Kern, David M., et al. "Neighborhood Prices of Healthier and Unhealthier Foods and Associations with Diet Quality: Evidence from the Multi-Ethnic Study of Atherosclerosis." International Journal of Environmental Research and Public Health, vol. 14, no. 11, 2017. doi.org/10.3390/ijerph14111394.

Sun, Yangbo, et al. "Association of Normal-Weight Central Obesity with All-Cause and Cause-Specific Mortality Among Postmenopausal Women." *JAMA Network* Open, vol. 2, no. 7, 2019. doi:10.1001/jamanetworkopen.2019.7337.

"The State of Obesity 2018: Better Policies for a Healthier America." T*rust for America's Health*, 2018. www.tfah.org/report-details/the-state-of-obesity-2018/.

"Chapter 2: Grocery Stores Encouraging Full-Service Grocery Stores to Locate in Underserved Areas and Promote Healthier Foods." *CDC,* 9 Jun. 2022, https://www.cdc.gov/nccdphp/dnpao/state-local-programs/pdf/healthier-food-retail-guide-chapter-2.pdf

Addressing Our Nation's Substance Abuse Epidemic

Big Picture:
Substance abuse continues to be neglected as a national health issue; with approximately 130 Americans dying every day from opioid overdose. This proposal recognizes addiction as a disease and takes a health-oriented approach to solving our nation's substance abuse epidemic.

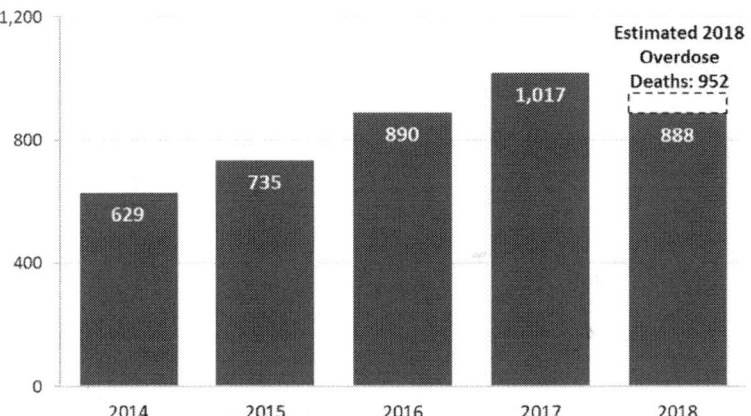

Note: Data from 2018 is preliminary and underestimates total overdose deaths. There are 888 confirmed overdose deaths in 2018 with more cases pending the cause of death. Many of these pending records will be drug overdoses. An estimation of the approximate number of 2018 overdose deaths is represented by the black dotted line above the confirmed 2018 deaths.
Source: West Virginia Health Statistics Center, Vital Statistics System, Sept. 04, 2019.

Graphic From: "Gov. Justice – DHHR Data Suggests West Virginia Overdose Deaths Appear to be Declining." *West Virginia Department of Health & Humans Resources.* 5 Sept. 2019. This graph illustrates an increase in the amount of overdose deaths in West Virginia over a four-year period, followed by a slight decrease in 2018.

Operative Definitions:
1. **The 2018 SUPPORT Act:** The Substance Use Disorder Prevention that Promotes Opioid Recovery and Treatment for Patients and Communities Act. This comprehensive, bipartisan legislation addresses the opioid epidemic with a very broad scope including treatment, prevention, recovery and enforcement. It also addresses the role of Medicaid in helping each state provide medical services related to substance abuse.
2. **Medication-assisted treatment:** The use of medication combined with counseling and behavioral therapies to take a holistic approach to substance use disorder treatment.
3. **Naloxone:** A medication designed to rapidly reverse opioid overdoses. It binds to opioid receptors to block the effects of opioids and reverse the symptoms.

Important Facts and Statistics:
1. Nearly 21 million Americans struggle with at least one substance related addiction, but only 10% receive treatment.
2. Alcohol and drug addiction cost the U.S. economy over $600 billion annually.
3. More than 90% of people who have a substance use disorder started to drink alcohol or use drugs before they were 18 years old.

6-Point Plan:
1. **Double the amount of funding allocated to medication-assisted treatment programs.**
Psychosocial interventions and counseling are a critical aspect of the treatment regimen for opioid addictions. Fully optimizing psychosocial treatments, particularly different forms of cognitive behavioral therapy, requires expanding access to medication-assisted treatment (MAT) programs. MAT combines psychosocial therapies and medication (methadone, buprenorphine or naltrexone) to

effectively inhibit opioid addiction, blocking receptors in the brain and therefore controlling withdrawal symptoms during recovery. As there is a shortage of providers who administer MAT nationwide, expanding and increasing funding in MAT programs across all providers would counteract this scarcity.

2. **Increase federal grants by 10% for nonprofit organizations (NGOs) that are actively confronting the opioid crisis.**
Increasing federal grants to these NGOs will provide the necessary funds for research, treatment and prevention concerning the opioid crisis. Increasing federal grants can serve as an incentive for other NGOs to further assist in the crisis.

3. **Impose a federal opioid registration fee.**
Set a fee on opiate producers and sellers based on Minnesota's opiate fee policy, a regulation requiring opiate manufacturers that sell, deliver or distribute opiates to pay a fee. Resulting revenue must be allocated to rehabilitation and treatment programs to complement federal and state-level funding.

4. **Reform drug addiction education.**
The Department of Health and Human Services (HHS) must require that medical schools remove training material that associates addiction with certain racial or social groups. In addition, require medical schools to teach future physicians the impact of and alternatives to opioids, establishing opioids as a last-resort treatment option.

5. **Introduce guidelines for opioid prescription.**
Standardization of prescriptions lacks an evidence-based approach and allows for the wrongful administration of opioids. By introducing standardized guidelines created through previous

patient data and surgeon consensus, doctors will be more conservative with prescriptions and less likely to over-prescribe/prescribe opioids in unnecessary cases. Research indicates that opioid prescriptions will reduce by over 50% through the introduction of an evidence-based approach.

6. **Make Naloxone more available.**
Make Naloxone available over the counter. Along with education on the correct usage of opioids, this will reduce accidental overdoses. Additionally, states must require high schools to carry Naloxone. This would add a negligible cost to the Department of Education's Safer Schools programs, which already target drug use and abuse in schools.

Why This Initiative is Important:
Less than 20% of Americans who need addiction treatment actually receive the treatment. Expanding options and requirements for coverage will increase its accessibility. Fifty percent of those suffering from addiction have mental health issues; in 80% of those cases, mental illness precedes substance abuse. As a result, treating mental health is a necessary preventive measure. Holding doctors and manufacturers accountable for opioid production and distribution will curb the loss of life from prescription drug abuse. Recognizing addiction as a treatable illness and increasing treatment access will help tackle America's opioid epidemic and reduce the billions spent on opioid misuse.

Economic Impact (from our student economist team):
- New federal costs are covered by new revenue and savings. Costs will decrease over time alongside addiction.

- Opioid abuse alone costs $80 billion annually in direct costs and up to $500 billion when both implicit and explicit costs are considered.
- Meaningful numbers could not be calculated for this proposal's effect on the federal deficit.

To learn how our student economists came up with this economic impact, send an email to info@ournationalconversation.org and ask for a more thorough description of their methodologies.

Final Thought for Now:
***"Penalties against drug use should not be more damaging to an individual than the use of the drug itself." —* Jimmy Carter**

Acknowledgments:
The following student(s) worked on this nonpartisan proposal: Catheryn McDowell, Vanderbilt University; Andrew Jarvis, University of Pennsylvania; Sophie Brown, Boston University; Pablo Herrera, Baylor University; Polina Lissin, Boston University; Marisa Kim, Vanderbilt University; Sumiko Sato, University of San Diego; Karen Huynh, University of California Los Angeles; Maui Wabe, Mira Mesa High School.

The following individuals worked with our student interns and contributed expertise, wisdom and moral support in the development of this proposal:
1. Payal Patel, M.D., M.P.H.: Assistant Professor of Internal Medicine, University of Michigan. Ann Arbor, MI.
2. Ricardo Ramos, M.D.: Family medicine doctor, Community Care Health. Selma, CA.
3. Lorena Ramos, M.A.: Founder and therapist, She is Strong and Mindful. Chicago, IL.

Note: Not all participants agree with every aspect of this proposal. To arrive at a proposal that takes multiple views into account requires compromise and difficult decisions. For individual commentary on this proposal, and more detail, go to OurNationalConversation.org. We invite you to add your comments as well.

Sources:

Bossert, Nikki, et al. "State Opioid Taxes." *Taxnote*, vol. 93, no. 12, Sept. 16, 2019, p.1151. tax.kpmg.us/content/dam/tax/en/pdfs/2019/state-opioid-tax-state-tax-notes-sept-2019.pdf.

Brown, C. S., Vu, J. V., Howard, R. A., Gunaseelan, V., Brummett, C. M., Waljee, J., & Englesbe, M. Assessment of a quality improvement intervention to decrease opioid prescribing in a regional health system. BMJ Quality & Safety, Vol 30. No 3., (2020). 251–259. https://doi.org/10.1136/bmjqs-2020-011295

Bruckner, Tim A et al. "State-level education standards for substance use prevention programs in schools: a systematic content analysis." *The Journal of adolescent health: official publication of the Society for Adolescent Medicine* vol. 54, No. 4 (2014): 467-73. doi:10.1016/j.jadohealth.2013.07.020.

Chandler, Redonna K, et al. "Treating Drug Abuse and Addiction in the Criminal Justice System: Improving Public Health and Safety." *JAMA,* Jan 14, 2009. pp. 183–190. doi:10.1001/jama.2008.976.

Kaafarani, H. M., Eid, A. I., Antonelli, D. M., Chang, D. C., Elsharkawy, A. E., Elahad, J. A., Lancaster, E. A., Schulz, J. T., Melnitchouk, S. I., Kastrinakis, W. V., Hutter, M. M., Masiakos, P. T., Colwell, A. S., Wright, C. D., & Lillemoe, K. D. "Description and impact of a comprehensive multispecialty multidisciplinary intervention to decrease opioid prescribing in surgery." Annals of Surgery, 270(3), 452–462. (2019). https://doi.org/10.1097/sla.0000000000003462

"Medicaid Expansion." *NAMI,* 9 Jun. 2022, nami.org/Advocacy/Policy-Priorities/Improve-Care/Medicaid-Expansion.

"Opioid Overdose Crisis." *National Institute on Drug Abuse: Advancing Addiction Science,* 27 May 2020. www.drugabuse.gov/drug-topics/opioids/opioid-overdose-crisis.

"Reversing the opioid epidemic." *American Medical Association,* 23 Aug. 2019. www.ama-assn.org/delivering-care/opioids/reversing-opioid-epidemic.

"Understanding the Epidemic." *Centers for Disease Control and Prevention,* 19 Mar. 2020. www.cdc.gov/drugoverdose/epidemic/index.html.

Foreign Policy and Defense

"Our military strength is a prerequisite to peace, but let it be clear we maintain this strength in the hope it will never be used."

- Ronald Reagan

Let's Fix America

Reforming U.S. Immigration Policy

Big Picture:
Immigration policies have been a subject of extreme contention since the inception of the United States. However, the data is clear: with smart immigration reform, America will see huge increases in GDP, while setting ethical and humane standards for national immigration policy.

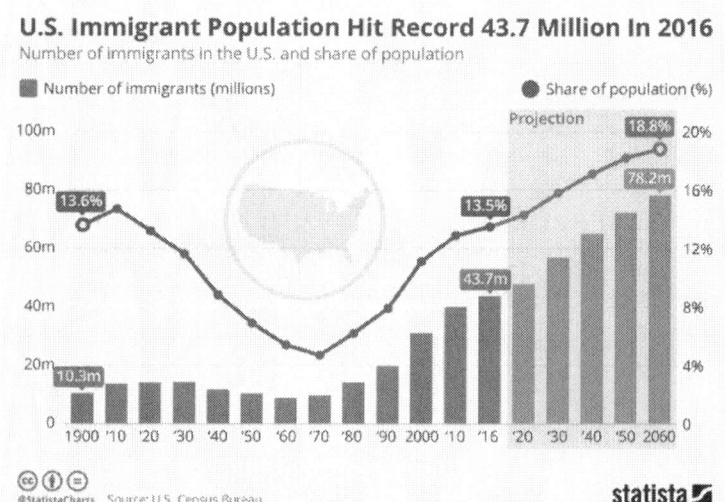

Graphic From: Niall McCarthy. "U.S. Immigrant Population Hit Record 43.7 Million In 2016." *Statista*. 19 Oct. 2017. This figure illustrates the increase and subsequent percentages of immigrants as a portion of the United States population since 1900. The graphic shows a sharp increase in both the number of immigrants in the U.S. and the percentage of the American population which they hold.

Operative Definitions:
1. **Amnesty**: The process of releasing certain individuals from criminal liability; pardoning.

2. **DREAM Act**: A bipartisan bill introduced in 2001 that provides temporary conditional residency, the right to work and a pathway towards citizenship on the condition that they attend college or serve in the U.S. military for a minimum of two years while exhibiting good behavior.
3. **Immigration and Customs Enforcement (ICE):** An agency within the Department of Homeland Security. Its main division focuses on arresting, detaining and deporting unauthorized immigrants within the U.S.

Important Facts and Statistics:
1. Between 2014 and 2017, the U.S. gave $750 million to the Northern Triangle countries of Honduras, Guatemala and El Salvador.
2. It is estimated that there are between 10.5 million and 12 million undocumented migrants in the U.S., and that they have a lower rate of criminal convictions than native-born Americans.
3. People traveling as families constituted the majority of apprehensions at the southwest border of the U.S. in 2019. This marks a shift from the previous immigration apparatus in the U.S., which was oriented towards individuals and young males.
4. The US Bureau of Animal Industry erected the first fence along the frontier in 1909 to stop the trans-border movement of cattle. Border towns erected fences during the 1910s to help channel people into designated crossing points.
5. The US began the installation of border fences to restrict the movement of unlawful immigrants and drugs in 1993 when President Bill Clinton mandated the construction of a barrier between San Diego and Tijuana.
6. The Secure Fence Act of 2006 authorized the construction of 700 miles of border fencing and vehicle barriers, which was completed in 2011.

6-Point Plan:
1. **Provide unauthorized immigrants who have no criminal record with a path to permanent residency.**
This will be available only to undocumented immigrants with no felony charges who register with authorities within six months of the policy coming into force, including those under the DREAM Act. This will help immigrants integrate into society and contribute economically to the country, encouraging a level of involvement in U.S. society which will help ease tensions between immigrant and non-immigrant communities.

2. **Revamp and finance the existing Executive Office of Immigration Reform (EOIR).**
Under the status quo, this agency's primary role is to conduct removal proceedings in immigration courts and pass formal judgments on appeals which arise from these cases. The U.S. should hire 540 more immigration judges over the next three years to accelerate the immigration hearing process. This will be further pushed by establishing a minimum number of cases for judges to hear in a given period. The wait times for citizenship and the lawful permanent resident process must be limited to ensure no one is left waiting too long. The EOIR must also permit spouses and families to immigrate together. Increasing transparency and making all forms available online and in multiple languages will ease this transition.

3. **Reorient the goals and purpose of ICE.**
Focus our ICE agents on deporting criminal unauthorized immigrants. Charges of felonies, domestic violence and willful failure or refusal to depart must be prioritized; this ensures that ICE resources are utilized effectively. In addition, ICE needs to

adopt higher ethical standards, particularly at migrant detention facilities where the human rights of detainees have been violated. Such a policy will prohibit family separation and see increased internal and external inspections, as well as medical, religious and legal services. This will help to ensure the safety of migrants within our borders and return the U.S. to a point of moral authority.

4. **Increase aid to El Salvador, Guatemala and Honduras by $250 million per year for long-term stabilization.**
Many immigrants come from the countries El Salvador, Guatemala and Honduras. Providing more assistance will decrease the number of immigrants to the U.S. This aid will be used to help ensure elections are fair, giving people more of a voice in their countries and more reason to stay. The aid will continue until the number of immigrants drops to below a level that is manageable by border protection authorities. The conditions for this aid must be specific, based on clear and tangible governance reforms in the governments of Guatemala, Honduras and El Salvador, rather than broad goals. Creating incentives for the Central American governments to curtail emigration with increased investments in job markets and infrastructure would increase the quality of life in the region and decrease migration patterns north. In addition, grant opportunities will be made more accessible to local organizations with the goal of addressing the water and material shortages, gang violence and other ills that are the root cause of illegal immigration. Proposals will be advertised and accepted to submit in Spanish.

5. **Reallocate $1 billion in funding from punitive immigration policies to job-focused programs, and another $1 billion to Customs and Border Protection.**
Immigration policy funding is better spent on helping immigrants become useful members of society than it is on punishing them. We should use the funds to grant healthcare access to qualified immigrants. Alongside these programs, extra funds will expand training facilities and increase digital surveillance at the Mexico-U.S. border.

6. **Increase funding for more prominent border infrastructure.**
It is true that a nation without a border is not a nation. Despite increased funding for EOIR and Central America and the reorienting of funds for ICE, it is still critical to ensure that the US border maintains a physical presence and is able to deter illegal immigration. Greater focus must be paid towards legal paths towards citizenship. A weak southern border will neutralize any foreign investment the U.S. makes towards Central America and will further incentivize unauthorized crossings into the U.S. Although increased surveillance and training facilities will help deter illegal immigration, physical barriers must be maintained in order to decrease pressure for border security from record levels of crossings.

Why This Initiative is Important:
This proposal will grant amnesty to unauthorized immigrants who do not have criminal records, while also addressing the fiscal impact of immigration. Immigration is a key component to boosting the economy. These policies aim to restructure the immigration system in a way that prioritizes the safety and national security of the United States. Further national security will be maintained with secure border

Let's Fix America

infrastructure. Once the government implements policies geared towards granting citizenship to more immigrants, there will be an increase in the number of taxpayers, leading to more funding for education, healthcare and infrastructure.

Economic Impact (from our student economist team):
- Estimated effect on the annual federal deficit: + $5.75 billion

To learn how our student economists came up with this economic impact, send an email to info@ournationalconversation.org and ask for a more thorough description of their methodologies.

Final Thought for Now:
"I had always hoped that this land might become a safe and agreeable asylum to the virtuous and persecuted part of mankind, to whatever nation they might belong." – George Washington (1788)

Acknowledgments:
The following student(s) worked on this nonpartisan proposal: Victoria Ely, University of Southern California; Grace Richardson, Point Loma Nazarene University; Leon Langdon, New York University; Marco Wertheimer, Lafayette College; Connor O'Neill, Lafayette College; Cameron Olbert, University of Edinburgh.

The following individuals worked with our student interns and contributed expertise, wisdom and moral support in the development of this proposal:
1. Kemal Kirisci: Director of the Center on the United States and Europe's Turkey Project, Brookings Institute. Washington, DC.

Let's Fix America

2. Erin Corcoran: Professor of Global Affairs, Notre Dame; Executive Director, Kroc Institute for International Peace Studies. Notre Dame, IN.
3. Ann Lin: Professor of Immigration Law, University of Michigan. Ann Arbor, MI.

Note: Not all participants agree with every aspect of this proposal. To arrive at a proposal that takes multiple views into account requires compromise and difficult decisions. For individual commentary on this proposal and more detail, go to OurNationalConversation.org. We invite you to add your comments as well.

Sources:

Ernst et al., "US Foreign Aid to the Northern Triangle 2014–2019: Promoting Success by Learning from the Past", *Wilson Center*. Dec. 2020, https://www.wilsoncenter.org/sites/default/files/media/uploads/documents/US%20Foreign%20Aid%20Central%20America.pdf

Gramlich J. and Noe-Bustamante, L., "What's happening at the U.S.-Mexico border in 5 charts", *Pew Research Center*. 9 Nov. 2021, https://www.pewresearch.org/fact-tank/2019/11/01/whats-happening-at-the-u-s-mexico-border-in-5-charts/

Kamarck, E. and Stenglein, C. "How many undocumented immigrants are in the United States and who are they?", *Brookings Institution*. 12 Nov. 2019, https://www.brookings.edu/policy2020/votervital/how-many-undocumented-immigrants-are-in-the-united-states-and-who-are-they/

Mallinder, L.. "Amnesty and International Law", *Oxford Bibliographies Online Datasets*. 2018 https://doi.org/10.1093/OBO/9780199796953-0172

Nixon, R. and Qui, L., "What is ICE and Why Do Critics Want to Abolish It?", *New York Times*. 3 Jul. 2018, https://www.nytimes.com/2018/07/03/us/politics/fact-check-ice-immigration-abolish.html

North American Integration and Development Center, "No DREAMers Left Behind: The Economic Potential of DREAM Act Beneficiaries" Aug. 2018, https://www.cccie.org/wp-content/uploads/2010/08/NAID_No_DREAMers_Left_Behind.pdf

Nowrasteh, A., "New Research on Illegal Immigration", *Cato Institute Blogs*. 13 Oct. 2020, https://www.cato.org/blog/new-research-illegal-immigration-crime-0

Boosting Cybersecurity

Big Picture:
Maintaining America's cybersecurity and integrity as a global power is crucial. It is necessary to take practical steps to guarantee national security through effective counterterrorism measures and protection of cyber information, both public and private.

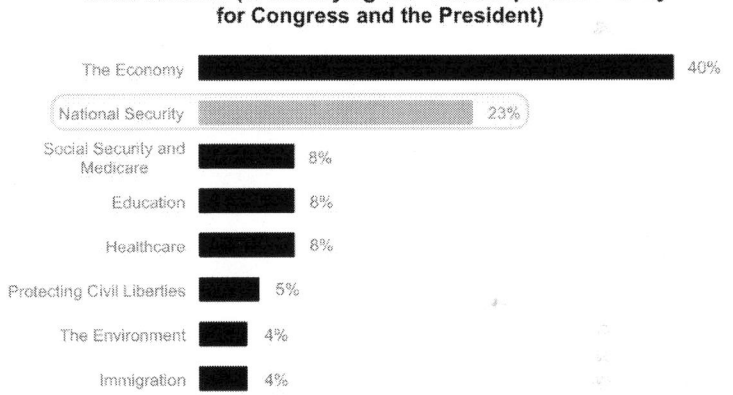

Graphic From: *Issue Salience (% Identifying the "Most Important Priority" for Congress and the President). Thirdway.org.* 8 Sept. 2020. This graph illustrates that national security is the second most important issue to voters when considering candidates for political office.

Operative Definitions:
1. **Cybersecurity:** The practice of defending computers, servers, mobile devices, electronic systems, networks and data from malicious attacks.
2. **Cyber hygiene:** Practicing safe online behaviors. This includes protecting personal information and avoiding illegal activities.

3. **U.S. Cyber Command (CC):** One of the 11 branches of the Department Of Defense. Designed to coordinate and bolster U.S. cybersecurity.
4. **Congressional oversight:** The review and monitoring of federal agencies, programs and policy implementation, which grants the legislative branch authority to inspect and review the executive branch and its agencies.
5. **Ethical hacking:** Authorized or legal attempt to gain unauthorized access to a computer system, application or data.
6. **Huawei:** China's leading multinational technology company, founded in 1987.
7. **United Nations Relief and Works Agency (UNRWA):** A UN agency with specific intentions of supporting the relief and human development of Palestinian refugees.

Important Facts and Statistics:
1. Globally, 30,000 websites are hacked daily. 64% of companies worldwide have experienced at least one form of a cyberattack. There were 20 million breached records in March 2020 alone.
2. Nearly 87% of terrorist incidents from 2001 to 2012 across the globe were domestic. That is, the impact was felt by the citizens of a country where the terrorism took place.
3. Twelve countries accounted for almost 79% of global terrorism incidents. Most of these countries were developing nations.

4-Point Plan:
1. **Strategize in cybersecurity with both federal agencies and private firms, keeping regulations at a high standard.**
Create a cybersecurity standard law with U.S. Cyber Command (CC) leadership. Specifically, enact preventive security software through CC. Since many government personnel make avoidable

but costly mistakes online, this software will prompt pop-ups prior to risky choices, such as opening spam.

2. **Upgrade outdated legacy software and ensure high data protection standards.**
With technology becoming ever more prevalent and complex in all workplaces, cybersecurity risks have also become more complex. It is important for government software to be upgraded and to attract the best talent in the cybersecurity field. This is critical not only for national security reasons, but also to ensure that American tax dollars are not being exploited by malicious actors. High data protection standards are critical. Including lessons on how to report cybercrimes in technology class curricula would create a more reliable base of citizens that could help protect key government cyber infrastructure. Moreover, it would be important to form an international cyber defense coalition with established allies that sets data protection standards. This will safeguard American data stored abroad and build a united front against cybercrime.

3. **Investigate federal security personnel and programs at least once every year.**
Security will be subject to congressional oversight through congressionally-funded, ethical hacking to test the security of current programs.

4. **Address Chinese influences by developing competitors to Huawei services.**
Commit $2 billion to help allies stimulate development of non-Huawei 5G services in U.S.-allied countries. Doing so will reduce China's ability to obtain American security information through

allies, as Huawei is a Chinese carrier network with a history of spying on users and threatening the West.

Why This Initiative is Important:
This initiative integrates finance, international affairs and data management principles to ensure that these national security strategies are well-coordinated. It also makes short and long-term goals to address the most pressing cybersecurity concerns. It takes strategic action against U.S. rivals that threaten our freedoms and democracy. This plan also encourages cooperation with trusted allies, reducing burdens on domestic government personnel. Lastly, it pushes America to work with key agencies, such as the U.S. Cyber Command and the United States Relief and Works Agency, which manage national cybersecurity capabilities and support economic development abroad. These measures will help prevent cyberattacks on critical infrastructure, classified information and private data.

Economic Impact (from our student economist team):
- Estimated effect on the annual federal deficit: + $2 billion.
- Improved security yields, and increased growth, trade and investment and will generate long-term returns.

To learn how our student economists came up with this economic impact, send an email to info@ournationalconversation.org and ask for a more thorough description of their methodologies.

Final Thought for Now:
"And it's one of the great paradoxes of our time that the very technologies that empower us to do great good can also be used to undermine us and inflict great harm." – **Barack Obama**

Acknowledgments:
The following student(s) worked on this nonpartisan proposal: Sarah (Lillian) Schaeffer, Pennsylvania State University; Royce (Rice) Williams, University of California, Davis; Michelle Liou, Mountain View High School; Cole Woody, John Foster Dulles High School; Marco Wertheimer, Lafayette College; Connor O'Neill, Lafayette College; Cameron Olbert, University of Edinburgh.

The following individuals worked with our student interns and contributed expertise, wisdom and moral support in the development of this proposal:

1. David Kawesi-Mukooza: Executive Assistant, Office of Chief of Naval Operations; Commander, U.S. Navy. Norfolk, VA.
2. Michael T. Rawls: Deputy Commander, NATO forces in Iraq; Brigadier General, U.S. Air Force. Germany.
3. Ben Taylor: Director, National Security Council Counterterrorism for ISIS; Lieutenant Colonel, U.S. Army. Washington, DC Metro Area.
4. Dennis Murphy: Retired submarine commander in the US Navy
5. Patricia Sullivan: Professor of Political Science, UNC Chapel Hill; Director, Triangle Institute for Security Studies. Chapel Hill, NC.
6. Clay R. Fuller: Expert, Global Initiative against Transnational Organized Crime; Professor of Political Science, Western Carolina University. Washington, DC.
7. Annita Nerses: Vice President and General Manager, Intrepid Networks LLC. Indianapolis, IN.
8. Chris Conley: Consultant, Sigmatech; Former Captain, U.S. Coast Guard. Colorado Springs, CO.

Note: Not all participants agree with every aspect of this proposal. To arrive at a proposal that takes multiple views into account requires compromise and difficult

Let's Fix America

decisions. For individual commentary on this proposal and more detail, go to OurNationalConversation.org. We invite you to add your comments as well.

Sources:

Bandyopadhyay, S. and Younas, J. "Trade and Terror: The Impact of Terrorism on Developing Countries", *Federal Reserve Bank of St Louis.* 11 Dec. 2017, https://www.stlouisfed.org/publications/regional-economist/fourth-quarter-2017/impact-terrorism-developing-countries

Byman, D.L.,. "The assault on the US Capitol opens a new chapter in domestic terrorism", *Brookings Institution.* 19 Jan. 2021, https://www.brookings.edu/blog/order-from-chaos/2021/01/19/the-assault-on-the-u-s-capitol-opens-a-new-chapter-in-domestic-terrorism/

Jagannathan, M.,. "Data breaches soared by 17% in 2019: 'We also saw the rise of a significant new threat'", *MarketWatch.* 29 Jan. 2020, https://www.marketwatch.com/story/data-breaches-soared-by-17-in-2019-but-theres-some-good-news-too-2020-01-29

Jones, S. G., Doxsee, C., and Harrington, N. "The Escalating Terrorism Problem in the United States", *Center for Strategic and International Studies.* 17 Jun. 2020, https://www.csis.org/analysis/escalating-terrorism-problem-united-states

"Stop Domestic Terrorism", *Scientific American.* 17 Feb. 2021, https://www.scientificamerican.com/article/stop-domestic-terrorism/

Let's Fix America

Mitigating U.S./China Tensions and Reducing the Potential for Military Conflict

Big Picture:
China's increasing geopolitical rivalry with the U.S. over the militarization of the South China Sea, siding with Russia against Ukraine, human rights abuses against the Uighur people, ongoing trade disputes centered around intellectual property theft and an alleged "debt trap" diplomacy have set the course for further conflict in the years to come. This proposal seeks to mitigate the chances of conflict with China.

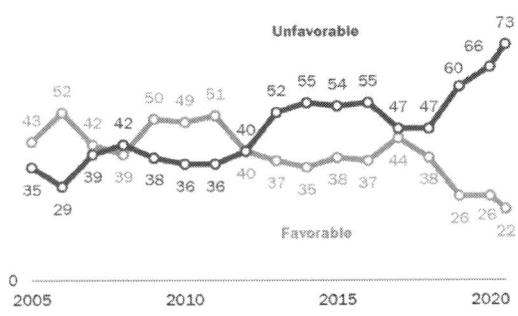

Graphic From: Silver, Laura, Kat Devlin, And Christine Huang. "Americans Fault China for Its Role in the Spread of COVID-19." *Pew Research Center.* 30 July 2020. This figure illustrates the rise in unfavorable opinions of China by people in the United States before and after the onset of the COVID-19 pandemic.

Operative Definitions:

1. **The Quadrilateral Security Dialogue ("The Quad"):** Encompasses the nations of Australia, India, Japan and the U.S. It is principally focused on maintaining security and enhancing economic opportunity within the Indo-Pacific region. The Quad, as an institution, serves as a point of agitation for China, who has called it an "Asian NATO" due to its perceived containment of Chinese economic and military influence within the Indo-Pacific region.
2. **Indo-Pacific Partnership for Maritime Domain Awareness (IPMDA):** A maritime initiative aimed at providing satellite data that is a "near-real-time, integrated, and cost-effective maritime domain awareness picture" used to enhance security against territorial intrusions, dark shipping and more.
3. **South China Sea (SCS):** Currently viewed as the area with the most potential for conflict due to numerous territorial claims by Malaysia, Vietnam, Brunei, Philippines and Taiwan, all overlapped by China's so-called "9-Dash Line." Contains large amounts of fish stock and untapped energy reserves.
4. **Belt and Road Initiative (BRI):** A Chinese implemented global infrastructure development initiative seeking to transform international trade within both the Indo-Pacific maritime region and Eurasia. Also known as "One Belt, One Road" policy.

Important Facts and Statistics:

1. China's maritime strategy centers around the development of international deepwater ports that enable expansion and protection of naval routes. According to the late U.S. National Security Advisor Robert McFarlane, as of now, China owns 96 ports around the world, with 100 more planned in at least 60 nations.

2. Roughly 80% of global trade is carried out by sea, and the total volume carried through the South China Sea ranges between 20-30%, according to David Uren of ASPI.
3. As outlined by the Center for Strategic and International Studies, $5.3 trillion in goods and shipping transits the South China Sea each year, which contains 40% of the energy and petroleum products important to sustaining regional and Chinese economic development.

5-Point Plan:
1. **Coordinate with Institutional Allies.**
   While the Quad is a relatively young organization, its primary focuses on naval activity, security, economy, health and climate issues will increase its importance as a point of cooperation in the Indo-Pacific region. As the institution grows in capabilities and potential membership, its increased importance will allow the organization to better and more effectively coordinate with institutional allies and members, serving as an alternative partner for nations currently experiencing difficulties with China.

2. **Clarify the QUAD's peaceful initiative without compromising its defensive posture.**
   China primarily sees the Quad and U.S. support of Taiwan as an attack against their interests. As a defensive institution focused primarily on the security of the Indo-Pacific region, this cannot be true unless China has aggressive intentions. Proving that the Quad is an organization initiated for peace and international stability will aid in gaining legitimacy, while also providing assistance to potential partner nations within the SCS.

3. **Strategic ambiguity on the Taiwan issue.**

The issue of the U.S.' unofficial support for Taiwan has escalated in recent months due to Russia's invasion of Ukraine. While China continuously claims to meet any support for Taiwan with the appropriate measures, it would be wise to maintain strategic ambiguity in U.S.-Taiwanese relations. Providing official support for Taiwan may embolden it to continue with independence rhetoric that would further anger China, possibly pulling the U.S. into an unnecessary conflict.

4. **Support individual countries in the Indo-Pacific region.**
   Providing economic support that will promote economic development for certain nations may result in increased security in the Indo-Pacific. For instance, increasing trade, investment and military ties to the Philippines would, in the long term, help them push back against increasingly dangerous encroachments by the Chinese navy and its so-called "People's Armed Forces Maritime Militia," which has exposed Chinese naval and economic ambitions in the area. The above-mentioned IMPDA may serve as an important foundation for further cooperation with other nations in the future.

5. **Provide a sustained alternative economic development model for the region.**
   In order to effectively compete with China's Belt and Road Initiative, the U.S. must provide an alternative funding institution that would meaningfully aid developing nations within the region and help capture economic growth. The Build Back Better World initiative recently launched by U.S. and G7 partners would provide this alternative, particularly due to the involvement of U.S. International Development Finance Corporation and the U.S. Trade and Development Agency.

Let's Fix America

Why This Initiative is Important:
The Indo-Pacific region is one that will likely take on increasing relevance in the future due to the economic and strategic implications the region can have. The competing territorial claims over small islands that promote exclusive economic zones are already causing small skirmishes and diplomatic disagreements. To prevent a globally destabilizing conflict, it is important for the U.S. and partners to facilitate international cooperation in the area, especially when it comes to determining, as a region, how to sort out competing territorial claims in an equitable manner. In the meantime, the U.S. should not seek to confront China, but simply provide a stabilizing, ethical and inclusive forum for regional powers to facilitate continued peace and prosperity for the Indo-Pacific region.

Economic Impact (from our student economist team):
- Meaningful numbers could not be calculated for this proposal.

To learn how our student economists came up with this economic impact, send an email to info@ournationalconversation.org and ask for a more thorough description of their methodologies.

Final Thought for Now:
"To leave the present and future leaders of China isolated, nurturing their resentments and even hatred of the United States because of what they consider to be unjustified actions against China is senseless and counterproductive." – Richard Nixon

Acknowledgments:
The following student(s) worked on this nonpartisan proposal:
Matthew A. Reyna, University of California, Irvine

Let's Fix America

Note: Not all participants agree with every aspect of this proposal. To arrive at a proposal that takes multiple views into account requires compromise and difficult decisions. For individual commentary on this proposal and more detail, go to OurNationalConversation.org. We invite you to add your comments as well.

Sources:

Freund, Eleanor. "Freedom of Navigation in the South China Sea: A Practical Guide." *Belfer Center*, June 2017. https://www.belfercenter.org/publication/freedom-navigation-south-china-sea-practical-guide

"Fact Sheet: Quad Leaders' Tokyo Summit 2022." *White House Statement and Releases*, 23 May 2022, https://www.whitehouse.gov/briefing-room/statements-releases/2022/05/23/fact-sheet-quad-leaders-tokyo-summit-2022/

"How Much Trade Transits the South China Sea?" *China Power*, CSIS, 25 Jan. 2021, https://chinapower.csis.org/much-trade-transits-south-china-sea/

Martinson, Ryan D. "Manila;s Images Are Revealing the Secrets of China's Maritime Strategy." *Foreign Policy*, 19 Apr. 2021, https://foreignpolicy.com/2021/04/19/manilas-images-are-revealing-the-secrets-of-chinas-maritime-militia/

Uren, David. "Southeast Asia will take a major economic hit if shipping is blocked in the South China Sea." *Australian Strategic Policy Institute*, 8 Dec. 2020, https://www.aspistrategist.org.au/southeast-asia-will-take-a-major-economic-hit-if-shipping-is-blocked-in-the-south-china-sea/

Stearns, Scott. "Challenging Beijing in the South China Sea." *Voice of America*, 31 July 2012, https://blogs.voanews.com/state-department-news/2012/07/31/challenging-beijing-in-the-south-china-sea/

Xie, John. "China's Global Network of Shipping Ports Reveal Beijing's Strategy." Voice of America, 13 Sept. 2021, https://www.voanews.com/a/6224958.html

Let's Fix America

The Israeli-Palestinian Conflict: Can We Achieve a Breakthrough?

Big Picture:

Coupled with a pro-Israel proclivity that initially supported America's Cold War strategy, domestic political factors have largely sustained America's unshakable support for Israel. Though the deadlock persists, the American public and public officials have shown signs of increased support toward the plight of Palestinians. Thus, it is incumbent on American officials to rethink the foreign policy measures that sustain the cycle of human rights abuses and ongoing violence in the Israeli-Palestinian conflict, acknowledging both the needs of the Palestinians and the security concerns of the Israelis.

Recent Trend in U.S. Views on Israel and the Palestinians

	2018 %	2019 %	2020 %	2021 %
Favorable ratings				
Israel	74	69	74	75
Palestinian Authority	21	21	23	30
Mideast sympathies				
More with the Israelis	64	59	60	58
More with the Palestinians	19	21	23	25
Neither/Both/No opinion	16	20	17	17
U.S. pressure to make compromises				
More on the Palestinians	50	--	--	44
More on the Israelis	27	--	--	34
Both/Neither/No opinion	23	--	--	22
Palestinian statehood				
Favor	47	50	55	52
Oppose	39	39	34	37

Polls conducted in February of each year

GALLUP

Graphic From: *February 2021 Gallup poll measuring U.S. support for Israelis versus Palestinians.* This poll indicates growing support towards Palestinian Authority in the West Bank as well as decreasing sympathy for Israelis in the Israeli-Palestinian conflict.

Operative Definitions:
1. **UNSC:** United Nations Security Council
2. **PNA:** The Palestinian National Authority, which is a quasi-state established during the Oslo Accords (see below) to administer the domestic policies of the Palestinian people. Should Palestine become its own state, this is the entity that will likely become the Palestinian government.
3. **Two-state solution:** A highly popular policy advocated by most US presidential administrations to acknowledge Israel and Palestine as two separate states.
4. **Oslo Accords (1993):** Series of agreements that were intended to achieve a larger peace agreement between Palestine and Israel. The Clinton administration mediated the process.
5. **West Bank:** Contested area between Israel and the PNA. Initially under control after the First Arab-Israeli War, Israel recaptured the territory in 1967. The West bank is split into territories occupied by Israel and 'islands' that are administered by the PNA.
6. **Golan Heights:** Contested region north of Israel. Part of the eastern Golan Heights is administered by Syria, whereas the majority of it is administered by Israel since its occupation of the area after the Six-Day War in 1967.
7. **The Gaza Strip:** A Palestinian territory under political control by the Islamic fundamentalist group Hamas, which has controlled Gaza since 2007.
8. **Abraham Accords (2020):** An agreement between Israel, the United Arab Emirates and the United States in which Israel and the United Arab Emirates agreed to the normalization of peace and to greater economic cooperation. The Trump administration mediated the process.

Important Facts and Statistics:
1. 1948: First Arab-Israeli War resulted in the creation of the State of Israel after Arab defeat.
2. 1967: Six Day War between Israel and an Arab coalition (Jordan, Egypt and Syria). Israel's speedy victory resulted in the capture of the Sinai Peninsula, the Gaza Strip, the West Bank, the Old City of Jerusalem and the Golan Heights.
3. 1973: Yom Kippur War fought when Egypt and Syria attacked Israel on the holiest day of the Jewish year in order to regain territory taken in 1967.
4. 1987-1993: The First Intifada, or Palestinian uprising against Israel, saw massive Palestinian protests against Israeli occupation in the first coordinated effort since 1948.
5. 1993: The Oslo Accords are signed.
6. 2000-2005: The Second Intifada began after Israeli Prime Minister Ariel Sharon visited the Al-Aqsa mosque, one of Islam's holiest sites, in Old Jerusalem.

6-Point Plan:
1. **Reopen the Palestinian Consulate in Jerusalem.**
Under President Trump, the Palestinian consulate in Jerusalem was closed and all aid was halted. There has not been enough direct communication with Palestinian Authority leaders in the West Bank on this matter. In October 2021, Israeli Justice Minister Gideon Saar commented that there was "no chance" the consulate dedicated to Palestinian affairs in Jerusalem would reopen. It is crucial that the U.S. press newly-reelected Prime Minister Netanyahu or risk closing the American embassy in Jerusalem.

2. **Emphasize combating regional and transnational terrorism related to this conflict.**

Transnational and domestic terrorist groups have long cited the Israeli-Palestinian conflict to be a fundamental grievance. The US should continue to prioritize anti-terrorist measures in their defense spending.

3. **Military aid should be conditioned on upholding human rights agreements.**
The U.S. gives $3.8 billion in unconditional aid to Israel annually, and President Biden recently approved a $735 million weapons sale to them as well. Israel has been the largest cumulative recipient of aid from the U.S. since WWII. President Biden should make any U.S. foreign aid legally conditional on respecting international legal norms, human rights and the halting of settlement expansion.

4. **Reconstruct Gaza.**
Israel's blockade of Gaza has led to a lack of medical resources, severe levels of unemployment, a lack of building materials, clean water, electricity and restricted freedom of movement. The May 2021 fighting left over 2,200 homes destroyed and infrastructure severely damaged. The U.S. must mediate negotiations between Israel and Palestine. To acknowledge Israeli security concerns while reinvigorating infrastructure in Gaza, the U.S. should exert its international influence and propose that, in return for some level of demilitarization of Hamas, Israel opens increased funds from Egypt and Qatar to contribute to the rebuilding of vital infrastructure in Gaza. The U.S. could draw from the international treaties established in the Abraham Accords between Israel and various Arab nations to facilitate these negotiations, placing greater international pressure on Israel and Palestine. Currently, only 10% of the estimated cost to rebuild has been allowed by Israel.

5. **Place an emphasis on international legal instruments.**
   The U.S. must stop hindering the potential of international organizations to provide relief or condemn illegal activity. It will be crucial to work bilaterally with the Middle East Quartet (U.S., EU, Russia, and the UN), which was suspended under the Trump administration. Respect and uphold the following: the 1949 Fourth Geneva Convention, UNSC Resolution 237 & 242 and the 2004 Advisory Opinion from the International Court of Justice. America must recognize its role in furthering injustices towards Palestinians through UNSC veto power, which has been used at least 53 times in the past five decades. They are overwhelmingly the sole veto against anything critical of Israel. Uphold the widely affirmed belief that settlement activity is illegal under international law.

6. **Prioritize the two-state solution.**
   President Biden and Secretary of State Anthony Blinken have indicated that the two-state solution is the only hope for resolution of this conflict. Support moderate Palestinians and Israelis in the Knesset. Incentivize more extreme Palestinians/Israelis to come to the negotiating table by highlighting the financial benefits for both sides in the next 10 years. Israel is projected to gain $123 billion versus $50 billion for Palestinians. The U.S. should press the need to compromise on borders, security, refugees and Jerusalem, as was most vigorously attempted during the 1990s Oslo Accords.

Why This Initiative Is Important:
This initiative underscores that America has a responsibility to show the world it is serious about protecting human rights and promoting democratic norms around the world. Foreign policy toward Israel has

largely been a repetition from one administration to the next. America is wasting resources and showing that all promises fall short by remaining fixated on foreign policy that neither advances peace nor stops violence from breaking out. America will show a commitment to international legal instruments that have been imperative in promoting peace and security. America can only project strength to the world by acknowledging where there have been shortcomings. It is the responsibility of American citizens to prove that public officials cannot be bought by powerful lobby groups and that inconsistent messaging between domestic and foreign policy can be deterred.

Economic Impact (from our student economist team):
- Estimated effect on the annual federal deficit: + $4 billion

To learn how our student economists came up with this economic impact, send an email to info@ournationalconversation.org and ask for a more thorough description of their methodologies.

Final Thought for Now:
"The question now is how to reconcile Israel's legitimate security concerns with the legitimate rights of the Palestinians. And that answer can only come at the negotiating table." – Ronald Reagan (1982)

Acknowledgments:
The following student(s) worked on this nonpartisan proposal: Breana Hume, University College London (MS); Samuel Keller, University of Maine (MA); Samuel Taylor, Brigham Young University (UT)

Let's Fix America

The following individuals worked with our student interns and contributed expertise, wisdom and moral support in the development of this proposal:
1. David Romney: Professor of Political Science and Middle East Studies, Brigham Young University. Provo, UT.

Note: Not all participants agree with every aspect of this proposal. To arrive at a proposal that takes multiple views into account requires compromise and difficult decisions. For individual commentary on this proposal and more detail, go to OurNationalConversation.org. We invite you to add your comments as well.

Sources:

Al-mughrabi, Nidal. "Gaza to Begin Rebuilding Homes Destroyed in May Conflict." *Reuters*, 26 Sept. 2021, www.reuters.com/world/middle-east/gaza-begin-rebuilding-homes-destroyed-may-conflict-2021-09-26/

Ambassador Hesham Youssef. "10 Things to Know: Biden's Approach to the Israeli-Palestinian Conflict." *United States Institute of Peace*, 10 Jun. 2021, www.usip.org/publications/2021/06/10-things-know-bidens-approach-israeli-palestinian-conflict.

Cheng, Amy. "Israeli Minister Says 'No Way' to U.S. Reopening of Consulate in Jerusalem." *Washington Post*, 13 Oct. 2021, www.washingtonpost.com/world/2021/10/13/israel-oppose-us-consulate-jerusalem/.

Conrad, Brooke. "How Much Does the US Spend on Israel and Palestinian Territories?" *WJLA*, Sinclair Broadcast Group, 26 May 2021, www.wjla.com/news/nation-world/how-much-does-the-us-spend-on-israel-and-palestinian-territories.

Cornish, Audie. "Liberal American Attitudes Are Starting to Shift on Israelis and Palestinians." *NPR*, 21 May 2021, www.npr.org/2021/05/21/999241551/liberal-american-attitudes-are-starting-to-shift-on-israelis-and-palestinians.

Fisher, Max. "The Two-State Solution: What It Is and Why It Hasn't Happened." *The New York Times*, 29 Dec. 2016, www.nytimes.com/2016/12/29/world/middleeast/israel-palestinians-two-state-solution.html.

Inc, Gallup. "Key Trends in U.S. Views on Israel and the Palestinians." *Gallup.com*, 28 May 2021, www.news.gallup.com/poll/350393/key-trends-views-israel-palestinians.aspx.

Mansoor, Sanya. "Pompeo Is Cracking down on a Movement to Boycott Israel. Here's What to Know about BDS." *Time*, 7 Dec. 2020, www.time.com/5914975/what-to-know-about-bds/.

Newton, Creede. "A History of the US Blocking UN Resolutions against Israel." *Al Jazeera*, 19 May 2021, www.aljazeera.com/news/2021/5/19/a-history-of-the-us-blocking-un-resolutions-against-israel.

Roberts, William. "Why Is the US Unequivocal in Its Support for Israel?" *Al Jazeera*, 18 May 2021, www.aljazeera.com/news/2021/5/18/short-answer-why-is-the-united-states-so-pro-israel.

Ross, Anthony C, et al. "The Costs of the Israeli-Palestinian Conflict." *RAND*, 2014, www.rand.org/pubs/research_reports/RR740-1.html.

Telhami, Shibley. "America Must Rethink Its Unique and Contradictory Advocacy of Israel's Jewishness." *Brookings*, 11 Jun. 2021.

World Bank. "GDP per Capita (Current US$) - West Bank and Gaza." *World Bank*, 2020, www.data.worldbank.org/indicator/ny.gdp.pcap.cd?locations=PS.

Preparing NATO's Long-Term Response to a Belligerent Russia

Big Picture:
The recent Russia-Ukraine conflict has clarified Russia's geopolitical intentions to revive Russian influence to the levels of its imperial past. This has spurred strategic coherence as well as a renewed rearmament regime within NATO. This proposal seeks to prepare NATO for a new era of revived power competition where regional security, both military and economic, will play a primary role in deterring would-be aggressors.

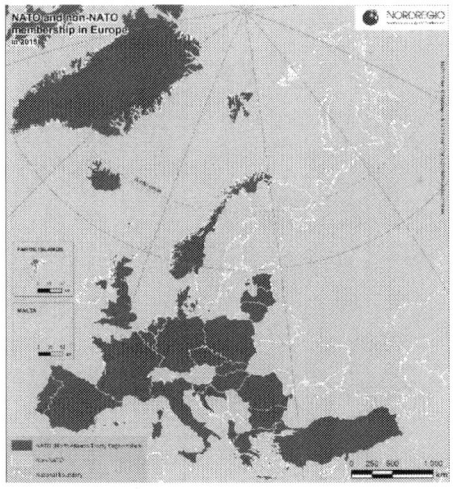

Graphic From: Rispling, Linus. "NATO and non-NATO membership in Europe in 2015." Nordregio. January 6th, 2016. This figure illustrates the current geographical and strategic makeup of NATO. Sweden and Finland have both applied for membership due to Russian aggression in the region, which has predictably drawn Russian condemnation.

Operative Definitions:
1. **NATO:** North Atlantic Treaty Organization. Alliance established to foster European political integration, prevent Soviet territorial expansion and to deter the type of militant nationalism that led to World War II. Sweden and Finland have recently applied for membership, further inviting Russian ire.
2. **Sanctions:** Tools of economic punishment (generally motivated by political purposes) utilized in a coercive manner to penalize states, individuals or organizations by halting economic activity in some manner.
3. **Western Nations:** Not necessarily a geographic term; alludes to nations with shared democratic, economic and cultural values. These include the U.S., European nations, Japan and arguably India.

6-Point Plan:
1. **Prepare for a long conflict.**
While Russia has suffered devastating battlefield losses, its ability to maintain its economy and energy exports in the face of sanctions is holding. Additionally, European nations will be reluctant to end their own purchases of Russian energy due to the severe economic losses they will face. To shift European dependence on Russian energy, the U.S. must facilitate the increase of natural gas and oil exports primarily to European allies. This will involve enhanced coordination with energy producers, shippers and storage logistics companies, while emphasizing natural gas use rather than strictly oil or coal to remain consistent with shared climate goals wherever possible.

2. **Continue international support for Ukraine.**

While the U.S. has provided nearly $50 billion in military assistance and financial aid to Ukraine, European nations must also step up in their support. U.S. stockpiles of highly effective weaponry, such as the Javelin missile, are dwindling, and will take years to replenish with current manufacturing and supply chain optimizations. The U.S. cannot shoulder this burden alone. It must push its NATO partners to contribute meaningfully to Ukraine's, and by extension, to their own long-term defense.

3. **Coordinate with allies to enhance regional security.**
While the U.S. is otherwise focused on geopolitical competition with China, European partners must take a stronger role in European security. While military budgets have been rapidly increased in nations like Germany, NATO's Rapid Response Force increase to 300,000 from 40,000 service members must be aided by the U.S. in areas such as training, strategic management and integration, and weapons production if capacity allows.

4. **Re-shore supply chains.**
This conflict has exposed underlying disagreements in the status quo order. U.S.-China geopolitical and economic competition, as well as India's desire to avoid taking sides, has disrupted supply chains and caused friction among the international community. In order to better combat and contain Russian aggression, the West must enact agreements that facilitate increased economic and military cooperation. Supply chains, particularly those involved in manufacturing and energy, are undergoing a period of reorganization. Ensuring that the majority of energy and manufacturing capacities are placed closer to home and in nations with friendly relations is critical to preventing prolonged energy and goods shortages in the years to come.

5. **Avoid international collateral damage.**
India has avoided taking sides in the conflict, and has in fact benefited from it in the form of cheap energy prices, primarily that of a $30/barrel oil deal with Russia, compared to the $100/barrel three-month average currently on the market. Currently, G-7 leadership is attempting to leverage its dominance of overseas shipment insurers to force any buyers of Russian energy to abide by a price cap. This is an untested method to indirectly impact Russian exports. To ensure long-term strategic maneuverability, the G-7 and associates must not indirectly harm nations and cause further divisions by making sure that methods used to disrupt Russia's ability to fund the war are targeted and as specific as possible to Russia.

6. **Expand U.S. energy production and refining.**
While U.S. energy production remains high, the critical issue is refining capacity. No new refineries of significance have been built in the U.S. since 1976, primarily due to heavy environmental factors and subsequent costs. If Europe cannot access cheap Russian energy, it is imperative that the U.S. make up the shortfall. This will require significant coordination between regulators and energy companies to facilitate the construction of energy infrastructure, including the transport of U.S. resources to Europe, that will account for long-term energy needs of our European partners. This effort will strengthen energy ties between the U.S. and Europe while contributing to improved economic and national security structure in the decades to come.

Why This Initiative is Important:
This conflict has largely exposed divisions within the world system led by the West. Sanctions on Russia are not having the intended effect due in part to many non-European nations' unwillingness to

participate in what they view as a European problem. While domestic concerns are prompting the U.S. to retreat from its position as the world's police, other nations within certain regions will be seen as critical partners in the future to maintain global stability. It will be important to enhance U.S.-European national security, but this cannot come at the cost of alienating would-be future partners such as India.

Economic Impact (from our student economist team)
- Meaningful numbers could not be calculated for this proposal.

To learn how our student economists came up with this economic impact, send an email to info@ournationalconversation.org and ask for a more thorough description of their methodologies.

Final Thought for Now:
"Today, our NATO Allies and the Alliance is as unified and determined as it has ever been. And the source of our unbreakable strength continues to be the power, resilience, and universal appeal of our shared democratic values." – Joe Biden (2022)

Acknowledgments:
The following student(s) worked on this nonpartisan proposal: Matthew A. Reyna, University of California, Irvine.

Note: Not all participants agree with every aspect of this proposal. To arrive at a proposal that takes multiple views into account requires compromise and difficult decisions. For individual commentary on this proposal and more detail, go to OurNationalConversation.org. We invite you to add your comments as well.

Sources:

Cancian, Mark F. "Will the United States Run Out of Javelins Before Russia Runs Out of Tanks?". *Center for Strategic & International Studies*. April 12, 2022. https://www.csis.org/analysis/will-united-states-run-out-javelins-russia-runs-out-tanks

IER. "Will Any New Refineries Be Built in the United States?". *Institute for Energy Research*. June 13, 2022. https://www.instituteforenergyresearch.org/fossil-fuels/gas-and-oil/will-any-new-refineries-be-built-in-the-united-states/

Rispling, Linus. "NATO and non-NATO membership in Europe in 2015". *Nordregio*. January 12, 2016. https://nordregio.org/maps/nato-and-non-nato-membership-in-europe-in-2015/

Sabbagh, Dan. "Nato to put 300,000 troops on high alert in response to Russia threat". *The Guardian*. June 27th, 2022. https://www.theguardian.com/world/2022/jun/27/nato-300000-troops-high-alert-russia-threat-ukraine

Quinn, Colm. "The G-7 Goes for Russia's Gold - and Oil Profits". *Foreign Policy*. June 27, 2022. https://foreignpolicy.com/2022/06/27/g7-oil-russia-gold/

Science, Environment & Technology

"I believe that this Nation should commit itself to achieving the goal, before this decade is out, of landing a man on the Moon and returning him safely to Earth."

- John F. Kennedy

Tackling Climate Change in America, Starting with Carbon Emissions

Big Picture:
The United States is second only to China in its production of greenhouse gasses, which is the leading cause of climate change in the world. It is time to prioritize combating climate change. The U.S. must reform its energy sources and set realistic goals to reduce fossil fuel consumption in a way that does not severely hamper economic growth over the next few decades. It is imperative that America utilize renewable energy to limit the extension of climate change.

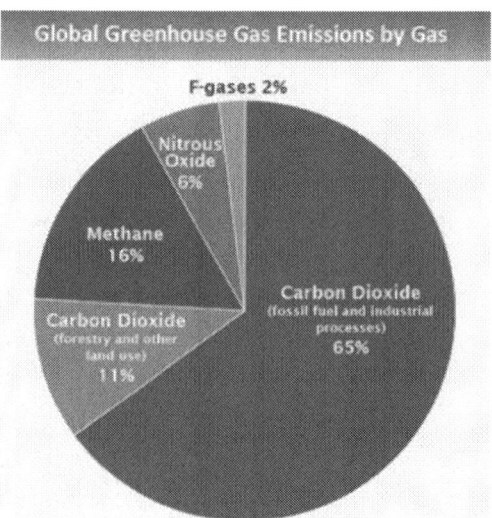

Graphic From: "AR5 Climate Change 2014: Mitigation of Climate Change." *Intergovernmental Panel on Climate Change.* 2014. This figure illustrates the proportions of certain greenhouse gasses in Earth's atmosphere, as well as some of their largest producers.

Operative Definitions:
1. **Fossil fuel:** A form of energy created from ancient organic matter, including coal, oil and natural gas. Fossil fuels are non-renewable because they take millions of years to form and cannot be replenished.
2. **Leadership in Energy and Environmental Design (LEED):** This independent certification system provides guidance on making new buildings efficient and retrofitting existing structures.
3. **Carbon footprint:** A measure of the carbon emissions released by a product throughout its life cycle. This includes the fossil fuel resources it takes to create, ship and consume the product.
4. **Concentrated animal feeding operations (CAFOs):** These massive livestock ventures confine thousands of animals to small indoor areas. The result is water and air pollution from excess manure.
5. **The Climate Action Rebate Act of 2019 (CAR Act):** This initiative intends to reduce carbon dioxide emissions by 55% by 2030 and 100% by 2050.
6. **Net-Zero:** Refers to the balance between the amount of greenhouse gas produced and removed from the atmosphere. Net-zero is reached when the amount added is no more than the amount taken away.
7. **Paris Agreement:** An international treaty created in 2015 that established various countries' commitment to fighting climate change. The treaty laid out goals for carbon emission reductions for each country involved.

Important Facts and Statistics:
1. In 2020, natural disasters and climate-related events cost the U.S. $95 billion.

2. Over 36 million American homes cannot meet their energy needs, making them vulnerable to negative health effects during extreme heat and cold.
3. Coal and tar sands, both types of crude oil, are the most carbon-intensive fossil fuels.
4. The CAR Act is an example of applying federal taxes to reduce carbon emissions. The CAR Act directs 70% of revenue into low- and middle-income communities through dividends.
5. 40% of food gets thrown away in America. Food waste causes 11% of global emissions.

5-Point Plan:
1. **Incentivize industries to reduce carbon emissions through a federal tax.**
Implement a federal carbon tax program to reduce carbon emissions. The flat tax will begin at $35 per ton of carbon dioxide and increase by two percent per ton every year. The revenue generated will be invested in energy assistance programs for low-income neighborhoods. This endeavor will allow these lower socio-economic areas to develop more successfully. Furthermore, a cap-and-trade program within industries will establish a limit on state-wide carbon emissions through the buying and selling of permit allowances. Emission limits will be set for various sectors. If a company meets its goals, it can sell its "right to pollute." This incentivizes rather than punishes, as companies will be encouraged to reduce emissions faster because they can profit off companies that need to buy more permits, allowing the free market to drive much of our reduction in carbon emissions. Still, punishment will occur where cheating is involved — fine and monitor companies that attempt to cheat the system by polluting without a permit, with the severity of these measures depending on the particulars of a given case. Establish carbon footprint

labeling requirements to increase transparency within carbon-emitting industries by requiring consumer goods to indicate the product's carbon footprint. This will let consumers have a substantial role in reducing carbon emissions.

2. **Develop strategies for energy-efficient building construction in urban and suburban areas.**
Encourage energy efficiency through the construction of "net-zero" and LEED-certified buildings in cities through cheaper permitting processes and property tax rebates. Invest in and subsidize the use of sustainable materials. Categorical grants from the federal government to states will allow this extension for public transportation.

3. **Localize agriculture.**
Increase regulation of CAFOs by reducing their size and density, with appropriate regulations set at the minimum sized CAFO farmers can affordably operate. These size regulations can be relaxed in cases where farmers use other methods to offset methane emissions caused by greater CAFO sizes. CAFOs must install anaerobic digesters, which are devices that reduce methane emissions from animal waste. Furthermore, to ensure anaerobic digesters are applied properly, CAFOs must be qualified via EPA guidelines and regulations listed on the official government website. Although smaller-scale facilities will limit the quantity of total food production, this effort would partner with food-waste limiting efforts, thereby lowering food demand. Following this, subsidize farms and CAFOs that use regenerative agriculture, which uses technology to revitalize used soil, allowing agriculture to improve land instead of degrade it. Shift existing subsidies from farmers that do not practice regenerative agriculture to those that do. Facilitate initiatives to educate and involve communities in

local agriculture ventures, including the creation of neighborhood gardens and information on partnerships with nearby farms. Offer workshops on home composting to reduce the amount of food waste that ends up in landfills. See *National Food Production and Distribution Policy*.

4. **Invest in renewable research and development.**
   Retire coal plants within 15 years while increasing renewable energy storage to fully replace carbon-based energy. Encourage solar energy firms to purchase municipality coal plants for decommissioning. Expand existing retraining programs for coal workers in renewable energy. All lost coal jobs will be regained in renewable energy firms, supporting 29 million better-paying, healthier jobs. Connect interregional lines for renewable energy. This policy will necessarily affect the livelihoods and personal lives of many involved in the coal industry. Investment in renewable energy jobs will help offset many of these negative effects.

5. **Establish a central grid in the United States.**
   Currently, there are eight organizations in the U.S. that each control a section of the power grid. A central grid will reduce imbalances and meet clean-energy goals. This will save $47 billion annually and create jobs. Require new natural gas plants to use the Allam Cycle, an innovative design that uses pure oxygen to burn natural gas. The carbon dioxide produced can be recycled, resulting in affordable power with zero emissions. Allow zero-emissions technology to receive innovation incentives. See *Innovation policy*. Create competition between nuclear energy firms to design advanced, safe nuclear plants. Standardize plant designs to reduce costs and timelines. Provide financial support for facilities to research and develop thorium energy, which is more abundant than uranium and produces less volatile waste.

Why This Initiative is Important:
Greenhouse gas emissions are the leading cause of man-made contributions to global warming. Mitigating consequences like extreme weather, rising sea levels and natural disasters are critical in safeguarding America's future. Taxing carbon will increase federal revenue, generating more funds to support environmental initiatives, research and programs for low-income communities. Investments in renewable and nuclear energy will create new jobs, providing increased financial stability and economic stimulation. The effects of climate change hurt people of low socioeconomic status the most. With policies such as a carbon tax, money will be reinvested back into the communities most affected by climate change.

Economic Impact (from our student economist team):
- Estimated increase in annual federal spending: $210 billion.
- Estimated increase in annual federal revenue: $52.8 billion.
- These proposals would save the American people nearly $2.5 trillion over 10 years.
- Encouraging the development of efficient, climate-friendly energy solutions will foster long-term economic growth.

To learn how our student economists came up with this economic impact, send an email to info@ournationalconversation.org and ask for a more thorough description of their methodologies.

Final Thought for Now:
"The climate crisis is both the easiest and the hardest issue we have ever faced. The easiest because we know what we must do. We must stop the emissions of greenhouse gasses. The hardest because our current economics are still totally dependent on burning fossil fuels, and thereby destroying ecosystems in order

Let's Fix America

to create everlasting economic growth." — Greta Thunberg
(2019, *No One Is Too Small to Make a Difference.)*

Acknowledgments:
The following student(s) worked on this nonpartisan proposal: Pragya Jain, American University; Ellery Saluck, Washington University in St. Louis; Marianne Swan, State University of New York College at Oneonta; Yoni Ferbank, Syracuse University; Gabby Ostrov, University of Vermont.

The following individuals worked with our student interns and contributed expertise, wisdom and moral support in the development of this proposal:
1. Simon Nicholson: Co-Director, Institute for Carbon Removal Law & Policy. Washington, DC.
2. Ryan Hodum: Program Director, Southeast Policy at Energy Foundation. Washington, DC.
3. Anjali Tripathi: Research associate, Center for Astrophysics, Harvard-Smithsonian. Los Angeles, CA.
4. Anonymous expert who asked not to be identified.

Note: Not all participants agree with every aspect of this proposal. To arrive at a proposal that takes multiple views into account requires compromise and difficult decisions. For individual commentary on this proposal and more detail, go to OurNationalConversation.org. We invite you to add your comments as well.

Sources:
Amandeo, Kimberly. "Carbon Tax, Its Purpose, and How It Works: How a Carbon Tax Can Solve Climate Change." *The Balance,* 1 Aug. 2020, www.thebalance.com/carbon-tax-definition-how-it-works-4158043.
Amini, Adib, et al. "Cost-effective treatment of swine wastes through recovery of energy and nutrients." *Waste Management,* Nov. 2017, https://pubmed.ncbi.nlm.nih.gov/28864310/.
"Billion-Dollar Weather and Climate Disasters: Overview." *National Oceanic and Atmospheric Administration (NOAA),* 2022, https://www.ncei.noaa.gov/access/billions/overview
"Clean Energy Dc: The District Of Columbia Climate And Energy Action Plan." *Government of the District of Columbia.* Aug. 2018, https://doee.dc.gov/sites/default/files/dc/sites/ddoe/page_content/attachments/Clean%20Energy%20DC%20-%20Full%20Report_0.pdf.

Let's Fix America

Cummins, Ronnie. "What U.S. Farming Can Do to Stop Climate Change." *Yes Magazine,* 20 Feb. 2020, https://www.yesmagazine.org/environment/2020/02/20/climate-change-agriculture/.

Fischetti, Mark and Amanda Montañez. "Carbon Taxes Would Boost Jobs across the U.S." *Scientific American,* 1 Mar. 2020. https://www.scientificamerican.com/article/carbon-taxes-would-boost-jobs-across-the-u-s/.

"How Cap and Trade Works." *Environmental Defense Fund,* 2018, https://www.edf.org/climate/how-cap-and-trade-works

MacDonald, Alexander E., et al. "Future cost-competitive electricity systems and their impact on US CO_2 emissions." *Nature Climate Change,*, vol. 6, 25 Jan. 2016 pp. 526-531, doi.org/10.1038/nclimate2921.

Metcalf, Gilbert E. and James H. Stock. "Costing jobs or cutting emissions: What is the real impact of Europe's carbon taxes?" *Principles for Responsible Investment,* 6 Nov. 2020, https://www.unpri.org/pri-blogs/costing-jobs-or-cutting-emissions-what-is-the-real-impact-of-europes-carbon-taxes/6712.article.

Pillars, Roxanne. "Farm-Based Anaerobic Digesters." *Michigan State University,* 9 Jun. 2022, https://www.agmrc.org/media/cms/FinalAnearobicDigestionFactsheet_2E11FAB524 961.pdf.

Platt, Brenda and Colton Fagundes. "Yes! In My Backyard: A Home Composting Guide for Local Government." *Institute For Local Self-Reliance,* May 2018, https://sustainablect.org/fileadmin/Random_PDF_Files/Equity_Action_PDFs/Yes-In-My-Backyard-Full-Report.pdf.

Qian, Chad. "Three Carbon Tax Bills Introduced in Congress." *Tax Foundation,* 1 Aug. 2019, https://taxfoundation.org/carbon-tax-bills-introduced-congress"Reduced Food Waste." *Project Drawdown,* 9 Jun. 2022, www.drawdown.org/solutions/reduced-food-wast.

Dayaratna, Kevin, and Nicolas Loris. "A Glimpse of What the Green New Deal Would Cost Taxpayers." *The Heritage Foundation,* 25 Mar. 2019, https://www.heritage.org/environment/commentary/glimpse-what-the-green-new-deal-would-cost-taxpayers.

"Sources of Greenhouse Gas Emissions." *Environmental Protection Agency,* 2019. https://www.epa.gov/ghgemissions/sources-greenhouse-gas-emissions.

Incentivizing Environmental Protection

Big Picture:
Americans constitute only four percent of the world's population, yet produce 12% of global municipal waste. The U.S. should consider new approaches to combat overconsumption and pollution. Consumers, including individuals, companies and industries, should be encouraged to make sustainable, environment-friendly decisions and be held accountable for their actions.

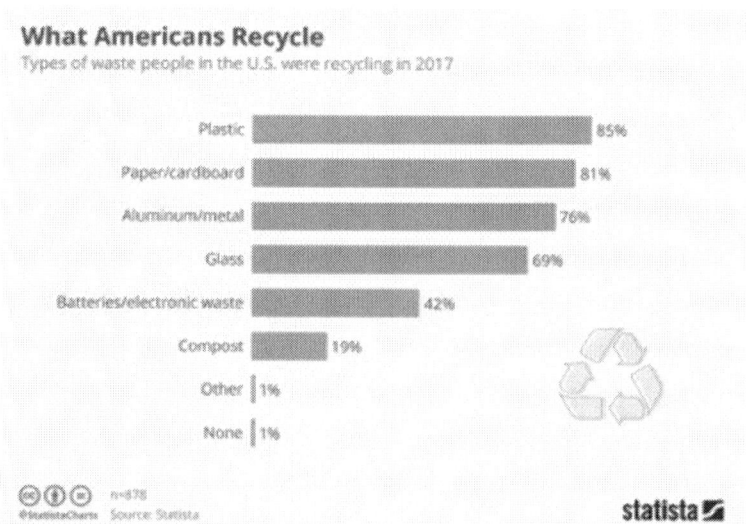

Graphic From: Niall McCarthy. "What Americans Recycle." *Statista*. 14 Nov. 2019. This figure illustrates the percentage of people who recycle certain items. Plastic is the most common, whereas items like batteries, electronic waste and compost are not nearly recycled as frequently.

Operative Definitions:
1. **Regressive tax:** A tax applied uniformly, taking a larger percentage of income from low-income earners than high-income earners.

2. **Climate change:** A progressive change in global or regional climate patterns associated with greater variability in weather and temperature. Climate change has been recognized as a threat, particularly since the mid-20th century, and the man-made contribution of climate change has been attributed to increased levels of carbon dioxide due to the use of fossil fuels.
3. **Environmental Protection Agency (EPA):** A U.S. federal government agency tasked with overseeing and protecting human and environmental health. Created under former President Richard Nixon in 1970.
4. **United Nations Intergovernmental Panel on Climate Change (IPCC):** A United Nations panel that puts forth the most current scientific assessments on climate change, explanations of its future risks, and mitigation and adaptation options.
5. **Food and Drug Administration (FDA):** Responsible for protecting public health by ensuring the safety, efficiency and security of various human and veterinary intake products and services.
6. **Occupational Safety and Health Administration (OSHA):** A sector of the U.S. department of labor responsible for inspecting and examining workplaces.
7. **U.S. Consumer Product Safety Commission (CPSC):** An independent agency which promotes the safety of consumer products, developing safety standards and conducting research on product-related illness and injury.

Important Facts and Statistics:
1. Since the 1950s, 8.3 billion metric tons of plastic have been produced. Half of that has been produced in the past 15 years alone.

2. Humans produce 150 million tons of plastic each year just for single-use items.
3. Two-thirds of American adults say the federal government is doing too little to address climate change.
4. Most Americans in all political and ideological groups think climate scientists should play some role in environmental policy decisions.

4-Point Plan:
1. **Incentivize the private sector to make sustainable, environmentally friendly decisions.**
Require firms to produce environmental profit and loss reports, detailing resource usage and pollution generated/reduced. The EPA will give each report a "grade" (on an A-F scale), available to the public, incentivizing businesses to pollute less. Those that receive failing "grades" (a D or lower) will have to pay the pollution tax on their revenue. See *point three for more details.* Invest $20 million in targeted local and state marketing campaigns to raise awareness and push personal responsibility for improved environmental protection.

2. **Incentivize high-polluting facilities to sign a community benefit agreement (CBA).**
Communities must agree with a company's plan to minimize and equitably distribute negative effects. Minority residents must be given suitable representation in this process, empowering locals in negotiating with these facilities to secure employment, support for urban development projects and protection against pollution. Require product manufacturers to partially fund the disposal of products. Within this CBA, facilities must agree to increase efforts in developing better techniques for managing waste. Federal and state agencies will allocate subsidies to these facilities to help

incentivize innovation, as far as budgets allow without increasing government spending.

3. **Impose taxes on plastic and pollution.**
Corporations must pay a five-cents federal tax on any single-use plastics they produce; businesses must pay a nickel for each non-recyclable or non-compostable piece of packaging they sell. During this time, the government will grant them subsidies to research innovative ways to create less detrimental methods for packaging. A maximum of five years will be allowed for the conduction of research toward these efforts. During this time, the U.S. Consumer Product Safety Commission will conduct internal investigations on the progress of said corporations' efforts. Medicinal products that must be single use, such as vaccines, will be exempted. As for the encouragement of private sector sustainability, impose a general pollution tax. This tax will go beyond just carbon and will be set at 10% of revenue for corporations that fail the EPA's report. *See point 1 for more details.* To ensure these taxes are not regressive, a pollution dividend utilizing half of the revenue collected by the taxes will be created to send to areas most devastated by private sector pollution.

4. **Establish direct communication between various environmental regulatory agencies.**
The U.S. House and Senate environment committees will hold biannual hearings with representatives from governmental agencies such as the EPA, FDA, OSHA and CPSC to share relevant updates and ensure each agency is briefed on the latest findings by the Intergovernmental Panel on Climate Change. This will allow the agencies to keep abreast of the latest scientific knowledge on climate change, and liaisons will be established

between the agencies to reduce redundancy and streamline public-private collaboration in environmental regulation.

Why This Initiative is Important:
Protection of the environment is critical given the impact man-made pollution and excessive consumption has on ecosystems and the climate. The solution will involve everyone from the public and private sectors. Public citizens will have a say in how private corporations treat the environment. The government will also play a key role by incentivizing private entities to refrain from polluting in the form of taxes and streamlined communication. The various independent government agencies responsible for closely related issues will be able to communicate directly with one another, allowing for unified missions that will put the environment on a path toward cleanliness.

Economic Impact (from our student economist team):
- Estimated effect on the annual federal deficit: - $29.5 million.
- Reducing pollution and promoting sustainable land management preserves resources for future economic stability.

To learn how our student economists came up with this economic impact, send an email to info@ournationalconversation.org and ask for a more thorough description of their methodologies.

Final Thought for Now:
"We have fallen heirs to the most glorious heritage a people ever received, and each one must do his part if we wish to show that the nation is worthy of its good fortune." – **Theodore Roosevelt**

Let's Fix America

Acknowledgments:
The following student(s) worked on this nonpartisan proposal: Aiden Merrill-Skoloff, Skidmore College; Ellery Saluck, Washington University in St. Louis; Zahra Said, University of California, Berkeley; Jessica Dine, Grinnell College; Rahul Hebbar, Rutgers University.

The following individuals worked with our student interns and contributed expertise, wisdom and moral support in the development of this proposal:
1. Dave Owen: Professor of Environmental Law, University of California, Hastings. San Francisco, CA.
2. Todd Myers: Director of Center for the Environment, Washington Policy Center. Seattle, WA.
3. Anjali Tripathi: Research associate, Center for Astrophysics, Harvard-Smithsonian. Los Angeles, CA.

Note: Not all participants agree with every aspect of this proposal. To arrive at a proposal that takes multiple views into account requires compromise and difficult decisions. For individual commentary on this proposal and more detail, go to OurNationalConversation.org. We invite you to add your comments as well.

Sources:
"Air Pollution Solutions." *UCAR Center for Science Education*, 2020, https://scied.ucar.edu/learning-zone/air-quality/air-pollution-solutions.

"About the Office of Policy (OP)." *EPA* 26 May 2021, www.epa.gov/aboutepa/about-office-policy-op.

Fischhoff, Maya. "How to Motivate People Toward Sustainability." *Network for Business Sustainability*, 22 Jun. 2020, www.nbs.net/articles/how-to-motivate-people-toward-sustainability.

Funk, Cary, and Meg Hefferon. "U.S. Public Views on Climate and Energy." *Pew Research Center Science & Society* 25 Nov. 2019, www.pewresearch.org/science/2019/11/25/u-s-public-views-on-climate-and-energy/"The Intergovernmental Panel on Climate Change." *IPCC*, 9 Jun. 2022, www.ipcc.ch/.

Lindwall, Courtney. "Single-Use Plastics 101." *NRDC*, 9 Jan. 2020, www.nrdc.org/stories/single-use-plastics-101.

Let's Fix America

"The Politics of Climate Change in the United States." *Pew Research Center Science & Society*, Pew Research Center, 4 Oct. 2016, www.pewresearch.org/science/2016/10/04/the-politics-of-climate/.

Simon, Matt. "Should Governments Slap a Tax on Plastic?" *Wired,*, 4 Aug. 2020, www.wired.com/story/should-governments-slap-a-tax-on-plastic/

Tiseo, Ian. "Global Waste Generation - Statistics and Facts." *Statista*, 26 Nov. 2020, https://www.statista.com/topics/4983/waste-generation-worldwide/.

Protecting Our Habitats and Endangered Species

Big Picture:
Deforestation, urbanization and climate change are tremendous threats to American wildlife. While America's various ecosystems provide more than $29 trillion in economic capital, biodiversity is rapidly decreasing and Earth's ecosystems face collapse. It is time to protect these habitats to ensure that plants and animals thrive and are not on the verge of extinction.

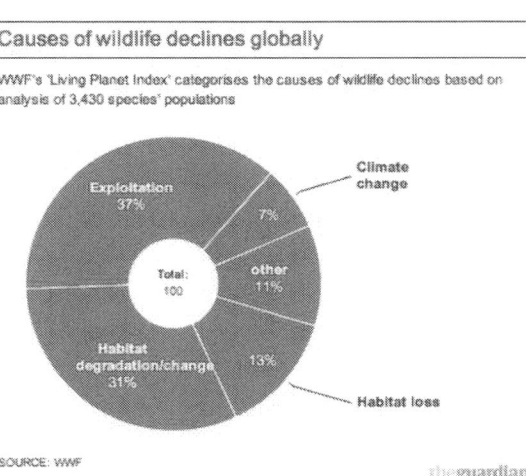

Graphic From: "Our Biosphere in Peril: 50% Decline in Wildlife Populations." *Public Citizen*. 2 Oct. 2014. This figure illustrates the major contributors - many caused by humans - to the decline in population of over 3,400 species since 1970.

Operative Definitions:
1. **Urban sprawl:** The rapid expansion of cities and towns, often characterized by low-density residential housing, single-use zoning and increased reliance on the private automobile for transportation.

2. **Biomimetic:** An approach to innovation that seeks sustainable solutions to human challenges by emulating nature's time-tested patterns and strategies.
3. **New Urbanism:** A planning and development approach based on the principles of how cities and towns were built for the last several centuries, with walkable blocks and streets, housing and shopping nearby, and accessible public spaces. New Urbanism focuses on human-scaled urban design.
4. **Light pollution:** The excessive or inappropriate use of outdoor artificial light. In addition to other damage, it impacts animal behaviors such as migration patterns, wake-sleep habits and habitat formation.
5. **Green infrastructure:** A biomimetic approach to infrastructure. Networks inspired by nature and the natural water cycle. Rain gardens, green roofs, trees and parks absorb water back into the Earth rather than transporting it through gray infrastructure (dams, seawalls, roads, pipes or water treatment plants). By utilizing green infrastructure, cities will be better equipped to handle extreme weather events.
6. **The Endangered Species Act (ESA) of 1973:** The primary law in the U.S. protecting domestic and international wildlife. The law allows individuals and organizations to petition to have a species listed as endangered.
7. **Fracking:** Drilling techniques used to extract natural gas from bedrock. Can pollute groundwater and air.
8. **Marine Catch Share System:** A regulatory system in which a certain portion or share of fish collected by a fishery is given to individual fishermen or fishing communities.
9. **National Park Service:** A government agency created under former President Woodrow Wilson in 1916 and tasked to protect national parks and monuments for recreational use. The service's responsibilities were expanded under former President Theodore

Roosevelt, who gave the agency the responsibility to oversee historical sites and a wider breadth of national monuments.

Important Facts and Statistics:
1. Forty-two percent of endangered species are at risk because of invasive species. These non-native species can drastically alter an ecosystem's balance and cost the U.S. over $1 billion each year in damages.
2. Bees are threatened by pesticides in their nectar, pollen and water supply. From April 2018 to April 2019, 40% of bee colonies died. Honeybees pollinate $15 billion worth of food crops every year, making their decline extremely concerning.
3. As of March 2021, over 1,200 species in America are listed as endangered.

6-Point Plan:
1. **Reduce the negative environmental impacts of cities.** Address urban sprawl through New Urbanism in city planning. Invest in public infrastructure, such as trees and parklets, with habitat conservation and efficient land use in mind. Introduce green infrastructure by applying natural water management practices that improve water quality without costly treatment plants. Through increased water storage, green infrastructure would help mitigate the effects of climate change. Minimize light pollution in cities through local lighting ordinances. Localities can establish lighting zones and curfews and invest in outdoor lighting that is less disruptive and more energy efficient. These ordinances will result in financial savings, improved public safety (for example, reduced glare will decrease car accident incidences) and healthier ecosystems.

2. **Incentivize landowners to make sustainable decisions.** Provide small property tax breaks to landowners growing resilient native plants for small businesses. Furthermore, educate homeowners to shift towards non-toxic alternatives to pesticides, including insecticidal soaps and plant-based horticultural oils. Consolidate landowner compensation programs for protecting endangered species into one state initiative. Programs include the Wildlife Habitat Incentives Program and the Environmental Quality Incentives Program, which incentivize landowner action. Merge these with environmental groups' efforts into a fund for purchasing habitats from landowners.

3. **Regulate and monitor land use and development.** Implement wildlife-friendly zoning regulations. Reduce the effects of habitat fragmentation by requiring buffer zones around land desirable for development, adding zoning areas for wildlife. Local and state governments will sell vacant public land to wildlife conservation organizations for habitat preservation. Enact stronger hydraulic fracturing (fracking) regulations, including bi-annual inspections of sites. Inspection results will require publication for the public to increase transparency. Invest in research and sustainable energy development in communities, especially in areas where fossil fuel development occurs.

4. **Revise the Marine Catch Share system to be more equitable.** Reform and promote the Marine Catch Share system, which uses shares to determine who receives fishing privileges in an area. Currently, small fishermen are allotted few shares, resulting in job losses. While the system itself has improved fisheries and marine ecosystem safety, it must designate areas for the public and for small fishermen to ensure equity.

5. **Strengthen the Endangered Species Act of 1973.**
    The central law geared towards conservation, the ESA, has been criticized for being insufficiently flexible and cost-effective. Reform it by increasing states' roles in recovering species and by applying market-based approaches to private conservation and expanding universal regulations. This entails establishing public funds to reward sustainable practices or private funds to pay landowners who manage their land in ways that maximize ecosystem services. Assigning economic value to ecosystem services is another way to reward responsible land management.

6. **Establish long-term environmental projects in rural and urban schools.**
    As most Americans live in cities, there is a growing disconnect between students and surrounding nature. The disconnect that exists in rural school districts must be considered as well. Environmentally engaged students are more likely to actively preserve their environment. Projects should engage students in the nature that cities have to offer, potentially highlighting aspects of nature like wildlife, water runoff or park rehabilitation. An allocation of funding from the state government will help the success of this endeavor. Schools will collaborate with local nature clubs, environmental awareness organizations like the Boy and Girl Scouts of America or the Sierra Club, and museums or parks departments on projects.

Why This Initiative is Important:
This proposal addresses the major challenges faced by American wildlife and offers comprehensive protection guidelines. By highlighting the importance of educational programs and developmental flaws, this proposal supports wildlife conservation through awareness and actionable change. Prioritizing conservation

through market-based and property-rights-based initiatives lets landowners, fishermen and farmers have significant economic incentives to conserve the environment. This plan satisfies the conservation interests of most Americans, addressing key issues in wildlife conservation such as endangered species, fracking and habitat fragmentation.

Economic Impact (from our student economist team):
- Increased costs in reducing urban sprawl would be offset by the consumer savings brought by long-term sustainability.
- Revising the Marine Catch Share system will preserve and bring back fishing jobs to our coastlines.
- Protecting species and habitats is essential to maintaining healthy tourism and employment opportunities.
- Estimated effect on the annual federal deficit: - $400 million

To learn how our student economists came up with this economic impact, send an email to info@ournationalconversation.org and ask for a more thorough description of their methodologies.

Final Thought for Now:
"Unless we practice conservation, those who come after us will have to pay the price of misery, degradation, and failure for the progress and prosperity of our day." – Gifford Pinchot (1910, The Fight for Conservation)

Acknowledgments:
The following student(s) worked on this nonpartisan proposal: Pragya Jain, American University; Ellery Saluck, Washington University in St. Louis; Marianne Swan, State University of New York College at Oneonta; Yoni Ferbank, Syracuse University; Gabby Ostrov, University of Vermont.

Let's Fix America

The following individuals worked with our student interns and contributed expertise, wisdom and moral support in the development of this proposal:
1. Jonathan Wood: Senior Attorney, Pacific Legal Foundation. Washington, DC.
2. Anjali Tripathi: Research associate, Center for Astrophysics, Harvard-Smithsonian. Los Angeles, CA.
3. Andrea K.I. Hall, Quality Control, Compliance, and Sustainability Coordinator in the canned seafood sector, Sausalito, CA

Note: Not all participants agree with every aspect of this proposal. To arrive at a proposal that takes multiple views into account requires compromise and difficult decisions. For individual commentary on this proposal and more detail, go to OurNationalConversation.org. We invite you to add your comments as well.

Sources:
"Invasive Species." *The National Wildlife Federation,* 9 Jun. 2022, www.nwf.org/Educational-Resources/Wildlife-Guide/Threats-to-Wildlife/Invasive-Species

Smitley, David, et al. "How to control invasive pests while protecting pollinators and other beneficial insects." *Michigan State University Extension,* 1 May 2019, https://www.canr.msu.edu/news/how-to-control-invasive-pests-while-protecting-pollinators-and-other-beneficial-insects

Toothman, Jessika. "How Light Pollution Works." *HowStuffWorks* 9 Jun. 2022, https://science.howstuffworks.com/environmental/green-science/light-pollution.htm#pt1

"We Could Do a Lot More to Regulate Fracking." *Natural Resources Defense Council,* 18 Jul. 2018. www.nrdc.org/stories/we-could-do-lot-more-regulate-fracking

"Wildlife Habitat Fragmentation." *The Wildlife Society,* May 2014, wildlife.org/wp-content/uploads/2014/05/Wildlife-Habitat-Fragmentation.pdf

Let's Fix America

Economic Scorecard: Do the Numbers Add Up?

In this "scorecard," we show the economics for each proposal, and then a grand total (close to $300 billion in annual deficit reduction, at least during the next decade). Our student economics team was unable to project the annual change to the federal deficit for proposals marked "N/A." Our students are quick to say these projections are based on limited information, assumptions that cannot be considered definitive, and the still-developing economic knowledge of students. Still, our students think the projections are, at least, directionally on target and give the reader a rough idea of where the proposals may stand economically. For more information about the methods that went into calculating these numbers, please send an email to info@ournationalconversation.org and ask.

Chapter	Proposal	Annual net change (+/-) in federal deficit	Chapter Totals
Governance	Restoring Trust in Elections	+ $34,500,000	
Governance	Reforming Congressional Rules	N/A	
Governance	Increasing Congressional Effectiveness	+ $530,000,000	
Governance	Increasing Lobbying Transparency	+ $2,061,000	+ $566,561,000
Economics	Mitigating Inflation	+ $58,000,000,000	
Economics	Addressing U.S. Debt and Deficits	- $116,000,000,000	
Economics	Creating Sustainable Tax Reform	- $277,900,000,000	
Economics	Reducing Poverty	N/A	
Economics	Sustaining Social Security	- $113,350,000,000	- $449,250,000,000
Infrastructure	Creating Affordable Housing	- $4,000.000.000	
Infrastructure	Rethinking Transportation in America	+ $5,620,000,000	
Infrastructure	Disaster-resilient Infrastructure	+ $5,100,000,000	+ $6,720,000,000
Social Issues	Overhauling Media Landscape	+ $60,000,000 (one time grant)	

Social Issues	Creating New Foundations for K-12 Public Education	+ $15,000,000,000	
Social Issues	Combatting Homelessness in America	+ $7,926,000,000	
Social Issues	Incentivizing National Service	- $20,000,000,000	
Social Issues	Promoting Entrepreneurship	+ $125,000,000	+ $3,111,000,000
Justice and Public Safety	Creating a More Egalitarian Justice System	- $420,000,000	
Justice and Public Safety	Balancing Gun Control and Civil Liberties	+ $10,500,000	
Justice and Public Safety	Law Enforcement and Minority Groups	N/A	- $409,500,000
Healthcare	Improving Access to U.S. Healthcare	+ $6,500,000,000	
Healthcare	Reducing the Costs of Healthcare	N/A	
Healthcare	Tackling Obesity in America	- $34,000,000,000	
Healthcare	Reforming Women's Reproductive Healthcare	+ $110,000,000	
Healthcare	Getting Serious About Providing Mental Healthcare	N/A	
Healthcare	Solving Our Nation's Substance Abuse Epidemic	N/A	- $27,390,000,000
Foreign Policy and Defense	Reforming U.S. Immigration Policy	+ $5,750,000,000	
Foreign Policy and Defense	Mitigating US/China Tensions and Potential Conflicts	N/A	
Foreign Policy and Defense	The Israeli- Palestinian Conflict; Can We Achieve a Breakthrough?	+ $4,000,000,000	
Foreign Policy and Defense	Preparing NATO's Long-Term Response to a Belligerent Russia	N/A	
Foreign Policy and Defense	Protecting Public and Private Cyber Information	+ $2,000,000,000	+ $11,750,000,000
SE&T	Tackling Climate Change in America, Starting with Carbon Emissions	+ $157,200,000,000	
SE&T	Protecting Our Habitats and Endangered Species	- $400,000,000	
SE&T	Incentivizing Environmental Protection	- $29,500,000	+ $156,770,500,000
			Grand Total: - $298,131,439,000

Let's Fix America

The Baby Boomers & Gen Z: Many Similarities, Many Differences

Hi there, this is Jeff Hall again, newspaper dinosaur. I'm back to write the final three chapters of this book. In this "first last" chapter, I want to make some observations about the many similarities — and many differences — between the Baby Boomers and Gen Z.

In the next, second-to-last chapter, I will spell out where I see ONC going from here.

And then, in the final chapter, I will acknowledge all the fine people who have contributed to this effort so far (and ask *you* to join this effort, as well).

Let's start by exploring the parallels between Boomers and Gen Z. By the time my Boomer contemporaries and I graduated college, we had experienced the Cuban Missile Crisis (complete with "duck beneath our desks" exercises). We cried after the assassinations of JFK, Dr. Martin Luther King Jr. and Bobby Kennedy.

We witnessed race riots, the ravages of Vietnam, political rallies that became violent, oil spills and choking air pollution. We lived through Watergate and saw, on live television, the only U.S. president to ever resign, in disgrace. We thought things couldn't get any worse than that.

Gen Z has experienced the Great Recession, climate change, hyper-partisanship, the "forever wars," mass shootings on campuses (with their own duck, cover, run and hide exercises) and the excesses of social media. Today's students have seen the rise in student debt, the college admissions scandals, white supremacist rallies, the life-threatening COVID-19 pandemic and the Black Lives Matter protests that erupted after the murder of George Floyd.

The Russians invaded Ukraine, and now there is talk of possible nuclear war for the first time in a very long time. Inflation, after going into hibernation for many decades, is now back with a vengeance. Roe v. Wade recently got overturned. The mass shootings continue.

We are once seeing acts of political violence, reminiscent of what the Boomers experienced in the sixties and seventies. Gen Z witnessed a marked shift in governance and style when Donald Trump was elected president. His administration ended with accusations about a stolen election and the unprecedented Jan. 6 attack on the Capitol.

Whether you like Donald Trump or not, we can all agree his was not a typical presidency. For many, the Trump years gave hope and voice to forgotten Americans; others found the Trump years exceedingly traumatic. The fact we are so divided as a country came into much sharper focus in recent years.

Young Americans are told regularly that their standard of living will be below that of their parents. The arrival of social media has, without a doubt, had a huge impact on Gen Z. Social media isn't going away, but I'm thankful, as a Baby Boomer, we didn't have it in our day.

Because of social media, I think many of today's students are fearful that anything they say or do could come back to haunt them. That has a chilling effect, I believe; it's hard to propose big ideas — or really put yourself out there at all — when you fear ridicule.

We Boomers were much freer (and, I think, more creative) in our day. We were inspired early on by President John F. Kennedy, who told us to "ask not what your country can do for you — ask what you can do for your country." Kennedy started the Peace Corps in 1961, and this was the era of early space flight — a rather thrilling time.

We had The Beatles and all the great bands; art was very experimental. We had the free speech movement. Star Trek was a very popular show that caused us to ponder the future with wonderment and hope. We staged the first Earth Day in 1970. In the sixties and seventies, CBS news anchor, Walter Cronkite, was often referred to as the "most trusted man in America." What media personality today comes close?

We patted ourselves on the back when Nixon resigned and the Vietnam War ended; we thought our protests brought about these results (without a doubt, they contributed). I think, when Vietnam ended, we figured we were "done." We had completed our assignment, and it was now time to get back to some kind of normalcy (that is, cut our hair and get a job). This accounts for, I think, the lack of continued follow through on the part of the Boomers. I think we thought America was now back on a good course, and problems would get solved in due time.

We *thought* we were making progress when it came to race relations in America. We *surely* made progress when it came to women's rights. We were, as a generation, quite *hopeful*. *Anything* seemed possible.

By comparison, today's students seem quite anxious.

Quite often during our ONC deliberations, our Gen Z students will talk about their mental health, anxiety and stress; they sometimes request time off or a delay in achieving a deadline. Some of my

Boomer colleagues and I don't always know how to respond to this. In our day, we were taught to suck it up and keep marching. We didn't talk about our emotional health when we were in college. That was all kind of taboo.

As much as I would like to say this future generation is amazing and will fix everything, I don't think reality will be that simple, *especially if an entire generation is stressed out and fearful.* At a time when we desperately need innovation and courage, our young people seem cautious — almost to a fault. They've been traumatized. Adults need to listen, engage and do something proactive. It's not realistic to expect our youth to figure this out on their own. *These are our children.*

I've asked my students to come up with a public policy proposal to address mental health issues among today's youth. We didn't have time to write that proposal; check OurNationalConversation.org to see when something appears. Better yet, if you are a mental health professional and want to weigh in, we'd like to hear from you.

Every generation is called upon to face its challenges. Our Founding Fathers — many quite young at the time — took it upon themselves to start a revolution against the most powerful empire on Earth. In the 1860s, our country was ravaged by civil war, fought mostly by young soldiers.

Back in the 1920s, young suffragettes marched for women's right to vote. The Greatest Generation — many in their teens and twenties at the time — faced the Depression and World War II. In the 1950s and sixties, young Black Americans and the Freedom Riders, including many white supporters, had to fight for the right to vote and the right to get a decent seat on a bus or in the cafeteria.

We never heard much from gay individuals in the sixties and seventies; they were still "in the closet." Generally speaking, women weren't really welcome in the workforce in the 1970s. They had to fight their way in. Those with disabilities had to do the same.

While America isn't perfect, I'm guessing most Americans alive today would choose to live now rather than in any earlier time. Despite America's current issues, our society is possibly fairer and more inclusive than it has ever been. Surely the technology and our material standard of living are better. So, we *have* made progress. We just need to make *more* of it — especially social progress — and we need to make it *faster*. Then we need to *hold onto it*.

Despite all this progress, our politics have moved in the opposite direction.

Things have become increasingly toxic and dysfunctional in recent decades, which makes *any* progress hard to achieve. When Boomers were coming of age, senators and congressmen used to address each other using words like, "my esteemed colleague from the State of Mississippi." There were some liberal Republicans and some conservative Democrats. Tip O'Neill, Democratic Speaker of the House used to join President Ronald Reagan, a Republican, for cocktails. The drumbeat of progress seemed quiet but steady.

Today, by contrast, we are consumed by anger — hate, even. Politicians rarely cooperate across the aisle. Is anybody really happy with the current state of affairs? What can change this dynamic?

David Gergen, presidential advisor to four presidents, argues in his new book, "Hearts Touched with Fire," that it's time for our older leaders to step aside and make room for the new. I think he's right. When you think about it, it has *always* been young people who bring

Let's Fix America

about social change. So, we *need* Gen Z to emerge strong from this current low.

If Gen Z and Millennials can rise above all they have faced growing up — and all that they will continue to face — they will be a very strong generation, indeed. They must pass through the "crucible" David Gergen describes — and come out, intact — and stronger, *on the other side.*

This won't be easy but there are reasons to be hopeful this is possible.

Gen Z does diversity incredibly well. I see *zero* evidence of racism among Gen Z. Wouldn't it be nice if, in their lifetimes, Gen Z could put race to bed as an issue in America? Think about how much creative energy that would free up. As older people die off and the young take over, this could all happen almost effortlessly.

Gen Z is naturally collaborative, as well. I detect almost *no* competition or jockeying for position among our students. They really do work well together. I just can't imagine today's young Americans entering positions of responsibility and engaging in all the "performative politics" we see among our adult elected officials today.

I think snarky tweets will be viewed by Gen Z in the future the same way people nowadays look at the bell bottoms we Boomers wore in the seventies — or maybe even *more* harshly. Bell bottoms and long sideburns cause us to chuckle; divisiveness by design is serious business.

Gen Z's extraordinary ability to collaborate makes me think that, over time, as the oldsters die out, America's divisive ways will simply disappear.

There are signs a political turnaround has already started — but maybe this hasn't sunk in, yet (or maybe it's not really happening, yet). In 2021, a big infrastructure bill was passed with bipartisan support. After the Russians invaded Ukraine, there was huge bipartisan support for providing the Ukrainians with weapons. In the aftermath of the Uvalde (Texas) campus shooting, there was bipartisan cooperation on introducing some reasonable gun safety measures.

The Inflation Reduction Act that got passed in summer of 2022 includes features to reduce both pharmaceutical costs and the deficit. Another bill, designed to shore up chip manufacturing in the U.S., recently passed with bipartisan support. That's a change.

There was also a recent stinging verdict against Alex Jones, purveyor of online hate and lies spread via his "Infowars" platform. A jury just awarded the parents of young children killed at Sandy Hook nearly $1 billion in punitive damages. I think this Alex Jones verdict offers hope that the dark side of media will finally get reined in.

If you are running a podcast or blog or website that monetizes hate, one day you might have to pay big damages to your victims. That should give the hate-for-profit crowd pause. I hope it does. I have always thought it was individuals, and not platforms, who were ultimately responsible for content.

A new group of Democrats, Independents and Republicans just announced they want to start a third, centrist political party called "Forward." I don't know if Forward will take off or not, but, clearly, many are fed up with the traditional two parties. Ranked Choice Voting is starting to take hold. That holds the promise of reducing extremist politics.

Let's Fix America

Maybe a golden era of sobriety, logic and common-sense problem-solving is about to begin. Let's hope so. But, as the old saying goes, "24 hours is a long time in politics." Things can change in an instant. Elections have a huge impact; as we go to press with this book, it appears there was no decisive shift brought about by the midterm election (November of 2022). Our government remains divided.

Just as the stock market can't go up — or down — forever, the political pendulum eventually swings in a new direction. It's time for problem-solving to become widely viewed as more important than political party. As young people assume positions of power, they will *see to it*. Today's young Americans don't care about political parties. They care about survival!

Another Big Generational Difference: How We Say Things

There is a bias among many young Americans, I think, that leads a significant majority of them to believe liberal conclusions and solutions are the only conclusions and solutions that can and should be discussed — and, therefore, there is no need to even consider conservative points of view. This, of course, has come to be known as *political correctness* or *cancel culture*.

I recall it being very different when we Boomers were in college. Most of us were quite liberal, but we *loved* dorm-room debates that went late into the night. We *wanted* to hear all sides (and then do our best to win the other person over). All the intellectual ferment was incredibly stimulating.

It's not so easy for today's students. Every word is scrutinized. You have to say things just right. This spilled over into ONC. For example, at the insistence of one of our students, we had long talks about whether or not to use the term, "Latinx," (as opposed to Latino or Hispanic). One of our Hispanic students convinced us, using polling data, that *most Hispanics* in our country actually don't like the term, but the person arguing we use it persisted.

To resolve this issue, we decided to follow AP Style in the writing of this book, and, right now, the more traditional terms (Hispanic, Latino, Latina) are preferred by AP. The pro-Latinx student wasn't happy with this decision, but we simply had to keep moving. This particular conversation could have dragged on and on.

And then there is the issue of "ghosting;" sometimes, I said things I thought needed to be said to the students, only to be met with a wall of silence. Several times, when pressed on an issue, our students acted as if they hadn't heard what I said, or hadn't seen my email or text message left in Slack. They simply went blank on me.

If we are to have a national conversation that includes tackling tough issues, it helps when all parties are willing to, at least, *engage*. Sometimes, difficult conversations lead to better outcomes that could not have occurred without having had the difficult conversation in the first place. I find Gen Z to be conflict avoidant. I don't like conflict, either, but Gen Z takes it to a whole new level.

Gen Z: Tough Enough?

I do think Gen Z needs to focus more on results and less on process. Talks among Gen Z typically go on *way* too long. Everyone must be heard. Nobody wants to offend. At some point, it's time to bring the conversation to a close, make a decision and take action. You can't always achieve one hundred percent consensus.

But if the group never decides, nobody is offended; the moment the group decides, someone will be unhappy. Gen Z really doesn't like making others unhappy. I keep urging the students to decide and move on; if the decision turns out to be wrong, they can always adjust. This is really hard for them. Decision making under conditions of uncertainty is definitely something Gen Z needs to learn.

If today's young Americans don't seem competitive compared to earlier generations, it's important to note the rest of the world maybe isn't yet as enlightened. We clearly live in a competitive world, and there are people and countries out there that would love to take America down. I'm not sure Gen Z sees this.

Maybe the next generation from all around the world will adopt a "kumbaya" approach to international relations, and we'll finally achieve world peace. This is what the Baby Boomers wanted, too. Unfortunately, history tells us this won't be the case. The current international climate is increasingly scary. Weapons of war are far more powerful. I don't think anyone is predicting world peace anytime soon.

We had several students from other countries participate at ONC. In general, their contributions have been quite productive. It's often the case that America can learn from the successes of other countries.

I remember one conversation about healthcare in which a German student had us in awe, as he described how easy and inexpensive it was to receive medical treatment in Germany. You just walked in off the street, received treatment and then walked out without paying. He simply couldn't understand America's healthcare system at all, and I think most Americans would agree with him!

Let's Fix America

I urge all Americans to consider the following: *Quite often, our foreign students seem to love America even more than our American students.* Our foreign students really *want* America to succeed; they fear, if America goes down, their countries will be dragged down as well, and America won't be able to do anything to help.

Many non-U.S. students think America is still a role model for other parts of the world. They know we suffer hyper-partisanship, and they want to help us overcome it. They see a direct self-interest in all this. In contrast, some of our American students seem almost ashamed to be Americans. I remember feeling this way too, back when I was a college student, backpacking in Europe. This was at the height of the Vietnam War, and Europeans were appalled by what we were doing in Vietnam. We were often asked to explain why the U.S. was in Vietnam when we couldn't understand it ourselves.

One final observation about our foreign students and our first-generation American students: they work hard. I mean, they work *really, really hard.* They've got something to prove. They aren't here to simply add one more little thing to their resume.

I urge young Americans to not give up on America. We've seen dark times before, but history tells us we always rise. One day soon, you will be in charge. What will you do with this awesome opportunity — and responsibility? What will you do to make you and your children proud to call yourselves Americans?

Just as I talk about the Baby Boomers passing the baton, one day you will be called upon to do the same.

Jeff Hall, Editor & CEO

Let's Fix America: Only a Conversation Starter

As was discussed in the introduction to this book, the purpose of these 34 public policy proposals is to start a conversation about how we can all work together to improve America. Our students took this assignment very seriously. Now, it's your turn.

We Want Your Ideas

There is a PROPOSALS section of our website where citizens can comment on and critique proposals, as well as submit proposals of their own. If you have ideas, go to OurNationalConversation.org and look for the PROPOSALS button up near the top of our web page.

You will be able to upvote and downvote what you see and interact with others who are interested in the same topic. We will host sub-communities around specific topics (healthcare, infrastructure, etc.). Think of OurNationalConversation.org as "the people's voice" — *your* voice.

Ideas proposed on OUR NATIONAL CONVERSATION's platform will change over time as conditions and thinking evolve. I hope, within a few years, the ONC community will have solved *hundreds,* if not *thousands,* of thorny problems together. This is a marathon, not a sprint. We won't solve all of America's problems overnight. New issues we can't imagine today will take the place of the ones we solve together in coming years.

America has always had issues and always will. We are human beings; we are imperfect. So, some form of "Our National Conversation" will *always* be needed. With today's digital tools, a new kind of digital town hall based on civility becomes possible. We are just getting started with this and hope ONC will facilitate needed conversations for years to come. There will always be something in need of fixing.

Where ONC Goes from Here

My student interns and I have received a lot of positive feedback about this project. That has inspired us to think of ways we can conduct OUR NATIONAL CONVERSATION on a grander scale. We want to become financially self-sustaining quickly, so we can remain vital and journalistically independent.

We don't want special interests to try and push us to become too liberal or too conservative. Publications that are broke often fall to temptation. Be can't fall to temptation, in my view. Neutrality is key to our potential success — and survival.

We have lots of ideas that we are kicking around regarding how we can become viable as an enterprise. Let's talk about all that in greater detail sometime next year; we need to get up and running first. But here's a preview.

As has been noted, many of the proposals you see in "Let's Fix America" are very balanced, not very controversial — maybe a bit vanilla. For those of us who prefer more razzle-dazzle, we will address this in a second book we are working on. We're calling it our "Moonshot Edition."

This book will be filled with wildly imaginative and futuristic ideas that aren't practical today but *could be* one day. If you found "Let's Fix America" boring, we're going in the opposite direction with our second book. We now have solid ideas for literally 10 new books. Our students are excited to continue the journey.

In addition to our books and our website, we want to produce a TV show — or a streaming video production — *also* called "Let's Fix America." Young Americans will pitch ideas they think will make America a better country. In this show, older experts with real-world experience will weigh in on the students' proposals.

We already shot a TV show pilot episode. I'm, of course, biased, but I do think people will actually watch our show. Maybe a network or cable outlet will pick it up and distribute it far and wide. If you are a TV executive, please get in touch.

We obviously can't count on a TV or cable network to adopt us, so we are exploring using video-friendly platforms, such as YouTube, Snapchat, TikTok, Instagram and Twitch. Young people don't watch much traditional TV anymore, and we need to embrace these new platforms. We'll figure it out (or our young people will, anyway).

One of our interns, Benny Rosenzweig (Princeton), said that ONC needs to "be more than just talk." He argued, with great passion, that ONC needed an *action* division. We're adding that to our website and calling it "Get Involved." In our Get Involved section, there will be a place for interested individuals to find volunteer opportunities with local, national and even international causes.

We want to set up ONC chapters on high school and college campuses across America. Many of today's students are weary of all the political correctness, intolerance and "cancel culture" that exists on campuses today. At ONC, we want to provide an alternative, making healthy give-and-take possible everywhere. We want to start college campus chapters; this is where we think we have a chance to really take root.

Today's students seem very nonpartisan to me. I think they are turned off by both major political parties. But they do care about policy — and results. They want a safe space to discuss politics and public policy. We will try and help provide this for them.

America's challenges go deeper than just policy disagreements. It's clear to me there is something emotionally, spiritually and culturally amiss in our country. We'll have to get to that later. To start, we decided to work on public policy proposals because it seemed like this could be a "confidence-building" exercise. If we can actually sit down and solve problems together — which we have shown is possible — maybe we can start to trust one another again. Then, over time, we can try and solve tougher problems.

For ONC to work, it has to be widely embraced by citizens. This is really a *movement* we're hoping to build — one based on facts, civil exchange and practical problem-solving. The energy is there; the vehicle has, up until now, been missing.

For ONC to become truly impactful, we need to get the word out. You can help with that.

10 Ways You Can Help ONC — The "Big Ask"

There are lots of ways that you can help make ONC the big deal it ought to become. Here's a list of action items for your consideration:

1. **If you represent a media outlet and want to interview some of our bright students, get in touch.** We live in a media-driven world. Eyeballs are important. Meet some of America's future leaders, interview them and introduce them

to your audiences. Let America know there's a new path forward.

2. **Buy one copy of "Let's Fix America" for yourself and *additional copies for others*.** Give them away as gifts to those you think will be interested. Go to Amazon and look for "Let's Fix America." If you want to pay for 535 copies that we'll send to every member of Congress, send an email to info@OurNationalConversation.org. The same goes for think tanks, academics and media outlets. You buy the books, and we'll get them distributed. We also sell branded merchandise with the ONC logo (stickers, coffee mugs, baseball caps, T-shirts, hoodies, etc.) on our website. Look for the "STORE" button.

3. **Into social media? If you like ONC, spread the word among your friends and followers.** One tweet from just the right person could put us on the map. You can find us on Twitter (@OurNatlConvo) or on Facebook (facebook.com/ournationalconversation). Our Instagram and TikTok are both @ournationalconversation. Our YouTube Channel can be found by searching for OUR NATIONAL CONVERSATION. Find us on Snapchat by searching "ournatlconvo." On LinkedIn, look for OUR NATIONAL CONVERSATION (ONC). Into social media? Do your best to come up with some creative social media posts that will get shared.

4. **If you have anything to do with your company's marketing plans, consider buying advertising on our site (and/or our other media platforms).** You can show America you support what we're doing here by advertising on

our website, on our podcast or in our newsletter. You could also sponsor one of our initiatives. We are very open to win-win proposals.

5. **If you are a young American with leadership potential and want to intern with us, please contact us. If you are an older, established professional and want to work with our students, contact us.** Everyone really likes the exchange; it's fun and intellectually stimulating.

6. **If you want to provide scholarships and/or stipends to our students who come from challenging socio-economic circumstances, send us an email.** We've had some great intern prospects who couldn't join us — or couldn't stay with us too long — because they had to make money and couldn't afford to take on an unpaid internship.

7. **If you have a good cause or project that could benefit from our students getting involved, reach out.** If you'd like publicity for *your* project — remember, we're a media company — send us some background information (and a video link if you have it) to: info@OurNationalConversation.org.

8. **If you want to host an ONC event or campus chapter, let's talk.** If you want to host a local version of OUR NATIONAL CONVERSATION in your city or country, we can make our platform available to you, and you can tailor it to your needs (for a reasonable fee).

9. **Consider *investing* in ONC.** We have taken ONC as far as we can on our own; it's time to do this right. We want to

raise $1 million via a crowdfunding campaign. In the early stages, especially, most of the money will go toward marketing. Much of our initial marketing will target high school and college students. They are the ones who helped build ONC, so they are already invested in the idea. If we succeed on campus, ONC could take off from there (that's how Facebook did it). Send an email to info@OurNationalConversation.org, and we'll tell you more about our financial needs and the investment opportunity as we see it. We'll need to raise more money soon enough, but $1 million surely gets us started.

10. **We are open to any and all good ideas.** If you have something you'd like to propose, send an email to info@OurNationalConversation.org.

It's Up to You. It's Up to Me. It's Up to Us

Civility, fairness, accuracy and balance in the media might seem like radical new ideas. But civility, fairness, accuracy and balance are actually very *old-fashioned* ideas in desperate need of a comeback.

When we first started assembling ONC's intern team in the spring of 2020, I told a Zoom room filled with approximately 65 interns, who were just e-meeting each other for the first time, that we were about to build a nonpartisan media outlet, publish a book filled with student-generated policy proposals and produce a TV show — and that, one day, people in high places would pay attention to all this.

While most of these students were thrilled to take part in this adventure — most internships are quite boring by comparison — I could tell some were skeptical. And, like most new ventures, this turned out to be much harder and take much longer than we anticipated. It took us two years to get to this place. We thought we'd be up and running by the end of our first summer.

But here we are. We didn't give up, and now we've built something that has the potential to change the tenor of our country's political conversations for years to come. As ONC seems more real in the minds of our students, I can tell their confidence levels are rising. This gives me great satisfaction. Our students are seeing that they really *can* do this. Now, we just have to convince the *rest* of America!

I have a strong feeling one or two of our interns will go on to become president one day. Some definitely have the potential. I hope I'm still here to see it — and that my former intern invites me to the inauguration. I hope ONC inspires them to continue on the journey ahead — and that the ONC platform helps facilitate needed conversations.

It's time for Boomers to pass the baton — and for Gen Z and the Millennials to grab it — and then *run like the wind.*

God bless America.

Jeff Hall, Editor & CEO
Editor@OurNationalConversation.org

Acknowledgments: Plenty of Appreciation to Go Around

As of this writing (Fall 2022), we've had over 400 students and 175 established professionals participate in our adventure. We also have a lot of friends and formal and informal advisors. There's a long list of wonderful people who need to be acknowledged for jumping in the way they have.

I want to give special recognition to **Brynn Shaffer**, our first student book editor (a senior at Loyola Marymount in Los Angeles). Getting something started from scratch requires a very heavy lift, which she provided in spectacular fashion. She was partnered up with **Ashwin Prabu** (student director of our "policy shop" at that time — now a sophomore at Stanford).

Aiden Merrill-Skoloff (Skidmore) and **Vidhi Prasad** (UC Berkeley) did a lot of work driving the book project. When Ashwin got into Stanford, **Brooke Ballhaus**, a high school student from rural Virginia, took over as our student general manager and continued to push the book along (like Ashwin, she also got into Stanford the following year).

The reins were recently handed over to **Sam Taylor**, a freshman at Brigham Young. Sam is now our student managing editor, and, with the help of **Sara Ghiorzi** (Southern New Hampshire University), **Brandon Cowit** (University of Michigan), **Jake Sell** (Colorado State University), **Margaux Shearer** (Lehigh University), **Anosha Raziq** (University of Maine) and **Stephanie Shiflett** (already out of school), Sam and his team were able to finally wrestle this beast to the ground.

Let's Fix America

Interns, **Ashlyn Kehoe** (Trinity College Dublin), **Elana Sederholm** (University of Minnesota) and **Gabby Klimov** (Calhoun High School, New York), helped us figure out printing, distribution and marketing.

At the end of each proposal, you'll see the names and schools of the students who worked on that proposal. A full list of all our students, their schools and their assignments while at ONC appears below. Let's start with the students, and then, after that, we'll get to the "Friends of ONC," our older, established professionals.

Our Student Interns

Tristan Wagner of Stanford University began brainstorming this idea with me in the Summer of 2017 — when we were calling this venture "SaveAmericaMovement.org." Tristan worked that summer from his home in Wyoming. Not only was he our first intern, but he was also our first *virtual* intern, long before going virtual was a thing.

In the summer of 2018, **Saba Nia** of Harvard Westlake High School (in Los Angeles) and **Brent Armistead** and **Surbhi Sachdeva** of Stanford came to LA, and we continued laying the conceptual framework. **Shivani Tripathi** of Exeter Academy pitched in virtually from afar. By this time, we had changed our name to "TheLatestPolitics.com."

In the summer of 2019, we continued to rely heavily on Stanford students. I attended Stanford years ago and know how to reach out to that school for the purpose of finding interns. **Lore Vasquez Olivera, Kai Kato, Joaquin Nicholas Garcia** and **Alexandra Popke** came to LA and did a lot of work that made us that much more prepared for what was about to unfold.

Let's Fix America

Because of what Lore, Kai, Joaquin and Alexandra did, we were able to move very quickly when COVID hit the following spring. The foundation had been laid. We obviously didn't predict COVID-19, but we were surely ready to ramp up when COVID shut down the world.

In the spring of 2020, with our new team of 92 interns assembled, we once again decided to change our name — this time to "OUR NATIONAL CONVERSATION."

We have kept ONC going since that time. Every semester, students leave, and new ones arrive. It's hard to get a consistent rhythm going, but we now have some rather sophisticated management systems in place — all built by the students — and we are getting better at making the transition every semester.

Here are our interns, in rough chronological order, starting in 2020 and continuing through the present day. The schools shown are where the students were when they interned at ONC. Many have since graduated.

Name	Team	School
Aakash Lilaramani	Technology/Programming	University of Illinois at Chicago
Adithya Ramanujam	Technology/Programming	Georgia Tech
Aiden Merrill-Skoloff	Governance; Infrastructure; Science, Environment & Technology	Skidmore College
Allan Babinar	Justice and Public Safety	University of California, Berkeley
Allison O'Donnell	Social Media/Marketing Outreach	University of Connecticut
Allison Potter	Healthcare; Polling	Elon University
Ally Small	Social Media/Marketing Outreach	Colorado State University
Alyssa Chacon	Marketing	California State University
Alyssa Crowe	Human Resources	University of Florida
Amanda Pasternak	Economy	Brandeis University
Andrew Jarvis	Healthcare	University of Pennsylvania
Andy Colando	Finance	Villanova University

Let's Fix America

Anna Engel	Justice and Public Safety	Indiana University Bloomington
Anna Pigford	Human Resources	Southern New Hampshire University
Armin Jorgenson	Infrastructure	University of California, San Diego
Asharon Baltazar	Development	N/A
Ashley Mullarkey	Futurist	Rhodes College
Ashwin Prabu	Infrastructure; Webisodes and Podcasting	Briar Woods High School
Brooke Ballhaus	Futurist; TV Show, GM	Wakefield School
Brynn Shaffer	Editorial; Book Editor	Loyola Marymount University
Caitlyn Scherrer	Polling	University of Wisconsin-Madison
Catheryn McDowell	Healthcare	Vanderbilt University
Claire Purdy	Human Resources	University of Michigan
Deaven Rector	Justice and Public Safety	Morehouse College
Derek Dzingle	Economy	Gonzaga University
Edna Vuong	Design; UI/UX	University of Pennsylvania
Ellery Saluck	Science, Environment & Technology	Washington University in St. Louis
Eoin Mills	Economy	Davidson College
Esther Kitavi	UI/UX	University of Houston
Gad Raganas	Futurist	Rutgers University Ernest Mario School of Pharmacy
Gizay Guler	Editorial	University of Milan
Grace Ellrodt	Healthcare	Bates College
Grace Richardson	Foreign Policy and Defense	Point Loma Nazarene University
Hritamber Chakraborty	Social Issues	Johns Hopkins University
Hyria Stuart	Editorial; Futuristic	Beijing University
Israd Mpeko	Marketing; Futurist; TV Show; Policies	N/A
Jake Musleh	Technology/Programming	University of Wisconsin-Madison
Jennie Leeper	Editorial	Indiana University Purdue University Indianapolis
John Strezewski	Social Issues	Johns Hopkins University
Joshua Ramos	Infrastructure	Texas Wesleyan
Karagan Knowles	Webisodes and Podcasting	Emerson College
Karli Tellis	Blue Ribbon Panel	Dickinson College
Katrina Harris	Editorial	Liberty University
Kyle Yuan	Finance	New York University
Kylie Kreitz	Futurist	Pennsylvania State University

Let's Fix America

Leonela Valenzuela	Social Media/Marketing Outreach	Loyola University Chicago
Linda Meyerson	Economy	UC Berkeley
Ileane Marquez	Polling	Texas State University
Marie Dishian	Economy	Centre College
Matthew Silberger	Foreign Policy and Defense	City College of New York
Meaghan Shea	Governance; Social Issues	Marist College
Megan Doherty	Webisodes and Podcasting	Emerson College
Mehak Rajpal	Foreign Policy and Defense	University of Southern California
Mikel-Lorenz Ilasco	Futurist	Glendale Community College
Mitchell Clarke	Economy	Virginia Tech
Monika Hossain (Pinky)	Design; UI/UX	University of Virginia
Nicholas Nafso	Polling	University of Michigan
Olivia Bronson	Justice and Public Safety	Barton College
Pablo Herrera	Healthcare	Baylor University
Pascal Lee	Webisodes and Podcasting	Kenyon College
Phoebe Webb	Governance	Texas A&M
Phyllis Feng	Social Issues	Centerville High School
Pragye Jain	Science, Environment & Technology; Social Issues	American University
Quinn Schott	Finance	San Diego State University
Rachel Kaufman	Social Media/Marketing Outreach	Brandeis University
Ralph Barsi	Economy	Texas Christian University
Rechelle Abalos	UI/UX	Long Island University
Rida Mahmood	Healthcare; Non-Profit/Fundraising	Queen's University
Royce Williams	Foreign Policy and Defense	UC Davis
Ryan Dexheimer	Futurist	University of Portland
Ryan Ishii	Healthcare	University of California, Santa Barbara
Samuel Greenberg	Polling	Elon University
Santiago M Rodriguez	Social Issues	University of Redlands
Sarah Schaeffer	Foreign Policy and Defense	Penn State School of International Affairs
Sarah Schmidt	Design; Technology/Programming; UI/UX	University of Central Missouri
Shree Khanolkar	Infrastructure; Science, Environment & Technology	Concord Carlisle High School
Shreya Budhiraja	Social Issues	Northwestern University
Siriveena Nandam	UI/UX	University of Miami
Sophia Welsh	Healthcare Policy	Mira Mesa High School
Sophie Brown	Healthcare	Boston University School of Public Health
Stefanny Garcia	Human Resources	CSU Stanislaus

Let's Fix America

Stella Bush	Economy; Infrastructure	Emory University
Steven Marshall	Technology/Programming	Youngstown State University
Thomas (T.J.) York	Governance; Polling	University of Southern California
Thomas Blandino	Technology/Programming	New York Institute of Technology
Tori Ely	Foreign Policy and Defense	University of Southern California
Vidhi Prasad	Economy; Foreign Policy and Defense	University of California, Berkeley
William-Brennan Merone	Economy	College of William & Mary
Zariya Jeffers	Justice and Public Safety	Clark Atlanta University
Zoe Benham	Futurist; Board Secretary; TV Show; College Campus Initiative	Robert Vela High School
Adam Brasher	Economy	Fordham University
Adolf Schmuck	Technology/Programming	San Diego State University
Ahmad Islam Ishakat	Foreign Policy and Defense	University of Jordan
Aiman Khan	UI/UX	Usman Institute of Technology
Aiza Gaffar	Futurist	Jasper High School
Alina Strileckis	Governance	Tufts University
Amos Afriyie	Programming	Ghana Technology University
Anna Porkus	UI/UX	College of New Jersey
Anoor Ajala	Social Issues	George Mason University
Benny Rosenweig	Economy; Futurist; Governance; TV Show	Princeton University
Courtney Clark	Infrastructure	Point Park University
Dasha Minich	UI/UX	Seattle Community College
Diego Andrades	Justice and Public Safety; College Campus Initiative; Business Development	University of Southern California
Ellie Tanaka	UI/UX	Seattle Central College
Emmanuela Esumanmba-Andoh	Social Issues	George Mason University
Ethan Hamilton	Infrastructure	Virginia Commonwealth University
Evelyn Gonzalez	Human Resources	UC Berkeley
Hannah Constandse	UI/UX	Stanford University
Jack Feenick	Social Issues; College Campus Initiative	University of Virginia
Jacqueline (Jacky) Flores	Social Issues	Florida International University
James DeLeonardis	Technology/Programming	University of South Carolina
Jared Jodts	Economy	Indiana University
Judy Lian	Technology/Programming; UI/UX	Towson University

Let's Fix America

Katherine Jacome	Video Production; Podcasting	Lindenwood University
Keri Thompson	Executive	Instructor, Emerson College
Kyle Kalindjian	Healthcare	N/A
Kyle Olson	UI/UX	San Jose State University
Leon Langdon	Foreign Policy and Defense	New York University
Lucas King	Social Issues	Washington and Lee University
Marisa Kim	Healthcare; Social Media	Vanderbilt University
Michelle Liou	Foreign Policy and Defense	Mountain view High School
Micky Braeger	Science, Environment & Technology; TV Show	DePaul University
Miles Jones	Science, Environment & Technology	Scituate High School
Nada Moghazi	Social Issues	North Carolina State University
Neel Bhat	Finance	New York University
Rahul Hebbar	Futurist; Governance; Science, Environment & Technology; TV Show; Business Development	Rutgers University
Rosalie Ramos	Technology/Programming	Kean University
Rudson (RJ) Varona	Programming	Southern Adventist University
Samuel Taylor	Social Issues	Brigham Young
Sara Irfan	Infrastructure	College of New Jersey
Sumiko Sato	Foreign Policy and Defense; Futurist; Healthcare; Editorial; Social Media	University of San Diego
Tiaira Bates	Front End Develpment	Towson University
Tim Antrim-Cashin	Economy	Columbia University
Tori Permann	Economy	New York University
Tyresa Jackson	Justice and Public Safety	Columbia University
Aissata Watt	Video Production	Colorado State University
Aleona McQueen	Graphic Design; Social Media	Claflin University
Amanda Clegg	Infrastructure	Texas A&M University
Angela Vitale	Video Production	Full Sail University
Anna Birman	Justice and Public Safety	William & Mary
Bowen Zhang	Economy; Futurist; Infrastructure	Thomas Jefferson High School for Science and Technology
Caroline Balan	Video Production	University of North Carolina Wilmington
Claire Dormitzer	Healthcare; Infrastructure	University of Maryland, College Park
Cole Woody	Foreign Policy and Defense; Futurist; Healthcare; TV Show	Dulles High School
Connie Xu	Healthcare	UC Berkeley
Diego Romero	Governance	Seton Hall University

Let's Fix America

Name	Topics	Institution
Esther Cash	Social Media	Biola University
Gabrielle (Gabby) Ostrov	Science, Environment & Technology	University of Vermont
Grace Madden	Social Issues	Dominican Academy
Haanbi Kim	Economy; Science, Environment & Technology	New York University (NYU)
Hannah Halladay	Futurist; Healthcare; Social Issues	Cornell College
James DeLeonardis	Technology; Programming	University of South Carolina
Jasmine Tan	UI/UX	The Ohio State University
Jessica Dine	Science, Environment & Technology; Editorial	Grinnell College
Katelyn Owens	Justice and Public Safety; College Campus Initiative	The Open University (UK)
Kayla Lim	Social Issues	San Diego State University
Lana Delasanta	Futurist; Governance; Infrastructure; Editorial; TV Show	University of Connecticut
Lina Puthengot	Futurist; Justice and Public Safety; Science, Environment & Technology	Erasmus University Rotterdam
Madeleine Polubinski	Governance	Princeton University
Mandy Musleh	Social Media	University of Florida
Marco Wertheimer	Governance	Lafayette College
Marianne Swan	Futurist; Science, Environment & Technology; Social Issues; Editorial	SUNY Oneonta
Marly Kaufman	Video Production	Emerson College
Max Phillips	Science, Environment & Technology	Colorado State University
Melissa Sahin	Governance	Anglo-American University (AAU)
Michelle Krolicki	Social Issues	California State University, San Bernardino
Nathan Simmons	Outreach	American University
Nidhi Nair	Economy; Editorial	University of Connecticut
Nikitha Amerishetty	Technology/Programming	University of Massachusetts, Lowell
Paul Samberg	Justice and Public Safety	University of Kansas
Rida Chaudhry	Governance; Editorial; College Campus Initiative	Queen's University
Riley Menzies	Business Development	Pasadena City College
Shreya Shesadri	Justice and Public Safety	Elisabeth Haub School of Law at Pace University
Sierra Rodriguez	Futurist; Justice and Public Safety; Social Issues	American University
Terron Jackson	UI/UX	University Preparatory School
Tyia Burnett	Social Media	SOAS University of London
Vania Cook	Governance	The University of Alabama

Let's Fix America

Name	Topic	Institution
Veda Kota	Healthcare	Rutgers University
Victor Suarez	Video Production	Valencia College
Victoria Permann	Economy	Oklahoma City University
William Duffy	Justice and Public Safety	University of Massachusetts Amherst
Yaxi Zheng	UI/UX	Columbia University
Yoni Ferbank	Science, Environment & Technology	Syracuse University
Zahra Said	Science, Environment & Technology	UC Berkeley
Andrew Arnold	College Campus Initiative	Washington and Lee University
Andrew Smith	Governance	George Washington University
Ariel Maldonado	Social Media	Florida International University
Avery Warmack	Governance	Lafayette College
Basma Elfandaki	Justice and Public Safety	American University
Benjamin Edelson	Justice and Public Safety	Princeton University
Benjamin Morris	Infrastructure; Foreign Policy and Defense	Harvard University
Cameron Olbert	Foreign Policy and Defense	University of Edinburgh
Christian Williams	Social Media	George Washington University
Connor O'Neill	Foreign Policy and Defense	Lafayette College
Deja Jackson	Social Issues	Lafayette College
Elena Carmona	Science, Environment & Technology; Justice and Public Safety	University of West Florida
Elizabeth Polubinski	Science, Environment & Technology	The Brearley School
Emma (Emile) Shah	High School Initiative	Martin Luther King High School
Fiona Simpson	Governance	Lafayette College
Harry Clennon	Foreign Policy and Defense	Kenyon College
Hasan Rasoul	Justice and Public Safety	Chaffey Community College
Ian Minsterman	Governance	University of California, Berkeley
Isabela Tasende	Economy	University of Notre Dame
Jack Feenick	College Campus Initiative	University of Virginia
Jacky Flores	Social Issues	Florida International University
Jacob Rossi	Video Production	SUNY New Paltz
Jasmine DeLeon	Foreign Policy and Defense	Seton Hall University
John Colson	Editorial	Wheaton College
Kailey Sjauwfoekloy	Justice and Public Safety	Georgetown University
Karen Huynh	Healthcare	University of California, Los Angeles
Kirsta Rodriguez-McKee	Human Resources	University of California, Santa Barbara
Krithik Vishwanath	Healthcare	Klein Cain High School

Let's Fix America

Lisa Green	Editorial	Lafayette College
Lucas King	Corporate Affairs	Washington and Lee University
Lucy Kade	Editorial	Lafayette College
Marco Wertheimer	Foreign Policy and Defense	Lafayette College
Mariana Paris	Justice and Public Safety	Patrick Henry College
Maui Wabe	Healthcare	Mira Mesa High School
Noah Dawson	Economy	University of Tennessee
Regina Arroyo	Infrastructure	University of Houston
Russell Reddecliff	Economy	University of Central Florida
Ryan Anderson	Governance	University of Mississippi
Sana Imam	Healthcare	George Washington University
Sasha Constandse	Social Media	Harvard University
Shreya Singh	College Campus Initiative	University of Georgia
Sofia Khalek	Foreign Policy and Defense	Lafayette College
Taylor Engel	Economy	Siena College
Theresa Kwong	Human Resources	University of San Diego
Thomas Adams	Foreign Policy and Defense	Georgetown University
Travis King	Governance	Lafayette College
Viviane Nguyen	College Campus Initiative	University of California, Irvine
William Reynolds	Science, Environment & Technology	Lafayette College
Alan Cunningham	Governance	Norwich University
Alero Adeniyi	Human Resources	Humber College Toronto Ontario
Alex Joplin	Social Issues	University of North Georgia
Alice Braga	Editorial	University of California, Los Angeles
Alicia Park	Economy	University of California Los Angeles
Allison Loudenback	High School Initiative	Parkway Central High
Ally Fox	Justice and Public Safety	American University
Amane Shuman	Justice and Public Safety	Florida International University
Ana Snyder	Healthcare	Stony Brook University
Anelise Walker	Governance	University of Colorado Boulder
Anna Sarah Langlois	Governance	New York University
Breana Hume	Foreign Policy and Defense	University of St Andrews
Chase Harness	Justice and Public Safety	Wright State University
Chloe Scott	Infrastructure	University of New Hampshire
Corina Ruelas	Justice and Public Safety	University of La Verne
Dalwin Corcino	Healthcare	Wheaton College
Diego Morales	Video Production	University of Central Florida

Let's Fix America

Dipin Subedi	Economy	University of Southern Mississippi
Dylan Vergara	Community	Chaminade College Preparatory High School
Ellen Dallaire	Social Issues	Wittenberg University
Emme Corson	Infrastructure	Virginia Tech
Eric Bleys	Infrastructure	Technical University of Munich
Erin Mahon	Foreign Policy and Defense	University of Virginia
Gabriella Klimov	Science, Environment & Technology	Sanford H. Calhoun High School
Gabriella Matos	Infrastructure	Barnard College
Gerald Shepard	College Campus Initiative	Notre Dame College
Gregory Koh	Foreign Policy and Defense	Graduated from University of Southern California
Guler Ceyda Ilhan	Newsletter	University of Padua
Hannah Snell	Video Production	Massachusetts College of Liberal Arts
Ian Elliott	Foreign Policy and Defense	Johns Hopkins
Ian Ogilvie	College Campus Initiative	California Maratime Academy
Jahon Mikal	UI/UX	Thinkful Code School
Jana Maleab	Economy	Northeastern University
Jodian Wickham	Human Resources	Fitchburg State University
Juan Quintero	Foreign Policy and Defense	Seton Hall University
Kasey Halbleib	Newsletter	Bloomsburg University
Kinsey Blackburn	Human Resources	The University of Texas at Arlington
Kira McClure	High School Initiative	Bethesda Chevy Chase High School
Laura Kim	UI/UX	UCSD
Leslie Sattler	Editorial	New York University
Lucas Silva	Video Production	Federal University of Espírito Santo
Lusadriana Ibarra	Justice and Public Safety	Arizona State University
Madeline Leung	Healthcare	The University of North Carolina at Chapel Hill
Mahanoor Nadeem	Governance	University of Baltimore
Maria Andrea Bojorquez	Social Issues	University of Arizona
Matt Manley	Social Media	Rowan University
Maurice Brantley Jr	UI/UX	Kent State University
Miranda Clapp	Video Production	University of Central Florida
Mohammad Ahmed	UI/UX	St. John's University
Nancy Eke	UI/UX	Cosumnes River College

277

Let's Fix America

Name	Topic	School
Nicholas Gillert	Infrastructure	Brandeis University
Nikki Dong	High School Initiative	Mineola High School
Raquel Chavez	Social Media	Independence University
Ryan Wu	Solve LA homelessness	Irvine Valley College
Shelli Vodovozov	Social Issues	Case Western Reserve University
Siera Joehnk	Social Media	Emerson College
Silvia Rafael	Newsletter	UPC Campus Monterrico
Simonas Bingleis	Foreign Policy and Defense	Villanova University
Sina Kermani	Foreign Policy and Defense	University of Minnesota
Stephany Vasquez	Governance	The City College of New York
Tabatha Fajardo	Social Issues	Stony Brook University
Thomas Liu	Video Production	Northern Illinois University
Travis King	Solve LA Homelessness	Lafayette College
William Gavin	Editorial	Quinnipiac University
Yijia (Christiana) Liu	Healthcare	Johns Hopkins University
Zelipha Gitari	Governance	University of Bridgeport
Sarah Allen	Social Media	Rowan University
Adam Johnson	Justice and Public Safety	University of Denver
Aditi Gotimukul	Human Resources	NMIMS University, Mumbai
Alex Bronowicki	Video Production	University of California, Riverside
Alex Sejas	Economy	University of Miami
Alexys Ewing	Infrastructure	George Mason University
Amula Redkar	Economy	UGA
Annie Portabella	Science, Environment & Technology	University of California, Santa Cruz
Cailey Davern	Social Media; Newsletter	DePaul University
Cayelynn Cruz	Human Resources	University of California, Irvine
Charlotte Chiang	High School Initiative	Palos Verdes Peninsula High School
Daryll Jackson	Justice and Public Safety	George Washington University
Elizabeth Bradley	Human Resources	Arizona State University
Gabriela Machado	Human Resources	Pepperdine University
Geo Tabet	Social Issues	University of Notre Dame
George Swithenby	Social Issues	Middlebury College
Grace Tuohey	Healthcare	George Washington University
Hannah Norton	Justice and Public Safety	Johns Hopkins University
Hayley Slohn	High School Initiative	Chaminade College Preparatory High School
Jennifer Osting	Foreign Policy and Defense	University of Kentucky
Jett Young	Governance	Miami University
Kallie Fox	Justice and Public Safety	Purdue University

Let's Fix America

Kallista Stamenov	Editorial	The University of Texas at Dallas
KeOndre Lane	Video Production	Mesquite High School
Klefy Kochuman	Newsletter	CSU East Bay
LJ Trevette	Foreign Policy and Defense	Georgetown University
Mallory Nichols	Editorial	Auburn University
Mara Bridwell	Science, Environment & Technology	University of Washington
Matthew Reyna	Foreign Policy and Defense; Science, Environment & Technology	University of California, Irvine
Michael Crampton	Infrastructure	University of California, Santa Cruz
Michael Joseph	Economy; Social Issues	New Milford High School
Min-Fang (Amber) Luo	Science, Environment & Technology; Social Issues	Suffolk University
Olivia Gambrel	Foreign Policy and Defense	University of Louisville
Olukayode "Kayode" Oladeji	Infrastructure	Carnegie Mellon University
Owen Braudrick	Infrastructure	University of California, Los Angeles
Rachel Cole	Social Issues	Walden University
Raheel Abubakar	Justice and Public Safety	George Washington University
Rhea Gandhi	Human Resources	California State University, Stanislaus
Robert Gan	Governance	UC Berkeley
Ruby Foxall	Science, Environment & Technology	Harvey Mudd College
Sahiti Karnati	Healthcare	New York University
Sami Tripasuri	Newsletter	California High School
Shefa Tarzi	Human Resources	Empire State College
Skylar Cowen	Governance	Plainview-Old Bethpage John F. Kennedy High School
Sofia Campanella	Script Writer	Hunter College
Suha Chowdury	Governance	University at Buffalo
Tahreem Ashraf	Editorial	Baruch College
Tatianna Staszkow	Healthcare	Wheaton College
Tina Cheng	Social Issues	Johns Hopkins
Uma Rao-Labrecque	Script Writer	Macaulay Honors College at CUNY Hunter
Wilson Schultz	Science, Environment & Technology	Gettysburg College
Yesica Martinez	Governance	University of California, Berkeley
Adam Allen	Healthcare	The University of Southern California
Alizia Gonzalez	Script Writer	University of San Francisco
Amruta Bhir	Healthcare	Monash University

Let's Fix America

Anahi Hernandez	Healthcare	University of Texas at Dallas
Anosh Matti	UI/UX	Washington and Jefferson College
Ashlyn Kehoe	Business Development	Trinity College Dublin
Audrey Kohlman	Science, Environment & Technology	Cornell University
Brandon Cowit	Editorial	University of Michigan
Brian Li	Economy	University of California Riverside
Carly Gegelman	Video Production	University of Minnesota
Caroline Xin	Governance	American University
Charlie Olsen	Action Network (Community)	University of Washington
Charlize Beronilla	Social Media	Santa Clara University
Cheuk-Yue (Karl) Cheung	UI/UX Design	University of California
Claire Park	Infrastructure	University of Southern California
Daamiya Ali Mir	Infrastructure	New York University
Dailuaine Esguerra	UI/UX	University of Nevada - Las Vegas
Dale Thomas	Business Development, Publishing and Content	Bradley University
Dana Lawrence	Science, Environment & Technology	Structuralia University
Danait Tzeggai	Healthcare	Eastern Virginia Medical School
Daniel Carvalho	Science, Environment & Technology	Haveford College
Daniel Cellucci	Video Production	Temple University
Danielle Meuret	Video Production	Southern Utah University
Diane Bao	Social Issues	University Of Texas
Elana Sederholm	Business Development, Publishing and Content	University of Minnesota Twin Cities
Ella Hutnick	Business Development	Northeastern University
Emily McGinn	Editorial	California Baptist University
Estefania De Caires	Science, Environment & Technology	Stevens Institute of Technology
Faith Rodgers	Scriptwriter	State University of New York at Plattsburgh
Finley Doyle	Script Writer	Yale University
Galen Heuer	UI/UX	UCLA
Gaytri Menon	Social Media	New York University
Grace Axlund	Infrastructure	Miami University
Grace Jang	Action Network (Community)	University of California, Berkeley
Guerdyna Gelin	Social Issues	Syracuse University
Hannah May	Foreign Policy and Defense	Columbia University

Let's Fix America

I-ting Chien	Action Network (Community)	Pennsylvania State University
Isabella Romeu	Justice and Public Safety	University of Chicago
Jack Fortner	Economy	University at Buffalo
Jagraj (Jack) Atwal	Healthcare	University Of Pennsylvania
Jeanelle Bailey	Video Production, Script Writer	City College of NY
Jesslyn Djaja	Video Production, Script Writer	De Anza College, UCLA
Kelsey Rogers	Social Issues	Temple University
Kennedy Files	Healthcare	Emory University
Kristin Sung	Business Development	University of California, Los Angeles
Krithika Bhardwaj	Business Development	Cornell University
Luke Pittman	Infrastructure	University of Missouri, Columbia
Luke Soule	Social Media	Cal Poly San Luis Obispo
Lyss Eng	Social Issues	Cornell University
Mariana Duque	Script Writer	Manhattan College
Mark Streiber	Economy	Boston College
Maryam Javed	Foreign Policy and Defense	University of Chicago
Matteo Roncaglia	Fundraising/ Crowdfunding	The Pennsylvania State University
Max Zimmerman	Social Media	Arizona State University
Michael Provoast	Foreign Policy and Defense	N/A
Misgana Ketema Asfaw	Infrastructure	
Mollie Duffy	Social Issues	Miami University
Muskan Singh	Business Development	George Washington University
Natalie Guo	Foreign Policy and Defense	High School for Dual Language and Asian Studies
Neesha Patel	Governance	UC Santa Barbara
Nidhi Yadalam	Governance	University of Massachusetts, Boston
Oishee Misra	Economy	UC San Diego
Oscar Infante	UI/UX	Torrens University Australia
Pooja Huded	Infrastructure	Vassar College
Rachel Mondelus	Video Production	Montclair State University
Rajen Upreti	Business Development, Public Relations	N/A
Rohan Krishnamoorthy	Foreign Policy and Defense	American University
Ruby Han	Advertising Sales & Sponsorships	UC Berkeley
Sahiti Agarwal	UI/UX, Moonshot Project	N/A
Sam Bingham	Action Network	Indiana University of Pennsylvania
Sandra Sosa	UI/UX	Jefferson High School
Shandra Ahsan	Healthcare	Yale University

Let's Fix America

Name	Topic	School
Sreenidhi Karnati	Science, Environment & Technology	Lufkin High School
Sukanya Mitra	Editorial	Boston University
Tania Ruedas Ortiz	Infrastructure	University of La Verne
Trung M. Vu	UI/UX	Community College of Aurora
Vedant Vamshidhar	Governance	University of Southern California
Vidith Iyer	Science, Environment & Technology	West Windsor Plainsboro High School South
Ying He	Economy	University of Michigan
Zara Jamshed	Action Network (Community)	Lebanon Trail High School (public high school)
Zhengmao Sheng	Infrastructure, U.S.-China Relations	Brandeis University
Abhinav Banerjee	Foreign Policy and Defense (Policy Shop)	Masaryk University
Alexander Richter	Foreign Policy and Defense (Policy Shop)	Archbishop Mitty High School
Alyssa Naigan	Business Development	Brown University
Anosha Raziq	Editorial	University of Maine
Aria Rashidi	Economy (Policy Shop)	Bard College
Ayesha Iqbal	Foreign Policy and Defense (Policy Shop)	Georgia State University
Brian Yip	UI/UX	N/A
Carson Gahagan	Business Development	Salisbury University
Cassandra Flandre-Nguyen	Infrastructure (Policy Shop)	Orange Coast College
Chip Myers	Moonshot Project	Middlebury Institute of International Studies
Christopher Montenegro	Business Development	Mount Saint Mary College
Christopher Plate	Podcast (Media)	Manhattan College
Clarisse Brown	Moonshot Project	Carnegie Mellon University
Corey Li	Moonshot Project	College of New Jersey
Domenic Maglio	Governance (Policy Shop)	University of Central Florida
Emerson Tsui	Governance (Policy Shop)	University of California, San Diego (UCSD)
Emily Fletcher	Science, Environment, & Technology (Policy Shop)	Rhodes University
Genesis Chicas	Podcast (Media)	Southern Methodist University
Gunneet Jammu	Human Resources	California State University San Bernardino
Hailey Sjoblom	Social Issues (Policy Shop)	University of California Santa Barbara
Jada Moylan	Social Media (Media)	University of Colorado Boulder
Jessica Torres	UI/UX	Santa Clara University
Jillian Coveney	UI/UX	Santa Clara University

Let's Fix America

Johanna Gustafsson	Human Resources	Baruch College
Jordan Francis	Video Production (Media)	Rowan College at Burlington County
Karabo Poloko	Social Issues (Policy Shop)	University of Botswana
Kealohilani Mendiola	Economy (Policy Shop)	University of Utah
Kendall Hoeszle	Graphic Design	Glendale Community College
Kharina Miramontes	Social Media (Media)	Palomar College/CSULB
Liza Howard	Human Resources	University of Southern California
Luzbelle Francisce de Castro	Video Production (Media)	University College Cork
Martin Clarke	Infrastructure (Policy Shop)	N/A
Naledi Mordaunt	Economy (Policy Shop)	St Peters College
Natalie Ruiz	Economy (Policy Shop)	University of California, Santa Cruz
Natnael Abate	Healthcare (Policy Shop)	Pennsylvania State University
Neel Taneja	Graphic Design	Netaji Subhas University of Technology
Ofkalera Gudina	Podcast (Media)	Minnesota State University Mankato
Olivia Barone	Script Writer (Media)	N/A
Rachna Raghavan	Social Issues (Policy Shop)	Brandeis University
Roberto Rodas-Herndon	Social Issues (Policy Shop)	Boston University
Salma Ibrahim	Foreign Policy and Defense (Policy Shop)	University of British Columbia
Samantha Adams	Graphic Design	The University of New Hampshire
Sarah Fadahunsi	Healthcare (Policy Shop)	Salisbury University
Skye Taylor	Science, Environment, & Technology (Policy Shop)	Bergen County Technical High School Teterboro
Stephanie Shiflett	Editorial	University of Georgia
Valeria Stefanutti Gan	Human Resources	Western Michigan University
Wesley Liu	Governance (Policy Shop)	Pacific Bay Christian School and Skyline College
William Sheehan	Infrastructure (Policy Shop)	Fordham University
Xiaolin Luo	Healthcare (Policy Shop)	University of California, Los Angeles (UCLA)

You might be asking: With all this help, why did it take so long to write this book? I often ask that, too. Students are busy; we can only get an hour or so a week out of them. Term papers, mid-terms, finals, boyfriends/girlfriends, vacations — there is always something that competes for their time. Plus, as described in this book, Gen Z likes to talk a lot. Decisions and progress come slowly.

We can push our interns only so hard. And then, every semester, just as we're really getting up to speed, it's time for the next semester to kick in, and we see a big turnover. We have to take a big step backward before we can begin moving forward again.

This first book represents only a tiny fraction of all that our students have done. We have around 350 proposals done, and we have teams working on podcasting, videos — all kinds of exciting stuff. "Let's Fix America" represents just the tip of the iceberg.

Friends of ONC — Our Established Professionals

Three individuals help guard and protect our nonpartisan mission. **Sandra Finley**, **Brian Thomas, M.D.** and **Ruben Navarrette** help make sure all sides are fairly represented.

Sandra Finley is one of my co-chairs of ONC. Sandra, President of the League of Black Women, is our resident progressive. She has been particularly helpful when it comes to addressing issues of recruiting for the purpose of achieving diversity. She is instructive in helping us understand racism and the role it plays in our society.

Brian Thomas, M.D., our senior policy director, is our resident conservative and national co-chair. He is a traditional Republican who is concerned about polarization in our country. Brian helps connect our students with policy experts. Brian knows something about nearly every facet of public policy you can imagine (and the history of every big agency and landmark bill).

Brian is a walking encyclopedia when it comes to public policy and asks our students excellent questions that cause them to really stretch. Brian is founder of The Candidates Network, a group of public policy enthusiasts. Many of these experts consulted with ONC's students. Brian is a "true believer" in the ONC mission. Brian is originally from Minnesota and currently resides in Pittsburgh, PA.

Ruben Navarrette, our third co-chair, is a syndicated columnist with The Washington Post Writers Group, a contributor to The Daily Beast, a member of USA Today's Board of Contributors and host of the podcast, "Ruben in the Center." He is fairly disgusted with both sides. Ruben helps keep us centered. Carlsbad, CA.

We are looking to add a Trump-follower and an AOC/Bernie Sanders type to this team. At ONC, our job is to set the tone — to show that civil conversations really are possible. They are. It can be fun, really — provided everyone treats each other with respect. *It surely helps to have a sense of humor.*

I'm **Jeff Hall,** Editor & CEO. I got ONC started. I'm a traditional newspaper professional (former VP, Los Angeles Times) who would like to see a return to civility in our political discussions. I worked at the White House for a year and I'm entrepreneurial. ONC is my fourth startup. I view myself as pretty moderate, politically. Over the years, I have voted for Democrats, Republicans and Independents. I vote for the person, not the party.

The following established professionals participated in many ways — reading proposals, participating in Zoom sessions, giving feedback to our students, advising members of our management team and providing moral support. Nobody involved in ONC has ever been paid (except some programmers).

Tom Johnson is the retired president of CNN and former publisher of the Los Angeles Times. Atlanta, GA. I worked for Tom at the LA Times. He is completely honorable in a world that often falls short. I love the guy.

Brian Churchill is a sergeant with the Los Angeles Police Department and runs a leadership training academy for the LAPD. He has consulted with our Public Safety student teams. San Pedro, CA.

Christine O'Donnell is a former television journalist who now runs a podcasting consulting company (see BrightSighted.com). She is helping us with our podcasts. New York City, NY.

Leo Wolinsky is the former managing editor at the Los Angeles Times and a board member at CalMatters.org. Los Angeles, CA. He is very smart about public policy matters, and he has a sense of humor — much needed these days.

Keith Newman is a veteran of the Silicon Valley scene with a deep background in media and technology. He has been involved in ONC since the beginning and loves the idea of connecting digital media and political discourse. If you are into tech, you will enjoy Keith's podcast, "The Look Back."

David Iglesias is a former U.S. Attorney from the State of New Mexico. He is a Republican and served in the George W. Bush Administration. He is now a professor of faith, politics and economics. He was especially helpful when it came to discussing how to best achieve team diversity and attract more Republican students.

I like to call our former general manager, **Mike Chirveno**, "Mr. Boring." He loves making the trains run on time. Mike replaced a lot of our "make it up on the fly" startup zeal with systems that will stand the test of time. Mike had to peel off recently for a paying gig, but I hope he returns one day.

Cindy Brown is our GM over at TheLatest.com. I surely hope she joins us over at ONC. She has the most common sense of anyone I've ever known. She lives just outside of Atlanta.

Dennis Murphy is a former nuclear submarine Captain and spent 17 years as a senior executive with Amgen, a global biotechnology company. He has worked with our Foreign Policy & Defense student team. Annapolis, MD.

Julie Fox Blackshaw is a great friend and supporter. She has always been a big supporter of this effort. Julie is very smart about a lot of things — and very practical, to boot. Pasadena, CA.

Joan Abrahamson runs a think tank, The Jefferson Institute. She was awarded a MacArthur Foundation "genius" grant. I started talking to her early on about ONC. She helped us work through issues of organizational structure. Los Angeles, CA.

Brad Phillips is a judge in the Superior Court of Los Angeles. He worked with our students on issues facing our electoral systems. Los Angeles, CA.

Let's Fix America

Dr. Thomas L. Datro is the Officer in Charge of the LAPD's Police Science and Leadership Section. He is a contributing member of the National Center for Biomedical Research and Training and a consultant with the Institute for Intergovernmental Research. Tom is the creator and host of the "Policing in America with Sgt. Tom" podcast. Los Angeles, CA.

Anjali Tripathi, Ph.D. is a research associate at the Center for Astrophysics, Harvard-Smithsonian. She has advised our Science, Environment and Technology group. Los Angeles, CA.

Ned Holland is a hospital and industry association counsel and board member, a private sector benefits and healthcare purchasing executive and a former assistant secretary of HHS (Obama Administration). Kansas City, MO.

Thanks to lifelong friends, **Ron** and **Don Poblenz** (twin brothers) and **Greg Moore** (also a twin), for making me watch FOX News whenever I visit them. I often recommend to my liberal and moderate friends that they watch FOX now and then. And to all my Republican friends: try a little MSNBC and CNN once in a while! *Better yet, come visit us at ONC and see all sides, all in one place, all the time!*

Patricia Rose Duignan and I went to high school together. She has always been a human dynamo. She worked for several years for George Lucas's Industrial Light & Magic, working on creating special effects for the original *Star Wars* movies (and several movies that followed). I've asked Rose to put her prodigious energies and creativity to work in helping get the word out about ONC. Berkeley, CA.

James Freeman is a real estate finance professional. He advised us on our efforts to come up with solutions to homelessness in Los Angeles. Los Angeles, CA.

Catherine Coleman is a recently retired professor of lawyering skills at USC Law School. She offered much editing advice in the early stages of this book. If there are any typos, it's not Catherine's fault. Someone else did that. Catherine (or "Cap," as we call her) simply doesn't do typos. Los Angeles, CA.

Sam Abrams is a professor of politics at Sarah Lawrence College and a visiting member of the American Enterprise Institute. He has consulted with us about Gen Z's relationship to politics. New York, NY.

Ed Holleran is the retired co-founder and CEO of Atlantic Broadband, a cable TV and broadband provider, later sold to Cogeco (Canada). He has worked with our student Economics team. Winchester, MA.

Randy Hull is an energy consultant at Mobility-Utility Hydrogen Solutions. He is the author of "Political Malpractice in America: Republic at Risk." He has worked with our student Infrastructure team. Philadelphia, PA.

Pam Jennings of Jennings Steine is our very patient CPA. She has been doing our books for years, going on faith that, one day, we'll turn this into a success. Maybe 2023 will finally be our year. Los Angeles, CA.

Jon Leader is also very patient. He has been our corporate attorney for years, giving us office space for much of that time. Jon is one of the keenest political minds I know. Los Angeles, CA.

Keri Thompson is an instructor of political communication at Emerson College. She is also an elected official (a "Selectperson"). She knows a lot about politics, media and social media and has a youthful approach our students adore. Cohasset, MA.

Claude Organ is a retired commercial banker at Union Bank. He has prior experience in lending and loan restructuring with Security Pacific Bank and Bank of America. He has spent time with our student Economics team. Del Mar, CA.

David Webster is a practicing attorney with a special interest in issues of governance and presidential history. He has advised our student Governance team. Lake Forest, IL.

Alan Kopit is the executive vice president and general counsel at MediLogix, LLC. He is the President of the ABA Retirement Funds. He gave excellent feedback to our student Governance team. Cleveland, OH.

Mike Campbell is an agriculture executive and a former administrator at the University of California, Davis. Mike worked with our students on several issues and appeared in our TV show pilot devoted to the topic of reducing food waste in America. Davis, CA.

Paul Huddle, executive director of Gathering of Men SoCal (GOMSC), leads men's Bible studies in Los Angeles and Orange Counties and works with over 200 churches throughout Southern

California. Prayers from one of his wonderful West Los Angeles groups provided much-appreciated encouragement.

Anne Mayfield is the owner of a marketing consulting company, Mayfield Consulting. She helps ONC come up with marketing plans. Charlotte, NC.

Rick McCay is a real estate investor. He invested real money in TheLatest.com, Inc., which gave birth to OUR NATIONAL CONVERSATION. Newport Beach, CA.

Ellie Tanaka is a graphic arts and website designer who did a lot of work on ONC's front-end design. Seattle, WA.

Harold S. Rosen worked at the World Bank for many years and then started the Grassroots Business Fund, which specializes in making micro-loans in some of the world's poorest regions. He worked with our students who are interested in international economics.

Dr. Jay Wagener is a psychotherapist. He has many keen insights into the emotional and psychological nature of America's divisions today. ONC will be exploring these issues in more depth in the future. Pasadena, CA.

Brad Baker is a serial entrepreneur, a financial whiz and one of the truly most interesting individuals I have ever met. Among his many adventures is deep-sea diving for ships, filled with gold, that sank hundreds of years ago. With high-tech robots, he often finds them (and then gets sued by the country where the gold came from centuries ago). These countries claim the gold is still theirs. Brad has advised our students on economic issues. Sarasota, FL

Andy Stewart is a good friend from Maine. He adds much color to our conversations and plays a mean guitar. Bangor, Maine.

John Chisholm, serial entrepreneur, past president/chair of the worldwide MIT Alumni Association and author of "Unleash Your Inner Company," advised us on publishing and logistics. He has also provided keen insights on how to best achieve diversity. San Francisco, CA.

Harrison Killefer works at a think tank (Mitre) in McLean, VA and has offered much good advice to ONC. Falls Church, VA.

If I forgot anyone, the fault is mine. Get in touch, and we'll add your name in time for our next press run.

Several of the "Friends of ONC" listed above spent a year participating in the White House Fellows program, as did I. The White House Fellows program is designed to give promising mid-career Americans, usually in their thirties, a one-year exposure to the highest levels of the federal government.

The White House Fellows program is completely nonpartisan: It is common for Republicans to serve in Democratic administrations and vice versa. The theory is, upon graduation, participants will go on to become better leaders in all walks of life. There is no doubt in my mind that my participation in the White House Fellows program helped inspire ONC.

While there is no direct connection between the White House Fellows program and OUR NATIONAL CONVERSATION, I believe ONC could become something of a "junior varsity" team for those

Let's Fix America

who might aspire to become White House Fellows (and, later, great leaders in their fields).

Several of my classmates from Harvard Business School (Class of 1978, Section F) also participated. Their businesslike thinking has been very helpful to our students. For a government or private sector program to work, it has to be practical, well run, cost-effective and self-sustaining. We put a lot of emphasis on that as our students put together their proposals.

Quite a few fellow journalists also pitched in. Our industry has been in a state of upheaval for a long time now — politically, economically and technologically. Thousands of reporting and editing jobs have evaporated in recent decades.

As old-fashioned newspapers shrink and new digital formats appear, eventually things will settle down. Without a doubt, there is something good about the democratization of media, and many new voices have surfaced in recent years — voices that would never have become known, pre-social media.

But today's free-for-all allows for a lot of partisanship, anger, hate, misinformation and disinformation. Many of us think this has all gone too far. But as they taught us back in Journalism 101, there is always another side to every story: some of my journalist friends think all this media rough-and-tumble is a *good thing*, really. All points of view now have their outlets; somehow or another, the news we need to know gets out. Secrets don't stay secret for long, that's for sure.

I'm all for getting all the news out there (so long as it's truthful). I'm all in favor of disseminating all points of view (if these opinions are based on facts). And I truly admire investigative journalists who take on those who deserve to be taken on. Truth should be every journalist's guiding light; it's not about us. We aren't the stars.

It's all the theater, fakery, bias and fighting that is hard for this traditionalist to embrace. Surely, we can do this better. We don't have all the answers yet at ONC, but, together, I think we can figure this out. I keep challenging our students by saying to them, "if social media is so bad, let's reinvent it and come up with a system people actually like." That's on our "to do" list.

Last, but not least, I especially want to thank my wife, Gail. She has been incredibly supportive of this effort, and, truly, she made ONC possible.

The very first time I met Gail at Stanford, back in 1972, we both said we wanted to change the world. That's how it was back then: we all pledged to do our part — even to people we had just met moments before — and we meant it.

Gail has certainly done her part, through her legal, mediation and judicial career. OUR NATIONAL CONVERSATION is my down-to-the-wire attempt to fulfill my "I want to help change the world" promise — made to Gail 50 years ago this year.

Better late than never, dear!

Gail isn't done yet, and neither am I, neither are you, neither are we. My students, some friends and I got something started. Now, let's keep it going.

Let's figure out how to build OUR NATIONAL CONVERSATION into something fair, truthful, unbiased, enlightening, benevolent and sustainable. Let's make ONC a national gathering place to hash things out.

It's time to unify. We are the *United* States of America — at our best when we work together. Let's see how far we get with this.

When the people lead, the leaders will follow.

Jeff Hall, Editor & CEO